Dorothea Bleek

Dorothea Bleek

A Life of Scholarship

A biography by Jill Weintroub

Published in South Africa by:

Wits University Press

1 Jan Smuts Avenue

Johannesburg 2001

www.witspress.co.za

First published 2015

978-1-86814-879-0 (print)

978-1-86814-882-0 (PDF)

978-1-86814-880-6 (EPUB North America, South America, China)

978-1-86814-881-3 (EPUB Rest of the world)

The publishers confirm that this work was subject to an independent, double-blind peer review process before publication.

Edited by Lisa Compton

Proofread by Ester Levinrad

Index by Margie Ramsay

Cover design by Abdul Amien

Book design and layout by Newgen

Printed and bound by Kadimah Print

Contents

Preface

The notebooks and associated papers collected in the 1870s and beyond by Lucy Lloyd and Wilhelm Bleek are inscribed in UNESCO's Memory of the World register. Since 1997, the Bleek Collection has been recognised as a documentary heritage of international significance. The landmark 1991 conference in Cape Town, the proceedings of which were published as *Voices from the Past: /Xam Bushmen and the Bleek and Lloyd Collection*, edited by Janette Deacon and Thomas Dowson, introduced an era of sustained cross-disciplinary interest in this unique collection of material that is most often described as ethnographic. Many academic and popular books, exhibitions and performances have since been created using the Bleek Collection and the interactions between Bleek, Lloyd and their prisoner interlocutors as reference and inspiration.

But my engagement with the collection pre-dated all that. It began in the early 1990s, when, as a reporter for one of Cape Town's daily newspapers, I interviewed Pippa Skotnes about her critically acclaimed art book *Sound from the Thinking Strings*. In that work, Pippa explored the final years of /Xam life and paid homage to the words of //Kabbo and to bushman cosmology through a series of etchings drawn from rock art motifs. The artworks were presented alongside contributions from Pippa's colleagues at the University of Cape Town (UCT), including poetry by Stephen Watson that drew on the /Xam notebooks and essays by archaeologist John Parkington and historian Nigel Penn.

I did not know then that my interest in the collection and the drama of its making would keep me busy for many years. While working on my MPhil at UCT in the early 2000s, I researched the story of Otto Hartung Spohr and discovered how his dedicated detective work and roots in pre-World War II Germany and Eastern Europe had played out in his study of German librarians at the Cape and of German Africana, and in his writings on the life of Wilhelm Bleek.

While employed as a librarian at UCT, Spohr travelled to archives in Germany in the 1960s and crossed the Iron Curtain while on the trail of material pertaining to Wilhelm Bleek. His obsession, described as 'some sort of madness', added much of the personal detail now taken for granted in the Bleek Collection, including the courtship letters between Wilhelm and his future wife, Jemima. As I read his correspondence, it became clear to me that Spohr's interest in Wilhelm Bleek was as much emotional as it was professional. The empathy he felt towards Wilhelm Bleek, combined with a profound nostalgia for the Eastern Europe he had been forced to flee in the 1930s, leapt out at me as I read his letters.

I began to realise how much Spohr's personal quest and his passion were embedded in a collection of documents that are now often mined for other reasons. This realisation led me to the person of Dorothea Bleek. Why had so little been said or written about her? Why was she the one labelled as 'racist' while Lucy and Wilhelm were celebrated as liberal thinkers ahead of their time? Was there nothing more that could be said about Dorothea's life?

Of the five Bleek daughters, Dorothea alone continued with her father and Lucy's bushman work. If it had not been for Dorothea's continued interest in bushman studies, her years of working alongside Lucy and her inheritance of the materials originated in Mowbray that have been a rich resource of creativity and intellectual labour for decades, the Bleek and Lloyd collection as we know it today may never have come into being.

I was intrigued by the silence around Dorothea. So began my journey through her archive, a journey that found me at times frustrated by her seeming lack of openness to new ideas, and at other times impressed by her determination to go into the field and see for herself. I began by reading Dorothea's 32 field notebooks in the Bleek Collection. Apart from two brief diaries recorded on early trips, much of the material in those pages is incomplete, ranging from vocabulary and grammar samples to fragmentary narratives that deal with topics ranging randomly from the weather to the names of stars to children dying of smallpox to snippets of genealogical and historical material, and including many blank or nearly blank pages.

Dorothea's notebooks show that classifying human bodies was a routine part of her bushman work. Delineating human 'types' on the basis of physical attributes, ways of life and language were intrinsic to her research. In addition to measuring such intimate spaces as nostrils, Dorothea dug up human skeletons and participated in making life casts drawn from live human models.

Dorothea's programme of physical measurement, photography and object collection took place alongside language sampling in a context in which such aspects were accepted as a routine part of scientific method that was in turn based on a stable and unchanging conception of 'race'. At the Iziko South African Museum, I looked through the many invasive images she (and other researchers) had taken of people she considered 'pure' examples of bushmen. I wondered about their determination and will to practice science according to the methods of the day that authorised such dehumanising activities.

But my research suggested there was another side to Dorothea. As with Spohr, it was the personal correspondence that allowed a private side of the person to come into view. Through reading her letters to Käthe Woldmann, I realised that Dorothea's scholarship and intellectual quest were driven as much by science as by a nostalgic attachment to the father she had barely known, and a passion and determination to continue the work that he and her beloved Aunt Lucy had begun. It was an expression of her loyalty and respect to their memory. Here, then, was a further example of the feelings, passions and desires that lay at the heart of the archive and of processes of knowledge making, but that were elided in public airings of such knowledge.

In Dorothea's case, it seemed that her scholarship led not only to the safe keeping and eventual preservation of the Bleek and Lloyd materials, but also to the continued presence of the notion 'bushman' in scholarly and popular minds. For all these reasons, I felt that Dorothea's contribution to southern African scholarship and to the history of thought in the emerging academy was worth exploring in detail. Without whitewashing her participation in methods of science and anthropology organised by and designed to produce racial knowledge, I argue in this book that Dorothea's place in the disciplinary histories of African studies, linguistics and anthropology in southern Africa in the early decades of the twentieth century ought to be recognised and acknowledged.

Jill Weintroub
Johannesburg
July 2015

Acknowledgements

The writing of manuscript versions of this narrative coincided with my relocation from Cape Town to Johannesburg at the beginning of 2011. For this born-and-bred Capetonian, adjusting to Gauteng was an interesting process. It was facilitated by Professor John Wright, my colleague at the Rock Art Research Institute (RARI), whose generous engagement in my writing and thinking over the past five years has added immeasurably to this book.

John must also be thanked for introducing me to former RARI director Professor Ben Smith, who offered me an Honorary Research Fellowship at the Institute. I am grateful to Ben for supporting my affiliation to RARI, and for facilitating, with Professors Karim Sadr and Helder Marques, my short-term Postdoctoral FRC Grant from the Faculty of Science at the University of the Witwatersrand in 2011. Thanks also to current RARI director Professor David Pearce who readily supported the extension of my fellowship, and in so doing enabled me to continue to benefit from a collegial environment as I finalised my manuscript.

The final draft of this biography was prepared with the support of the American Council of Learned Societies' (ACLS) African Humanities Fellowship Programme established with a grant from the Carnegie Corporation of New York. I was a recipient of an ACLS Postdoctoral Fellowship in the African Humanities Programme in 2011/12, and have benefited greatly from ongoing interaction and networking facilitated through that organisation.

My research on Dorothea Bleek began nearly 10 years ago as I embarked on PhD studies at the University of the Western Cape (UWC). I am grateful to my supervisor Andrew Bank for his close engagement with my research, and for sharing his impressive knowledge of the Bleek and Lloyd notebooks with me. Support for my PhD came via an Andrew W. Mellon-supported Fellowship in the Programme on the Study of the Humanities in Africa (PSHA) at the Centre for Humanities Research at UWC. I thank Professor Premesh Lalu, director of the Centre for Humanities Research, for providing a challenging space in which to grow my ideas, and Professors Leslie Witz and Ciraj Rassool of the History Department at UWC for their interest over the years.

Premesh arranged my Mellon-supported Visiting Scholar sojourn at the Interdisciplinary Centre for the Study of Global Change at the University of Minnesota (UMN) during 2010, where several draft chapters of this work were written. I thank Professors Helena Pohlandt-McCormick, Allan Isaacman and Eric Sheppard, Dr Karen Brown and Dr Jim Johnson for their interest and support during my visit.

At the University of Cape Town (UCT), Professors Nick Shepherd, Pippa Skotnes, John Parkington and Carolyn Hamilton have happily shared their time and knowledge at many different points on this intellectual journey. For their professionalism and friendly assistance, I thank Lesley Hart, Janine Dunlop, André Landman and Isaac Ntabakulu who helped in many ways with my research at UCT's Manuscripts and Archives Department, and Gerald Klinghardt and Petro Keene at the Iziko South African Museum.

Patricia Scott Deetz has been unstinting in sharing memories of her childhood home in Cape Town with 'Great Aunt D'. I appreciate the lengths to which she has gone to include the memories of her sister Anne Scott Roos in her responses to all of my queries. Those memories and her knowledge of Bleek-Lloyd and Scott family history have greatly enriched this book.

In addition, the insights gained from the letters Dorothea Bleek wrote to Käthe Woldmann have been an invaluable resource. I must thank José Manuel de Prada Samper for pointing out the presence of the letters to me, and Hannelore van Rhyneveld for translating them from their original German into English.

Many of the illustrations in this book are reproduced from collections held by UCT Libraries and Iziko Museums of South Africa. I thank Clive Kirkwood of Special Collections and Archives at UCT, and Lalou Meltzer, director of Social History Collections at Iziko, for their kind permission. Parts of the Introduction and Chapter 1 have appeared in a chapter entitled 'Colonial adventurer, loyal follower or problematic afterthought? Revisiting the life and scholarship of Dorothea Bleek', in *The Courage of //Kabbo: Celebrating the 100th Anniversary of the Publication of Specimens of Bushman Folklore*, edited by Janette Deacon and Pippa Skotnes (UCT Press, 2014). A version of Chapter 3 was first published as *By Small Wagon with Full Tent: Dorothea Bleek's Journey to Kakia, June to August 1913* (2011), in the Centre for Curating the Archive's Series in Visual Histories edited by Pippa Skotnes and Nick Shepherd. An earlier draft of Chapter 6 appeared under the title 'Sisters at the Rockface – the Van der Riet Twins and Dorothea Bleek's Rock Art Research and Publishing, 1932–1940' (*African Studies* 68 (3), 2009). It is reprinted with the kind permission of Taylor & Francis UK.

I am indebted to Wits University Press for supporting this publication. My thanks go to Veronica Klipp, Roshan Cader, Ester Levinrad and Corina van der Spoel for their enthusiastic reception of the manuscript biography that I submitted to WUP two years ago, and to Lisa Compton for helping me to streamline and fine-tune the narrative for presentation to awaiting readers.

Colleagues and friends who have offered encouragement and assistance or read drafts along the way include Elizabeth Bagley, Barbara Buntman, Michelle Coleman, Menán du Plessis, Gail, René and Kimberly Hochreiter, Anja Macher, Siyakha Mguni, Barbara Michel, Marcelle Olivier, Anne Wanless and Justine Wintjes. Thank you all. I am grateful to the two anonymous readers of the final manuscript whose thorough engagement and apposite suggestions have helped me to refine the final form of this work.

Lastly, I need to acknowledge the unfailing support and love of my family. Clive, Jonah and Kim, I could not have reached this milestone without you. And to my mom, Esther, in her 85th year, this work is dedicated with love and gratitude.

A note on terms and languages

As has been well documented, the term 'bushman' derives from the appellations 'Bosmanneken' and 'Bosjesmans' conceived in the minds of European travellers and early Dutch settlers at the Cape from at least the seventeenth century. The consequences of colonial expansion and its impacts on indigenous groupings and life ways, including the marginalisation of people identified as hunter-gatherers or foragers, have also been well documented. It is the elaborations of these processes and their playing out in various strategies of identity making and naming that are called to mind when thinking the category 'bushman'.

The scholarship of Dorothea Bleek is located within this evolving discourse. As this book suggests, Dorothea's work had bearing on the continued use of the term 'bushman' to designate a stable category of people defined by what were seen as unchanging cultural and physical attributes, and who were also regarded as 'ancient'. Such scholarship further contributed to the term 'bushman' being invoked to demarcate a particular area of disciplinary engagement in the South African academy of the early twentieth century.

My use of the term 'bushman' in this text includes an awareness of its historically contingent and contested meanings, and an acknowledgement of the shifting interpretations that have accrued to the term in the history of its usage. It also recognises its use in identity making in the present.

In this text, I follow Dorothea Bleek's terminology (though I dispense with her use of the capital B except where I am quoting her directly) in choosing to use the word 'bushman' to designate people she identified as such on the basis of language and physical attributes as was acceptable in her scholarly milieu. I use 'bushman' in preference to alternative terminologies such as 'San', 'Khoisan' or 'Khoesan', which are themselves historically and politically contingent and remain topics for debate among linguists who study southern African languages.

I also follow Dorothea's usage in regard to names given to groups defined on the basis of language, such as Naron (Nharo or Naro) or !Kung (!Kuŋ, !Xuŋ or !Kū), as well as to geographical locations such as Kakia (Khakhea) or the Tanganyika Territory (Tanzania). I do this in order to locate this work within the intellectual and geographical contexts that it is concerned to describe and explore.

I have chosen to use the word 'interlocutors' instead of 'informants' to refer to the bushmen and other people who shared their languages and folklore with Dorothea Bleek, and with Wilhelm Bleek and Lucy Lloyd before her. I do this to signal an awareness of the interview process as a conversation and a dialogue in which knowledge is shared among all participants rather than a one-dimensional method of knowledge extraction.

Languages

Linguists have continued to study the many diverse southern African languages sampled by Dorothea Bleek in the early decades of the twentieth century. These include 'bushman' languages such as

/Xam: This language, represented in the notebooks recorded by Wilhelm Bleek and Lucy Lloyd, was previously spoken across most of what is now the Northern Cape province of South Africa and parts of the north-eastern Cape stretching from Graaff Reinet to Oudtshoorn. Dorothea visited the Prieska and Kenhardt regions in 1910 and 1911 in search of descendants of Wilhelm and Lucy's 'Colonial Bushmen', and commented that their folklore was 'almost extinct'.

//Ng!k'e: Similar to /Xam, this language was recorded by Dorothea on trips to Mount Temple, the Langeberg and Lower Molopo regions of Griqualand West and Gordonia in 1911 and 1915. In addition, Dorothea recorded limited samples from **/'Auni** speakers as well as of **Xatia** (Kattia or ≠Keikusi) in the Lower Nossop area of the Kalahari. She described the latter as a dialect of the former. Together with **Masarwa** recorded at Kakia in 1913 and /Xam discussed previously, these were grouped as 'Southern Bushman' languages in Dorothea's classification system. A decade later, while travelling south of Sandfontein in Namibia, Dorothea sampled **/Nu//en** (or Nusan), a language described as similar to Masarwa. On the same trip, she described **!Ko** (!Xō) or **!Koon** (!Xóō) as a 'branch of /Nu//en'.

//Xegwi: Dorothea recorded limited samples of this language while at Lake Chrissie in what is now Mpumalanga. At the time (between 1913 and 1915) she wrote that the people 'had no name for themselves other than "Batwa", the Zulu and Swazi terms for "Bushman"'. She grouped it with the Southern languages.

Naron (//Ai kwe, Nharo or Naro) and Auen (//k'au//en): These languages form part of Dorothea's Northern and Central groups, and were recorded on trips to Sandfontein, close to the Botswana border in Namibia, between 1919 and 1922. Dorothea found Naron to be close to Nama (a Khoekhoe language still widely spoken by people living in Namibia), while Auen was similar to the !Kung spoken in southern Angola and in the region around Lake Ngami.

!Kung (!Kuŋ, !Xuŋ or !Kũ) and Hei//kum (Hai//Om): Dorothea recorded varieties of the !Kung language while travelling through Angola in 1925. She compared these with the samples Lucy Lloyd had recorded in the 1870s from a group of young men and boys from north of Lake Ngami who had spent some years at Mowbray. Dorothea categorised these languages as Northern, and noted that they were distantly related to languages in her Southern group. She obtained samples of !Kung and Hei//kum while interviewing prisoners at Windhoek prison. The Hei//kum, she wrote in her 1928 book, had lost their original tongue and spoke only Nama. Their name meant 'bush-sleepers'. Dorothea's 'Hei//kum' language is today described as a dialect of Namibian Khoekhoe.

On a trip to Tanganyika in 1930, Dorothea sampled a language she called **Hadza**. She classified it as Central because its speakers followed a hunter-gatherer or 'bushman' way of life, and because she thought its gender system was slightly similar to that of Naron. In contemporary linguistics Hadza is described as an 'isolate click language', and no evidence has been found to support Dorothea's suggestion of its relationship to Naron.

Dorothea's categorisation of 'Bushman languages' into three groups (Northern, Southern and Central) remains fundamental in contemporary linguistics, although subsequent scholarship has refigured terminologies, refined the relationships between families and groups, and redrawn genealogical and geographical boundaries between varieties and dialects. This is particularly the case in regard to those southern African languages previously described as 'Bushman' or 'Hottentot'. Dorothea and the linguists of her era drew distinctions based on non-linguistic features and their classifications were influenced by ethnographic characteristics such as whether the speakers of the language followed a hunter-gatherer or pastoral way of life. Thus, some of the languages previously included in Dorothea's Central

'Bushman' group are now recognised as having features in common with Nama, which is the best-known of the Khoekhoe dialects and is still widely spoken in Namibia and Botswana. Dorothea's Central languages are now classed as a branch of the Khoe family and are sometimes described as 'Kalahari' varieties. In contemporary linguistics, then, 'bushman' languages are subsumed within 'Khoesan' languages. Khoesan may be used as an umbrella term to refer to between 20 and 30 language dialects spoken in southern Africa that feature click consonants as regular speech sounds. The term may also refer to three genetically unrelated southern African language families now known as Ju (or Northern) languages, including Ju/'hoansi and !Kung spoken mainly in Botswana; Khoe (or Central) languages, including Nama and Naro, or Naron, spoken mainly in Namibia; and !Ui-Taa (or Southern) languages, spoken in South Africa. The latter family includes !Xóõ, the only surviving Taa language, and !Ui, in which N/uu (or N//ng) is the only surviving language.

Useful texts on southern African linguistics drawn on here include M. du Plessis. 2014. 'The Damaging Effects of Romantic Mythopoeia on Khoesan Linguistics'. *Critical Arts* 28 (3), 569–592; R. Mesthrie. 2002. 'South Africa: A Sociolinguistic Overview', and A. Trail. 2002. 'The Khoesan Languages', both in R. Mesthrie. Ed. *Language in South Africa*. Cambridge: Cambridge University Press, 11–26 and 42–43 respectively; and R. Vossen. Ed. 2013. *The Khoesan Languages*. Oxford: Routledge.

Guide to the pronunciation of clicks used in the spelling of names and languages in this text

/ indicates the dental click, in which the tip of the tongue is pressed against the back of the upper front teeth as in 'tsk, tsk'

! indicates the post-alveolar click, in which the tip of the tongue is curled against the roof of the palate and withdrawn suddenly, creating a cork-popping sound

// indicates the lateral alveolar click, in which the tongue is pressed against the upper palate and withdrawn as in the sound made when urging a horse on to greater speed

≠ indicates the palatal click, in which the blade of the tongue is pressed at the termination of the upper palate against the gums and withdrawn suddenly

Additional phonetic symbols used in the text

' indicates an ejective segment produced by a sudden arrest of breath

~ appears over a vowel to indicate a nasalised vowel or vowel sequence

ŋ indicates an 'ng' pronunciation or 'velar nasal segment' as in si<u>ng</u>

Further detail on orthography and pronunciation is available in J. Hollmann. Ed. 2005. *Customs and Beliefs of the /Xam Bushmen*. Johannesburg: Wits University Press, xvii; and W. Bleek and L. Lloyd. Eds. 1911. *Specimens of Bushman Folklore*. London: George Allen & Co, Preface, both of which have been drawn on here.

Map of southern Africa showing some of the locations to which Dorothea
Bleek travelled in the course of her research.

Introduction

Revisiting the life and scholarship of Dorothea Bleek

It is my wish that when a translation of the collection of my father and aunt is published, it is simply offered to the world, without comments or interpretations in whatsoever form.[1]

These words, penned in 1936 in a private letter to a friend in Switzerland, describe in a nutshell Dorothea Bleek's intellectual project that was her life's ambition. Dorothea devoted her life to completing the 'bushman researches'[2] that her father and aunt had begun in the sitting room of their home in Mowbray, near Cape Town, in the closing decades of the nineteenth century. For Dorothea, her bushman research was partly a labour of familial loyalty to her father, Wilhelm, the acclaimed linguist and philologist of nineteenth-century Germany and later of the Cape Colony, and to her beloved aunt, Lucy Lloyd, a self-taught linguist and scholar of bushman languages and folklore. Dorothea's research was also an expression of her commitment to a particular kind of scholarship and an intellectual milieu that saw her spending almost her entire adult life in the study of the people she called bushmen.

From the vantage point of the twenty-first century, how has history treated Dorothea Bleek? Has she been recognised as a scholar in her own right, or as someone who merely followed in the footsteps of her famous father and aunt by taking their 'bushman researches' out of their Mowbray home and into the landscapes of southern Africa at the beginning of the twentieth century? Was she an adventurer, a woman who stepped out of her colonial comfort zone and travelled across southern Africa driven by intellectual curiosity to learn all she could about the bushmen? Was she conservative and

1

racist, a researcher who belittled the people she studied and dismissed them as lazy and improvident? Or was she a scholar who believed staunchly in the importance of close observation, hands-on fieldwork and the collection of samples and evidence from the field? Did she make her own contribution to South African scholarship, or did she simply rewrite, repackage and publish the celebrated collection of folklore and ethnographic knowledge that was her family heritage? An examination of Dorothea's papers and personal letters suggests that she was a mixture of all of these things. She was a complex and contradictory character who warrants greater recognition in South African history and in relation to the much studied Bleek-Lloyd collection of bushman folklore in which the documentary records of her life and scholarship are now preserved.

This book examines Dorothea Bleek's life story and family legacy, her rock art research and her fieldwork in southern Africa, and, in light of these, evaluates her scholarship and contribution to the history of ideas in South Africa. The narrative reveals an intellectual inheritance intertwined with the story of a woman's life, and argues that Dorothea's project of producing knowledge about bushmen was also an emotional quest and an expression of familial loyalty. The collection of private correspondence preserved among her papers suggests that Dorothea's scholarship was motivated in part by her desire to honour the idealised father whom she barely knew, and to pay tribute to the aunt who had mentored her in the /Xam and !Kung languages and through whom she was able to access her intellectual inheritance. At the same time, Dorothea was concerned with a particular kind of scholarly inquiry in which language provided the key to understanding the 'soul' of a people, in her case the bushmen, who were seen as 'natural' and closest in evolutionary terms to the 'original' human. These intellectual and emotional strands woven together evolved into an archive that today bears the UNESCO designation *Memory of the World*, indicating its status as a documentary record of global importance that has been and still is consulted by historians, linguists, folklorists, anthropologists, archaeologists and rock art scholars, as well as the general public, from around the world.

But Dorothea's story begins some decades before she was born. Her father, Wilhelm Bleek (himself the son of a scholar and professor of theology), had grown up and completed his studies during the golden age of philology in Germany. Arising from the study of ancient Greek, Latin and Sanskrit manuscripts, philology in nineteenth-century Germany grew out of the endeavours of biblical critics to trace historical connections between written languages and peoples, and thereby to verify the textual authority of the Bible. Comparative philology emerged from the focus on theology as a discipline with a wider purview in which all the world's languages and peoples could be studied and compared. Thus, the young Wilhelm's studies in Berlin and Bonn explored theology and the classics as well as biblical languages including Hebrew, the languages of Africa, Sanskrit, European and Indo-Germanic languages and literature. He also took a course on Shakespeare. He received his doctorate from the University of Bonn in 1851.[3] His doctoral thesis had explored gender-denoting languages, and had attempted to find a link between the Khoekhoe languages (spoken by the Nama of south-western Africa) and the Hamitic languages of North Africa, drawing on comparative methods that were current at the time.[4] Wilhelm believed that the study of language could reveal clues to the origins, level of development and progress of humankind. His interest in 'click languages' in particular stemmed from their perceived primitivism, and the idea that the speakers of these languages were closest to animals on the scale of human evolution.

Determined to experience Africa for himself, Wilhelm joined Dr William Balfour Baikie's Niger expedition as official linguist in 1854, but had to return to England after contracting a tropical fever on the island of Fernando Po. His second attempt to visit Africa was more successful. As Bishop John William Colenso's translator, Wilhelm spent some 18 months studying the Zulu language and folklore in Natal, before arriving in Cape Town in 1856 to work as interpreter and librarian for Sir George Grey, governor of the Cape Colony. This move perfectly located Wilhelm for the 'bushman researches' that would captivate him for the rest of his life, and for meeting the young Englishwoman Jemima Lloyd, whom he married in November 1862.

The couple settled in Mowbray, near Cape Town. Jemima's sister Lucy joined the household some years later, in about 1869, and in time became a vital part of Wilhelm's bushman project. Historians and scholars from across the disciplines have written detailed accounts of the interactions between Bleek and Lloyd and the prisoner-interlocutors they studied.[5] Archaeologists, folklorists, historians, rock art scholars and academics from a range of other disciplines have studied the thousands of pages of notebook texts that Bleek and Lloyd generated, drawing on the narratives recorded in /Xam or !Kung with English translations. In the process they have contributed to an ever-enlarging body of critical scholarship that continues to stimulate debate, especially in relation to the analysis of oral literatures and in the interpretation of southern African rock art.[6]

The method of using prisoners as language interlocutors was not a new one for Wilhem Bleek. His interest in bushman languages had been piqued several years before by a visit in 1857 to Robben Island, off the coast of the Cape Colony, to interview prisoners from the Burgersdorp area in the eastern Cape Karoo.[7] The more systematic and intense Mowbray project began in 1870, when Wilhelm secured permission from authorities at Cape Town's Breakwater Prison to accommodate bushman prisoners at his home so that he could learn their language and folklore. From hesitant beginnings the project gathered momentum as communication and understanding between the researchers and their interlocutors improved with time.[8] By its close towards the middle of the 1880s, the project had generated 161 notebooks filled with narrations recorded using a special orthography, the system of symbols and alphabetical characters devised by Wilhelm to reflect the complex sounds including 'clicks' that he heard in his interviews.[9]

Some 100 years later, scholars have contrasted Wilhelm's narrowly comparative approach to language with Lucy Lloyd's empathetic interactions with her interlocutors and her sympathetic interest in their ways of life. Through Lucy, information about the use of plants and insects, the making of poisons and pottery, and beliefs and rituals associated with celestial objects entered the collection.[10] In contemporary writings, many scholars have recognised the project as a unique and heroic collaboration across barriers of race and society in the context of the extreme violence and dispossession characteristic of the frontier regions of the colonial Cape at the time.[11] Others have described Wilhelm Bleek as 'South Africa's first systematic theorist of racial difference', and have framed his intellectual approach and the research that he produced as foundational in terms of the discourses around race and language that were generated.[12] Notwithstanding these debates, the Bleek and Lloyd collection, as we have seen, bears the UNESCO appellation *Memory of the World*.[13] In this context, the notebook collection has been referred to as a 'Rosetta Stone which enabled scholars to decipher the meaning of southern African rock art' and contributed to 'advances…in the study of Australian and European rock art'.[14] Significantly – and controversially in regard to the limits forced upon the many and varied meanings residing in the /Xam words that were deployed to make up the phrase – vocabulary drawn from the notebooks has been incorporated in the motto of the coat of arms of post-1994 South Africa, alongside figures adapted from the Linton rock art panel.[15]

Aside from such public and high-profile references to the /Xam language, the story of the philological and ethnographic researches carried out by Wilhelm Bleek and Lucy Lloyd has been explored in many academic and popular publications, art installations, exhibitions and performances in South Africa since the 1990s.[16] But Dorothea's contribution has seldom attracted concentrated attention in these extensively researched, nuanced and vivid presentations. Despite her years of research, fieldwork and publishing inspired by the notebooks, Dorothea seldom receives recognition for taking charge of her family's intellectual inheritance, nor for carrying bushman research into the twentieth century. A short biography of Dorothea appears in the *Dictionary of South African Biography*, and there are references to her research and publishing in *Stories that Float from Afar: Ancestral Folklore of the San of Southern Africa*.[17] In edited collections arising from the landmark 1996 exhibition Miscast: Negotiating the Presence of the San, and the 1991 'Voices from the Past' conference that established the Bleek and Lloyd collection as a resource for international interdisciplinary study, contributions focused on the Mowbray project, with Dorothea featuring only in passing.[18] She is recognised for classifying bushman languages into three groups, a model that remains foundational to contemporary linguistics, and due attention is paid to her 1923 edited collection of stories from the notebooks published under the title *The Mantis and His Friends*, and to her submissions during the 1930s to the journal *Bantu Studies*. However, little attempt has been made to evaluate and appreciate her scholarship within the larger context of knowledge production and the emergence of fields of academic inquiry in the human sciences and languages as these developed in the first half of the twentieth century.[19] Finally, while Dorothea occupied the position of Honorary Reader in Bushman Languages at the University of Cape Town

(UCT) from 1923 until virtually the end of her life, in the definitive history of that institution she is mentioned only in a one-sentence reference to her 1928 monograph, *The Naron: A Bushman Tribe of the Central Kalahari*.[20]

Dorothea's early contribution to the systematic recording of rock art for research rather than antiquarian purposes and her several collaborative publications on the topic are rarely given a place in the history of rock art scholarship. When featured in academic or popular writing, she is characterised as an enigmatic figure who lacked the heroic insights that her father displayed towards the bushman subjects of his research. Equally, she is denied the empathy that Lucy Lloyd is celebrated for showing to the prisoners, in particular Dia!kwain and /Han≠kass'o, and for Lucy's sympathetic annotations of the drawings and watercolours produced by the !Kung youngsters who lived in the Bleek household in the late 1870s.[21] Rather, Dorothea is portrayed as feeling no sympathy towards the bushmen among whom she conducted her research, and dismissing them as 'idle' and 'improvident'.[22] She is taken to task for diminishing the importance of rock art by viewing it as a record of daily life and social history of the bushmen, or as merely 'art for art's sake' produced out of nothing more than a deep love of painting.[23] Little attention has been paid to Dorothea's views on the indigenous authorship of rock art, a position she stuck to in the face of the wave of thinking which questioned that notion during the 1920s and 1930s.[24] Neither is she credited for the trenchant statements she made about selectivity in regard to methods of rock art sampling and its effects on interpretation and meaning, nor for her early awareness of issues of interpretation and meaning evoked by the 'translation' onto flat paper surfaces of multidimensional, multi-hued images painted on rock walls.[25]

As an intellectual history this book asks, what kinds of knowledge did Dorothea Bleek produce during her lifetime? Her work, building on that of her father and aunt, contributed to ideas about 'bushmen', initially as race or type, and later as identity, in South African memory and landscape. Along with being an expression of familial loyalty, Dorothea's research was aimed at establishing evidence for the earlier, ancient and widespread presence of a 'pure' bushman race across southern Africa (and the continent as a whole). Her scholarship was steeped in the now discredited 'encroachment theory' elaborated by colonial government surveyor and rock art copyist George

Stow, and popularised by the historian George McCall Theal, in which the southern African past was narrated in terms of a conflict between groups of people who were racially defined.[26] In accordance with this thinking, Dorothea argued that the bushmen were the original inhabitants of southern Africa who had been 'swamped' by more powerful 'black races' from the north, and by 'white settlers' from the south. She devoted her life's work to perpetuating this idea through her research and publications.[27] It was a view she had grown up with. Both her father and Lucy Lloyd, as well as their colleague and correspondent George Stow, had supported this belief.[28]

Dorothea argued for the existence of a childlike and carefree bushman hunter whose ancient lifestyle was disintegrating under the pressure of modernity. This provided a context in which she could later situate the thousands of pages of /Xam and !Kung narratives that her father and aunt had produced, and that Dorothea continued to work on and publish from. Her first book, *The Mantis and His Friends*, offered selected translations of notebook texts in which the mantis, identified as the 'hero' or 'dream' figure of the bushmen, and members of his family played a part.[29] In the late 1920s she published two monographs, the first based on research she had done among the Naron, a group she identified as a 'bushman tribe of the Central Kalahari', and the second a comparative summary of bushman language research, including her own and that of her father and Lucy.[30] In addition, she published abroad, as her father had done before her, in scholarly journals.[31] In the 1930s she published an edited series of notebook translations in separate articles in the University of the Witwatersrand (Wits) journal *Bantu Studies*.[32]

Dorothea's work took place at a particular disciplinary moment in South Africa – at a point when academic research was beginning to be systematised but at the same time often remained haphazard, anecdotal and idiosyncratic in practice. The intellectual environment in Europe and the late colonial world remained premised on evolutionary understandings of race and social progress. Early fieldwork methods and practices were being applied across emerging and formalising academic disciplines – language and linguistics, archaeology and anthropology being the fields of study with which Dorothea's scholarship was mainly concerned. Dorothea's archived documents record in greater or lesser detail the various excursions she took during her career. Read together with her published work, these provide a sense of the texture of her fieldwork practice, and of the formal and informal methods and networks she used to structure her projects and to achieve her scholarly aims. This book examines the marginal status of her field methods and practice, and details the social, organisational and institutional networks she constructed through her fieldwork. It also describes the contributions of Dorothea's assistants and collaborators, both in the field and elsewhere, to the co-production of knowledge.

While acknowledging Dorothea's contribution to the colonial archive, this book argues that she was also a vital link in the preservation of the Bleek-Lloyd notebooks and additional materials. To dismiss her is to ignore how her scholarship contributed to early constructions of the notion of 'bushman' as a discrete field of study in the academy, not only in South Africa, but also globally. She did this by holding on to the notebooks, lexicon, rock art reproductions and other materials produced by her father and aunt and their interlocutors and collaborators, and also by adding substantially to this foundational knowledge base through her own fieldwork and writing. Dorothea continued to produce knowledge from the collected materials, thereby helping to keep the notion of 'bushman' on the table for discussion in both academic and public domains through the 1920s, 1930s and ultimately into the 1950s, when her bushman dictionary was finally published. Thus, her research contributed to holding open a space for the continued stereotypical understandings of bushmen as isolated and ideal hunters, tied to the landscape in a pristine idyll. It was into this space that the fictional writings of Laurens van der Post, alongside the famous ethnographies of researchers such as the Marshall family in the 1950s and 1960s and Marjorie Shostak in the 1980s, found a perfect fit.[33] These bodies of research have had far-reaching impacts on contemporary South African debates about identity, subjectivity and even land rights into the post-apartheid era.

Dorothea's rock art research, building on the earlier recording work of George Stow and on her father's exploratory and limited contribution just before his death, has largely been overlooked in the history of that discipline. Until very recently, the account of rock art as a discrete field of inquiry typically began with the contribution of late-nineteenth-century copyists such as Stow and Joseph Orpen, continuing through the activities of Harald

Pager, Bert Woodhouse and Alexander Willcox during the 1950s, before arriving in the 1970s with the contributions of David Lewis-Williams and Patricia Vinnicombe. The 1981 publication of Lewis-Williams's seminal work *Believing and Seeing: Symbolic Meanings in Southern San Rock Paintings* inaugurated an era in which interpretation of the art was linked to an expression of spiritual potency and to bushman understandings of the spiritual world through the practice of shamanism, in which ritual specialists reached altered states of consciousness in the trance and healing dances that could still be observed in bushman communities of the Kalahari.[34]

In this lineage, the contribution of Patricia Vinnicombe provided an interruption to an otherwise male-dominated narrative. Vinnicombe's research in the Underberg region of the uKhahlamba-Drakensberg in the 1950s culminated in her 1976 publication *People of the Eland: Rock Paintings of the Drakensberg Bushmen as a Reflection of Their Life and Thought*.[35] Yet Dorothea's earlier research across large parts of the country had established important benchmarks for the study of rock art that are being revisited in contemporary scholarship. Her findings around the authorship, age and historical relevance of paintings, and her attempts to situate paintings within the broader landscape and geography of shelters and overhangs, remain key areas of study in the discipline. Long before it was accepted practice, Dorothea used the notebook tales collected by her father and aunt to explain the meanings of some of the painted scenes she saw on the rocks. Further, she applied her field-based knowledge of weapons, clothing and beadwork, as well as of hunting practices and social life, to identify painted figures and scenes, thus inaugurating the early use of ethnography in rock art interpretation, a method that remains central, if contested, in contemporary scholarship.[36]

In light of the growing interest in the history of fieldwork, and in collaborations between fieldworkers and their assistants, Dorothea's many excursions across southern Africa should be acknowledged for their idiosyncratic qualities, and her methods and practices are noteworthy for several reasons. The semi-formal characteristics of the networks she made use of in the field add detail to histories of southern African fieldwork. Dorothea carried out her fieldwork at a time when, as Henrika Kuklick argues, a 'fundamental reorganisation of scientific work was underway'.[37] Quite apart from her gender, Dorothea inhabited a fracturing space which an earlier division between the work of the professional collector and that of the gentleman scientist ensconced in the city was breaking down, while the importance of the fieldwork experience grew.[38] It is apparent from Dorothea's correspondence and notes that she regarded fieldwork as an essential component of her scholarship, and that she believed that bushman language, folklore and culture could be meaningfully understood and interpreted only by those who had personal experience of the people in their landscapes. In addition, Dorothea's field methods aligned with the thinking emerging in British anthropology at the time, in which the fieldworker who became 'immersed...in an exotic culture could serve as a reliable research instrument'.[39]

In southern Africa in the first three decades of the twentieth century, Dorothea shared the developing space of fieldwork with the Cambridge-trained social anthropologist Winifred Tucker Hoernlé. In keeping with the thinking of the time, both scholars were motivated by a desire to 'salvage' what remnants of cultural information and material objects they could of the 'vanishing' peoples they studied. In line with this aim, both held in their minds the possibility of finding 'pure' examples of the 'tribes' they studied, respectively bushmen and Nama, and they employed photography and physical measurement as part of their work to document disappearing races. Both collected domestic objects, weapons and items of clothing in the field. They also recorded genealogical and historical knowledge from people perceived to be members of 'primitive' groups whose unique, pristine and previously unchanging life ways were disintegrating in the face of mixing with other groups, modernity and progress. Yet the detail of this kind of fieldwork method and practice has not been studied in any depth. While Hoernlé is credited with the title 'mother of social anthropology' in South Africa, she is recognised more for the calibre of students she trained during her tenure at Wits than for her pioneering fieldwork.[40] Likewise, Dorothea is rarely thought of as a fieldworker, being recognised instead for her language research, for her early classification (following her father) of bushman languages into three groups, and for her posthumously published *A Bushman Dictionary*. In general, however, neither Dorothea nor Hoernlé is credited for their months of research in the field at a time when fieldwork was being

10

established as a crucial method in the emerging discipline of anthropology in Europe, North America and Africa.

Given contemporary interest in fieldwork, research assistants and their role in the co-production of scientific knowledge, and in the formalising of academic disciplines and fields of study, it seems worthwhile to look at Dorothea's research through this lens. Scholars such as Henrika Kuklick, Nancy Jacobs, Jane Camerini and Lyn Schumaker have pioneered investigations into the history of the field sciences, and this examination of Dorothea's fieldwork is inspired by theirs.[41] The turbulent late-nineteenth-century European intellectual milieu within which Dorothea studied should be recognised for the complexity and nuance it brings to the history of scholarship in South Africa, especially in light of what Dorothea might have learnt during her tertiary studies in Germany and London about the quintessentially German practice of *Ethnologie* (ethnology) from its early proponents. Moreover, her maturing scholarship and intellectual contribution is noteworthy for what it says about the production of knowledge at the margins of the South African academy of the early twentieth century.

Dorothea's scholarship may be viewed as part of a process of establishing herself as central rather than marginal to the broader, mostly male-dominated work of knowledge making that was going on around her. Here use of the term 'marginal' is in line with Natalie Zemon Davis's conception of the margin as 'a borderland between cultural deposits' which may be rethought of as a locally defined centre.[42] Resisting easy oppositions, Zemon Davis examines notions of the 'marginal' by exploring the autobiographical writings of three seventeenth-century women whose lives and writings offer an illustration of 'the significance of writing and language for self-discovery, moral exploration and...the discovery of others'.[43] In one such autobiography, the Jewish merchant, wife and mother Glikl bas Judah Leib writes herself and her religion into the centre of a world that was for the most part constrained against her.[44] Dorothea's researches and writings fulfilled the same function, that of providing a space in which she could centre herself within a world of familial loyalty and shared intellectual tradition, and at the same time assert the belief that bushmen were the original inhabitants of southern African landscapes. For Dorothea, research and writing were dynamic processes by which she constantly reimagined and remade her identity and place in relation to her family inheritance on a personal level and, more publicly, in relation to the academy, its hierarchies and its institutionalised processes of knowledge making.

This argument is influenced by Dorothy Driver's reading of the Scottish artist and travel writer Lady Anne Barnard's diary entries of 1799–1800 and the suggestion that the people encountered and landscapes traversed were experienced and reflected upon in particular ways that impacted on Lady Anne's identity as a colonial woman traveller.[45] In Dorothea's case, her journeys through the landscape and her encounters in the field were experienced in the context of the sentimental and emotional freight she carried stemming from the work of her father and aunt, in relation to the people she regarded as the subjects of her research in the field, and influenced by her particular evolutionary understanding of the world and its peoples. As she processed her thoughts and feelings and produced them as knowledge, they in turn contributed to her identity making.

Yet while Dorothea was aware of debates centred on the emerging human and social sciences in Germany and Britain, her scholarship was cautious and wary of embracing what she considered to be some of the outlandish new theories of the early twentieth century. In her intellectual project, Dorothea held on to established ideas – especially those that were part of her family legacy and history. As will be shown in more detail, she was suspicious of what she called 'conjecture' that she read in the work of the 'devoted ethnographer and disgruntled patriot' Leo Frobenius.[46] She disagreed with his notion that an earlier, ancient civilisation was responsible for Great Zimbabwe, the stone-walled settlements of southern Africa, and some of its rock art. In letters to her friend in Switzerland, Dorothea showed that she was wary of the ideas connected to the esoteric spiritual sciences propagated by supporters of the anthroposophist Rudolf Steiner. Both these instances confirm that she was cautious and resistant to aspects of modern intellectualism, and that she chose not to venture into innovative thinking and thereby claim a larger intellectual space. Instead, she preferred to centre herself in a marginal world of family loyalty and empirical science. As will be seen in the following pages, Dorothea maintained institutional networks and contacts but remained peripheral in academic contexts. Nevertheless, her research made an impact in the field of bushman and African studies in South Africa and beyond. By preserving and continuing to work on the Bleek and Lloyd notebooks and other materials generated by her father and aunt, Dorothea influenced the course of disciplinary knowledge production during the early decades of the twentieth century. Through her own fieldwork and research, she kept a place open for a continued focus on the study of bushman life and languages throughout the twentieth century.

Her scholarly project led ultimately to the establishment of an archive of documents – the Bleek Collection – that provoked a paradigmatic shift in the study and interpretation of rock art during the 1970s and 1980s in South Africa and later globally, and one that has been drawn on increasingly in the postcolonial era as a source of precolonial San or 'First People' identities. Dorothea's major impact may well have been in donating the celebrated Bleek-Lloyd notebooks to UCT Libraries for public storage. Archived there, the notebooks and related materials have given rise to an 'industry' of knowledge making in academic and popular contexts, including fine art, theatre and storytelling, archaeology, anthropology, language studies and rock art interpretation.[47] Dorothea's contribution to the history of thought in South Africa ought to be located in this context.

This book presents a biography and traces a history of ideas. It examines the intellectual currents and theoretical paradigms that underlay a programme of research and scholarship which continued for nearly 40 years. It shows that Dorothea's scholarship was informed and influenced by her life story in varied and complex ways. In stitching together the personal and other documents and materials in the archive, this narrative is structured on the chronology and logic of the archive, drawing on Dorothea's field notebooks, personal correspondence, and published and unpublished materials to reveal a complex character whose scholarship and research was complicated by idiosyncratic personal and intellectual contexts. The archived record of Dorothea's fieldwork in southern Africa shows her engaging with the landscape and the people she found there in a myriad of complex and contradictory ways. Hers was a lifetime project to study the bushmen and to map their life ways and languages onto the landscapes of southern Africa. This biography focuses on Dorothea's life experiences as well as her intellectual lineages and suggests ways in which these impacted on her thinking, research practices and fieldwork as she traversed the landscapes of southern

Africa. The focus on the life of an individual allows a personalised biographical story to be constructed in contrast to a generalised view of the development of fieldwork as scientific practice in southern Africa. In so doing, it makes the argument that Dorothea's interest, inherited from her father and aunt, in what she and others termed 'bushman' people influenced the consolidation of disparate remnant groups of people into a defined object of research that made oral evidence and material objects available for study by a range of disciplines and discourses in both the sciences (for example, archaeology and linguistics) and the humanities (such as anthropology and folklore).

While her project was an expression of familial loyalty and the desire to pay homage to the memory of her father, whom she barely knew, Dorothea was also determined to keep in the public domain not only the work of her father, but also that of her aunt Lucy, with whom she shared a close intellectual bond. At the same time, Dorothea's scholarship unfolded within the context of a formalising intellectual landscape in South Africa as academic disciplines and fields of study established themselves in newly inaugurated universities and institutions of higher learning and research.[48] This book further places Dorothea's scholarship within the legacy of her schooling and tertiary education in Europe in the late nineteenth century. Dorothea was immersed in classical traditions of philology, and in the particular and individualistic development of ethnology and anthropology in Imperial Germany during the closing decades of the nineteenth century. Her intellectual antecedents resulting from inheritance and education impacted on her scholarship and the kinds of knowledge she produced, particularly in relation to notions evoked by the term 'bushman'. Dorothea's life story, viewed as a fixation with the bushman world studied and recorded by her father and aunt and their Breakwater prisoners at Mowbray, prompted her desire, perhaps even obsession, to continue the family project, with particular outcomes in regard to her scholarship.

On letters

The genre of biography occupies an in-between space. Poised between social history and literature, any individual biography may be either 'a work of record or an imaginative exercise', or perhaps a bit of both.[49] But, as Justin

Kaplan argues after Samuel Johnson, the expectation is that minute details of domestic life will be offered.[50] Often, private correspondence becomes the vehicle via which the biographer seeks to 'fix on certain illuminating occasions' or tries to 'penetrate the veil of unconscious or calculated deceptions' that people hang between themselves and the world.[51] Mary Beard reminds us of the difficulties that lie in unravelling documents, including personal letters, and that sensitive reading in archives is a 'tricky exercise'.[52] Rather than charting the history of Big Ideas and Grand Theory, Beard, biographer of the celebrated Cambridge classicist Jane Harrison, argues that space must be left to show 'the untidiness, vacillations, and day-to-day provisionality of the (real) life of the mind'.[53]

This intellectual biography of Dorothea Bleek follows Beard's suggestion that '[p]ersonal intellectual histories are never reducible to neat and straightforward teleologies' or stories that appear to have predetermined endings and conclusions.[54] The series of episodes drawn from the collected materials of Dorothea's life presented here are written against the grain of the 'assured certainty' in which most biographies strive to be written.[55] Contradictions of thought are brought to the surface, and ambiguities in experience and action exposed. While the temptation is to write the life of a person as a seamless chronological narrative that focuses mainly on events, with some attention paid to context (political, social, psychological), the intention here is to produce a biography that aims to 'show its working'[56] to some extent, through paying attention to the storied representation of the person, and the documents and sources consulted to obtain that narrative. Drawing again on Beard, an attempt is made to explore the possibility of biography writing in a manner that exposes the coherent story of a life as a loaded story, one that has been carefully selected, edited and retold by those with a stake in its telling.[57]

Moreover, in the tradition of Virginia Woolf, this biography is an exercise in 'life-writing', a term elaborated upon with reference to contemporary literary practice by the biographer and Oxford professor Hermione Lee.[58] Lee's biography of Virginia Woolf keeps words like *elusive*, *obscure* and *illusory* at the forefront even while providing an exhaustive chronology of the events, people and places in Virginia Woolf's life.[59] That Woolf herself produced novels, essays and diaries assisted Lee in her project of life-writing. Based on Woolf's prolific output as a writer, critic and journalist who left an archive of 'trans-Atlantically scattered hoards of manuscripts and letters, diaries and notebooks', Lee argues that a biographer could make a record of what 'Virginia Woolf said, felt, did and wrote on almost every day of her life'.[60] Yet, the paradox is clear: for Lee, so much remains unsaid. It is possible to resist the biographic impulse to describe, sum up, package and sell a life as a coherent, planned whole.[61]

It should be remembered that the personal details and domestic anecdotes now so familiar to Bleek and Lloyd scholars were added to the archived collection relatively recently, much of them during the 1950s. Correspondence, documents and photographs lifting the veil on Wilhelm Bleek's nineteenth-century childhood on the Baltic coast, his family relationships and early adult years, as well as on the Lloyd sisters' childhoods, family ties and education, and on the courtship and marriage of Jemima and Wilhelm Bleek, were drawn from collections of letters tracked down to various archives in Europe during the 1950s by the UCT librarian Otto Spohr.[62] Yet, in the mid-1990s, a UCT Libraries archivist noted that almost nothing personal relating to Lucy Lloyd, or to Dorothea Bleek, seemed to have outlived them.[63] Notwithstanding that statement, a trove of personal letters written by Dorothea Bleek can be found in the Käthe Woldmann Papers, held alongside the Bleek Collection in the Manuscripts and Archives Department of UCT Libraries.[64] These letters, written in German to Käthe Woldmann in Switzerland, span almost 20 years and provide a view of Dorothea's thoughts that is not available in any other documentary record. The letters are referenced consistently throughout these pages and have allowed the construction of a fuller picture of Dorothea's research and writing, movements and methods, and how she reflected on these.

Dorothea's letters to Käthe date from 1921, spanning Europe's tumultuous recovery from World War I, through the Great Depression of the 1930s and World War II, until Dorothea's death in 1948. They reach beyond Dorothea's death to involve her niece Marjorie Scott in correspondence related to the eventual publishing of the bushman dictionary in 1956. But while the biographer's privileged access to otherwise private correspondence may be an invasion, as Mary Beard and others have asserted, the intimate space of the letter allowed Dorothea to relax and express herself freely.[65] This has infinitely enriched this project of life-writing and enabled a more expansive presentation of a history of ideas.

No doubt Dorothea and Käthe were brought together through their shared fascination with bushman folklore and art. As will be seen throughout this book, their correspondence reveals an ongoing conversation addressing details of bushman language, cosmology and belief. It also gives insight into negotiations that eventually culminated in the publication of a German translation of Bleek and Lloyd folk tales in Basel, Switzerland. Käthe Woldmann's edited translations, titled *Das wahre Gesicht des Buschmannes in seinen Mythen und Märchen* appeared in 1938.[66] During the time of her correspondence with Dorothea, Käthe lived in Dornach, near Basel. Yet her ties to southern Africa were strong – her brother owned a farm in the then Orange Free State, and their correspondence confirms that Dorothea met Käthe's brother and niece on their farm while on a fieldwork excursion near Winburg in 1928.[67] Dorothea had apparently also met Käthe at an earlier time, although exactly where and when is not specified.[68]

Twenty years of regular correspondence has provided nuggets of information which has allowed this biography to be fashioned as a continuous progression from the beginning to the end of a life, even though unknowability remains at the core. The Bleek–Woldmann letters plot the course of a slowly developing friendship and interest in the domestic detail of each respective life. Throughout, Dorothea continued to address her friend as 'Miss Woldmann', and she signed herself 'D.F. Bleek', and sometimes 'Doris Bleek', 'Your (girl)friend' or 'Your loyal Doris Bleek'.[69] Without the Woldmann letters, there would be little to say about Dorothea's domestic arrangements beyond that she lived with her sister Helma and family at La Rochelle in Newlands, near Cape Town. In her letters to Woldmann, Dorothea noted details about her nieces (Helma's children Marjorie and Dorothy). Her oldest niece (Marjorie) married a cousin with business interests in Buenos Aires and went to settle there, but came back to deliver her baby in Cape Town.[70] The other niece (Dorothy) taught at a school in Cape Town, before marrying a British officer and going to live in India.[71] In her turn, Woldmann wrote about her brother and his children.[72] Besides their mutual friend Lötte Reinbach, Woldmann also kept in contact with Dorothea's sister Mabel Jaeger.[73] The letters reveal that Woldmann battled with ill health, possibly a form of rheumatism, throughout her life.[74] On the other hand, most of Dorothea's life in Cape Town was lived in a family home shared with her sister Helma (Bright) and her family. Correspondence shows that she was close to both of her nieces. Dorothy died of a brain tumour at the age of 31, but Marjorie Bright (Scott) remained extremely close to her 'Aunt Doris'. As a young woman, she helped her aunt record rock art from sites in the mountains close to Cape Town. Much later, when an established academic herself, she stepped in to make sure that the bushman dictionary was published after Dorothea's death.

Finally, a larger context for this biography-writing project is the flowering of the biographic genre as a means of narrating the past, and as a mode of writing in literary studies, in anthropology and other social sciences, and in feminist critique more generally.[75] For South Africa at least, the University of the Western Cape historian Ciraj Rassool has noted that '[h]eroic biography [has] become part of the order of society' and that 'biographic concepts of history' are expressed in 'virtually all spheres of life'.[76] In post-apartheid South Africa in particular, Rassool has argued that 'a biographic character was being given to the cultural landscape, with the life of leaders a central focus'.[77] Not only was biography, told in terms of individual lives, being used to narrate the past as a heroic struggle and a story of triumph over adversity, but this literary form was also being used as a means of nation building. Indeed, biography, 'conceived of in... conventional ways, [has been] confirmed as one of the chief modes of negotiating the past in the public domain, and [has become] a central feature of stories of resistance and reconciliation, recovered as the basis for nation-building in the new South Africa'.[78] Moreover, the biographic tradition in South Africa has taken on a particular – and gendered – character in which the focus has been on the lives of (mostly male) leaders and past struggle heroes.[79] Where 'the concepts of greatness and exemplary lives [have] seemingly seeped into the very veins of South African state and society since the 1990s', there is little place for biography writing aimed at exposing the contradictions and instabilities which underlie heroic life stories.[80] As far as male lives are concerned, their histories of thought have been subsumed within this 'political' context where public lives are portrayed at the expense of the private. Where women feature as biographic subjects, it is often within a literary or social perspective, although there are some exceptions.[81]

Feminist historians Dea Birkett and Julie Wheelwright suggest there are very few biographies of female figures, a scarcity that has crossed national boundaries.[82] They suggest that biography writing poses particular problems for feminist scholars when faced with the 'unpalatable facts', limitations and contradictions that are inherent within the character of the woman being portrayed. One way of addressing this problem is not to present a 'simple feminist heroine' but to write portraits of 'women rooted in their time' complete with the contradictions and challenges they faced.[83] The possibility for feminist scholarship rests in its ability to resist the distillation of a personality into a monolithic whole.[84] Instead of succumbing to pressure to portray the 'real' person, any good biography, feminist or not, should 'firmly grasp the cup of plenty that a person's life and their contemporaries' view of it represents'.[85] It is in this spirit that the life of Dorothea Bleek is here presented.

1 | Colonial childhood, European learning

Philosophy is just not my cup of tea. Of all the words of Goethe's that mean the most to me, are the ones he put into Mephisto's mouth:
Grey, dearest friend, is all theory,
And green is life's golden tree.[1]

Dorothea Bleek was born on 26 March 1873, the fourth in a line of five daughters. Soon after she was born, her family moved from their home, The Hill, to their new residence a short distance away in the same village of Mowbray, just outside colonial Cape Town. The rambling new property, called Charlton House, was located across from the existing student apartment complex, now known as Forest Hill, in the Main Road. Demolished in the 1960s to make way for a teachers' training college, Charlton House was just a few blocks from the Baxter Theatre in Rondebosch, on the edge of the middle and upper campuses of UCT, where Dorothea would one day hold an honorary readership.[2]

Dorothea was born into an unusual domestic situation. Her father, Wilhelm, was widely known within European intellectual circles despite his distant location at the Cape Colony. By the early 1870s his networks and correspondents included the leading thinkers and social scientists of the era, including his cousin the evolutionist and naturalist Ernst Haeckel, the philologist Max Müller, Charles Darwin and the English biologist Thomas Huxley. At the time of Dorothea's birth, Wilhelm's study of the 'click languages' of southern Africa had progressed, as had the process of collecting folklore from bushman prisoners who had been sentenced, mostly for stock theft and poaching, but in one case for murder, to hard labour at the Breakwater Prison. Some of the prison buildings, albeit repurposed, can still be seen along Portswood Road, close to Cape Town's glitzy V&A Waterfront entertainment and shopping complex. Wilhelm had obtained permission from the colonial government to have selected prisoners live at his home so that he could work intensively with them to study their language, folklore and cosmology. As is well known, Lucy Lloyd, the sister of Wilhelm's wife Jemima, became involved in the project. From early on, Lucy assisted Wilhelm with interviews and transcriptions and in time became schooled in the /Xam language and its nuanced phonetics. Lucy continued the project after Wilhelm Bleek's early death in 1875. She extended Wilhelm's narrow interests in grammar and folklore (and, ultimately, human origins), and recorded in her notebooks information about the bushmen's daily life, including hunting practices, the use of the environment, the harvesting of plants, the curing of skins, the production of household objects and materials, poison making, and details of cosmologies and belief systems.[3]

Lucy would become Dorothea's mentor and teacher, and the two collaborated on the publishing of *Specimens of Bushman Folklore* in 1911, the first public offering of tales from the Bleek and Lloyd notebooks.[4] Dorothea's mother, Jemima, contributed two notebooks to the collection, but her larger role was supportive. She continued to run the household and to support Lucy in the research project for nearly a decade following the death of Wilhelm. Also helping out, and a permanent fixture in this female-dominated household following Wilhelm's death, was the older Lloyd sister Frances (Fanny), who was Lucy Lloyd's constant companion.[5] Fanny took care of the youngest Bleek daughter, Helma (Hermione), who was born in December 1875, a few months after Wilhelm had died, leaving Jemima grief-stricken.

As an infant and toddler, Dorothea's awareness of her father must have been vague and later influenced by the memories of her mother and older siblings. Her babyhood would have been shadowed by her father's illness and her mother's worry. Wilhelm's health, never excellent, had deteriorated in the years preceding his death at the age of 49. He died in the early hours of 17 August 1875 when Dorothea was just three years old. The records confirm that Jemima was shattered by her husband's death, and that she was incapacitated by grief for months afterwards.[6] One can only imagine the atmosphere in the home during Dorothea's early years. Dia!kwain, the /Xam man who was living at Charlton House at the time, was sensitive to the sadness. Stories recorded by Lucy early in August narrate Dia!kwain's presentiments of death.[7] After Wilhelm died, Dia!kwain told a story about an owl visiting Charlton House, interpreting this as a visit by his 'master' to check on his little ones.[8]

Nevertheless, the 'bushman' work continued. The birth of Dorothea's youngest sister, Helma, in December 1875 may have brought some relief to the bereaved household. Dorothea would have been nearly five years old and much more aware of what was going on around her when /Han≠kass'o returned to Mowbray at the request of Lucy Lloyd. The family would have said goodbye to Dia!kwain and welcomed another set of interviewees, this time a Korana family, into their home.[9] Piet Lynx and his family stayed for close to a year, allowing Lucy to gather samples of their language. They were part of a rather more itinerant series of interviewees who were drawn on during this time. By now, Lucy's research methods had expanded to include the use of drawings, and sketches made by Dia!kwain and /Han≠kass'o entered the collection.[10] As far as Dorothea's biography is concerned, it is difficult to resist the temptation to mark these months and years as central moments in influencing the later tone and direction of her scholarship.

In the absence of documentary evidence, however, and given her location as a young girl in Victorian Mowbray, one can only imagine what kinds of interactions the six-year-old Dorothea would have had with the !Kung children who arrived in 1879. !Nanni, Tamme, /Uma and Da were from Damaraland (in what is now northern Namibia/southern Angola). The refugee boys were left in the care of Lucy by the explorer W. Coates Palgrave so that she could collect samples of bushman languages from the northern reaches of southwestern Africa, a project that had been part of Wilhelm Bleek's research agenda from the beginning.[11] Of all the interlocutors visiting the household, it was the presence of these youngsters that perhaps made the biggest impression on the young Dorothea. First, they were closest to her in age. Second, Lucy encouraged them to draw and sketch, and the young Dorothea may have been allowed to participate, or she may have watched as they produced the watercolours and drawings for which they are now most widely remembered. While in the Bleek household, the boys made illustrations of the flora, fauna and folklore of their home countries (Figure 1.3). These were annotated in detail by Lucy Lloyd.[12] The oldest, !Nanni, produced a map of his home country (Figure 1.4). He also told stories about his home to Lucy Lloyd. The youngest child, Da, remained in the Mowbray household until 1884.

So it is certain that the young Dorothea heard the !Kung language being spoken during the two or more years the youngsters lived at Charlton House. These years could have been crucial ones in directing the young Dorothea to her later scholarship. Dorothea gained further familiarity with !Kung vocabulary and grammar as she helped Lucy though the arduous process of editing and indexing a small percentage of the notebook texts prior to their publication in 1911. It may have been at that time that Dorothea learned of the boys' traumatic removal from their families and land and their insertion into the colonial economy. Perhaps that was the first time she properly looked at the drawings (and Lucy's annotations) produced by the youngsters, and closely examined the map that !Nanni had sketched of his country. In any case, Dorothea must at that stage have developed an ear for their language that was reinforced when helping Lucy with the manuscript for *Specimens*, and again years later when in the field. Dorothea's fieldwork from 1910 onwards suggests a level of familiarity with the languages that she was able to build on during subsequent trips.

Dorothea's association with the !Kung youngsters came to an end in her 11th year, when Jemima and her daughters left for Europe. Some details are available in the record to flesh out imaginings of what their life in Germany was like. Correspondence suggests the family had settled in Berlin by June 1884.[13] A studio portrait of Jemima and her daughters taken in Bonn confirms they were in Germany by 1886 (Figure 1.5). Family history suggests that the move may always have been part of Wilhelm and Jemima's planning. It was motivated by Jemima's desire that her daughters should, with the support of Wilhelm's relatives, receive the best education possible.[14] Jemima's support of Lucy's 'bushman researches' at Mowbray had delayed this move by almost 10 years. By then, the financial strain of having to support a large household with almost no income made the trip back to Europe a necessity.[15]

In Europe

Jemima and her daughters were able to draw on the support of members of Wilhelm's family in Germany. They set up home in Charlottenburg, a suburb of Berlin, but, according to correspondence and photographs in the collection, they also spent time in Bonn. They remained involved in the bushman work and continued to support Lucy, who, with Frances, travelled to Europe and London in 1887 to begin the process of publishing *Specimens*.[16] The Germany the family returned to in the 1880s was vastly different from the country their father had left three decades before. The post-1850s surge in industrialisation had seen rapid urbanisation as thousands moved to the cities. German universities had become world centres of study in both the humanities and the sciences. It was in this environment of growing affluence, urbanism, cosmopolitanism and intellectual vibrancy that Dorothea and her sisters completed their schooling and tertiary education. The family divided their domestic lives between Berlin and Clarens (Switzerland), spending six months of the year in each city.[17] According to notes recorded in the 1980s by Dorothea's niece Marjorie, the Bleek daughters 'went to school in both countries, becoming fluent in French as well as German, while speaking English at home'.[18] Years later, in correspondence with the Wits musicologist Percival Kirby, Dorothea would agree with his suggestion that 'bushman singing' resembled Alpine yodelling, remembering the 'very musical yodelling [she] used to hear in Switzerland & the Tyrol'.[19]

Family records show that each of the sisters achieved high levels of tertiary education. Margarethe (Margie) attended medical school in Zurich, but died in Italy on 16 December 1902 at the age of 31, of a fever contracted during her training.[20] The youngest, Wilhelmina (Helma), born in 1875 just months after her father's death, studied music and trained as a concert pianist.[21] Helma would return to South Africa, where she married and raised her family in Cape Town. She and Dorothea shared the family home, La Rochelle, in Newlands for most of their lives. Mabel (May) married Albert Jaeger in Berlin in 1899 and settled in Halle, which became part of East Germany after World War II. She died there in 1953.[22] Details are scarce regarding Edith Bleek. We know that she assisted with the editing and production of *Specimens*, and can surmise that she returned to South Africa with Jemima, Dorothea and Helma in 1904.[23] Edith and Dorothea collaborated to produce an essay for Helen Tongue's book in 1909.[24] But beyond that, the archive is silent.

Intellectual influences

There is little detail in Dorothea's papers regarding her teenage years and schooling apart from a single photograph that suggests that at some point she attended boarding school in Bonn. What is known is that she trained as a teacher and specialised in linguistic studies. Family memory suggests that Dorothea attended lectures at the School of Oriental Studies in Berlin and took classes in African languages in London, although no indication of courses competed and/or certificates obtained survive.[25]

Such uncertainties are intriguing when they are considered in the context of the intellectual climate of late-nineteenth-century Europe that formed the background to Dorothea's studies. Again, a single anonymous photograph (Figure 1.6) offers the suggestion that Dorothea moved with confidence in male-dominated circles and that she may have attained a level of scholarly recognition in Germany before her return to South Africa. Details are scarce, but the photograph album in which the undated image is preserved suggests it was taken at an 'anthropological or linguistics conference in Berlin'. The annotation was contributed by Marjorie Scott when she compiled the Bleek family album in the 1980s. It ties in with other documents, including research notes, published work and private correspondence, all of which suggest that Dorothea's commitment to the continued study of bushman language and culture throughout her life signalled her adherence to a particular aspect of the German humanist tradition that she may have imbibed during her early adult years – a moment in her early adult life that is caught and frozen in this intriguing photograph.

As this exploration of her research notes and publishing will demonstrate, Dorothea was wedded to fieldwork and observation as essential elements of the project of gathering knowledge that was observable and objective. She was suspicious of the 'armchair scholars' of Europe, and her faith in fieldwork may have been influenced by an implicit understanding that the human body could be used to record evidence in the field with the precision of a scientific instrument.[26] Given the timing of her tertiary education and her location in Germany in the 1880s and 1890s, Dorothea in all likelihood was exposed to the ideas of German thinkers and philosophers of the late Romantic period, among them the ethnologist Adolf Bastian. It is reasonable to suggest that Dorothea's early fieldwork in southern Africa should be located within the trajectories of early German philology and the emerging sciences of ethnology (*Ethnologie*) and anthropology, as well as a fascination with the *Volksgeist* (the idea that a people or nation could be identified by their unique spirit) theories of Johann Gottfried Herder. In the German tradition in which Dorothea found herself immersed, it was thought that language in particular provided a window on cultural difference and an indication of the essence of particular ('natural') lifestyles that needed to be sampled and correlated with their sophisticated ('cultured') counterparts so that a broader vision of humanity could be obtained.[27] These ideas animated the cosmopolitanist and humanist intellectual landscape in Germany during the late nineteenth century, when Dorothea would have been taking classes in Berlin and London.[28] While the precise details of Dorothea's education in Europe have not survived, a reading of her field notebooks – and, most persuasively, her private correspondence – suggests that her intellectual grounding and field practice followed the methods advocated by Bastian.

A crucial figure in the establishment of German anthropology during the nineteenth century, Adolf Bastian spent more than 25 years from the 1850s onwards travelling through the newly colonised world. Eventually, his vast collection of ethnographic material was shared between Berlin's Royal Museum and the Museum of Folk Art, which had been established to house his collections.[29] The aim of Bastian's travels was to unearth the 'elementary ideas' (*Elementargedanken*) of peoples that were hidden behind humanity's cultural diversity. These were not easy to discern. However, they could be observed through careful study of 'folk ideas' (*Völkergedanken*), which were patterns of thought of 'natural' groups of people that arose through their interactions with the environment or through contact with other groups. Such thought patterns would best emerge within identifiable zones such as river valleys, coastlines and mountain passes (and in Dorothea's case deserts), where geographical and historical influences shaped 'natural' peoples.[30] For Bastian, these interactions were the basis of all historical development and human history, and he argued that understanding the unique geographical and environmental contexts in which each culture (or *Volksgeist*) took shape was crucial for gaining insight into the universal character of the human being.[31] Thus, the analysis of differences among 'natural' people (*Naturvölker*), who were defined as the most isolated and simple societies without written

COLONIAL CHILDHOOD, EUROPEAN LEARNING

language, would reveal a set of seminal ideas from which every civilisation had grown.[32] These observations of the objective and 'natural' would provide evidence for the formulation of empirical laws regarding the effects of environmental and social conditions on the human mind. This model would in turn allow the construction of a scale that could be applied to the study of 'cultural' peoples (*Kulturvölker*), who were literate with a recorded past that historians and philologists could examine.[33]

The US historian H. Glenn Penny has described a generous 'cosmopolitanism' as one characteristic of the development of *Ethnologie* in Imperial Germany. This cosmopolitan spirit was, he suggests, swept aside in the early twentieth century by a wave of thinking that led to the development of new schemes for understanding society through the classification of groups and cultures along racial and evolutionary lines.[34] Andrew Zimmerman has argued for the presence of a strong 'anti-humanist' strain in *Ethnologie* as it took root in the burgeoning intellectual environment of nineteenth-century Germany that included a rejection of traditional concepts of humanity and a denial of human capacity to control actions and events. Zimmerman highlights the conditions in which objective methods of natural science were applied to the study of humans, and the processes of 'othering' (portraying certain groups of people as fundamentally different or alien) at work in German *Ethnologie*.[35] Grafted onto this empiricist and determinist mode was Dorothea's personal expression of familial loyalty that was played out in her (partly) nostalgic and sentimental research journey of language sampling and object collection among people she believed were 'dying out'. This research would in time contribute to the construction of the notion of 'bushman' as a formal field of study in the South African academic landscape as it emerged during the early decades of the twentieth century.

Dorothea's southern African research and fieldwork agendas suggest that she may have been influenced by this contradictory mix of cosmopolitan humanism on the one hand and the stringent objectivism derived from the natural sciences on the other. In the field, these contradictory approaches may be observed in her empathetic interactions with 'natural' people in contrast with other activities such as the measuring of body parts and the collection of human remains. Such modes of thought and action mingled with her childhood memories of the 'natural' people she had known in her own home. In addition, there would have been the emotional layer drawn from the association with an idealised father whom she barely knew, and with the childhood memories she shared with her sisters. Another influential layer of learning would be the many years of working on the notebook texts with Lucy, initially while they were in Europe, and then for a year or two back in Cape Town as Dorothea prepared for her first expeditions into the field.

A close reading of her research notes and fieldwork programme reveals a strong indication of Dorothea's insistence on the importance of fieldwork and the careful and comprehensive collection of as many samples and objects as possible from the field. Alongside her language work, a variety of objects now held at the McGregor Museum in Kimberley, the Iziko South African Museum in Cape Town, and in the Percival R. Kirby Collection at UCT's South African College of Music provide material evidence of Dorothea's inclusive approach to sampling.[36] Among many other objects, she collected beaded aprons and bags, ankle rattles made from springbok ears, a musical bow, ostrich-eggshell bracelets, hair ornaments, spears, and bows and arrows. Dorothea's letters indicate that she actively gathered materials and ethnographic information for Dr Louis Péringuey, director of the South African Museum in Cape Town from 1906. She also sent material to her friend and colleague Maria Wilman, the Cambridge-trained geologist, botanist and scholar of rock art who became director of the newly established McGregor Museum in Kimberley in 1908.

Dorothea's research methods resemble what the British social anthropologist Adam Kuper has described as the 'laundry list' approach to fieldwork favoured by Franz Boas, the German-born student of Adolf Bastian. While Dorothea travelled in southern Africa, Boas worked among the Inuit of the Pacific Northwest at the start of a career that would establish him as the founding figure of cultural anthropology in North America. Kuper, in his work on the intellectual history of anthropology, has suggested that Boas considered it best to let people 'speak' for themselves.[37] To achieve this goal, Boas assembled a 'magpie's collection of ethnographic titbits, ranging from accounts of ceremonies to descriptions of technical procedures, and including even gooseberry pie recipes'.[38]

Following a similar style, Dorothea collected snippets of folk tales from interviewees and paid particular attention to recording genealogies (family lineages), information about ritual dances and scarification practices, and historical traditions and myths, on which, in the German tradition, she (as her father and aunt had before her) and Boas laid great value.[39] Dorothea's 32 field notebooks offer a fragmentary mix of vocabulary and phrases in one or other of the languages she was sampling at the particular moment, with translations in English, interspersed at random intervals with biographical and genealogical notes about the particular person being interviewed, or about the person's immediate family and/or 'tribe'. Fragments of ethnographic information were common and concerned such topics as stars and their names, weather and seasons, and aspects of daily life including how food was obtained, cooked and eaten, the making of honey beer, ritual scarification, rites of initiation, how animal skins were cured for use as clothing, the preparation of sinews for use as binding, how poisons were made, and how and when dances were held.[40]

In regard to language sampling as well as documenting rock art, Dorothea's emphasis mirrored that of Boas. Both favoured the sampling and collection of materials rather than comparison or interpretation. Dorothea stated this preference unequivocally on several occasions in her private correspondence. The primary task was observation, collection and salvage. Others could do the comparative work later. In June 1928, for instance, she wrote: 'For me…the collection and recording of the remaining Bushman culture is of greater value than the exercise of comparing. That can be left to later generations to deal with, but what we do not record now will be lost forever.'[41] She reiterated this emphasis in November of the same year: 'I certainly do still have myths and legends, which have not been published, and a few that have not been translated. Over a period of time I am hoping to publish them all, however it is not possible to do everything at once, and when I am offered an opportunity to verify the language and customs from a living Bushman tribe, I defer the processing work on the data already collected.'[42] And once more in April of the following year: 'My goal is to write up as many Bushman languages and literatures as possible, before it is too late. The comparative work others can do later.'[43]

Dorothea's continued embrace of the study of language suggests she may have been influenced by an additional strand of scholarship in the early development of psychology that emerged in Germany in the mid-1800s.[44] There is nothing in what remains of Dorothea's written record that can confirm that she sympathised with the work of Heymann

Steinthal (1823–1899) and Moritz Lazarus (1824–1903), both of whom taught (philology and philosophy respectively) at the University of Berlin in the second half of the nineteenth century, and are credited with inaugurating the discipline of *Völkerpsychologie* (a branch of psychology based on research into communal and cultural products of human nature including religion, language and mythology) in the German academy.[45] However, Dorothea's research strategies suggest that, while following the methods inaugurated by Bastian as far as extensive fieldwork, detailed observation and the collection of objects belonging to 'natural peoples' were concerned, she (as did Boas) regarded the study of language as an essential component to the complete understanding of the *Volksgeist* (intrinsic spirit or culture) of a people.

It is tempting to argue that Dorothea may have been following the thinking of Steinthal and Lazarus, who sought to contest the anti-linguistic tone of the groundswell of materialist German anthropology taking hold after the 1870s.[46] It has been contended that, working against the increasing marginalisation of language by anthropologists bent on generating knowledge based on what could be viewed objectively, Steinthal sought to reframe linguistics as central to a human-centred study of 'natural peoples'.[47] For Steinthal, the social and bodily contexts of language provided privileged avenues through which an inquiry into the core of humanity in all its aspects could proceed.[48] There are moments in Dorothea's research and writings that suggest she was sympathetic to this line of thinking. But again, there are no direct references in any of her manuscripts, papers or publications to either of the proponents of *Völkerpsychologie* in Imperial Germany, nor to its dissenters such as Gustav Fritsch. Whether the debates around *Völkerpsychologie*, hardening materialist approaches to anthropology, and the place of linguistics within these seeped into her consciousness or impacted on her thinking as she completed her language studies and teachers' training in Berlin and London in the closing years of the nineteenth century remains tantalisingly unknown. That her field practices and scholarship decades later seemed to reflect and rehearse these older debates is intriguing and suggestive, and reason to ponder on the complexities of her archive.

Trips and notebooks

Dorothea's research was profoundly influenced by her late father's investigations into the languages of Africa. Also influential were the months and years she spent under the mentorship of Lucy in Europe, practising the /Xam and !Kung languages, learning about bushman cosmology, and translating notebook texts while preparing *Specimens* for publication.[49] Wilhelm Bleek had attempted to find a link between the languages of southern Africa (in particular the Nama language) and the Hamitic languages of North Africa and beyond, which he distinguished on the basis of their gender-denoting structure. While many of his propositions are now discredited, including his argument that the greater number of click sounds or plosive phonemes in /Xam meant that it was an 'ancient' language spoken by 'less civilised' peoples, these ideas remained current when Dorothea began her fieldwork in the early 1900s.[50] By the end of her time in Europe, Dorothea would have gained a deep knowledge of /Xam and !Kung folklore and built on the conversational introduction of her childhood, gaining fluency and grammatical knowledge in both languages. But she was not planning to stop at text-based study in her chosen field. In line with the approach of Bastian, fieldwork was to become an essential component of her research.

Carrying this mix of humanist ideas and theories of language expansion, Dorothea returned to Cape Town early in the twentieth century. She was a young adult now, aged just 31. Her mother and sisters Helma and Edith followed Dorothea back to South Africa in 1904 or 1905. It was a different country to the one they had left some 20 years previously. The nation was recovering from the devastating effects of the South African War. Being somewhat geographically removed from the conflict, the scholarly centre had remained in the erstwhile colonial centre of Cape Town. But there were links countrywide. Discourse remained dominated by a clique of male intellectuals whose late-nineteenth-century interest in the age and geology of southern Africa and the fossils and rocks buried there continued to hold sway.[51]

As soon as she was back on southern African soil, Dorothea took a teaching position at Rocklands Girls' High School at Cradock in the eastern Cape. Here she had an opportunity to take her bushman knowledge into the field for the first time. With fellow Rocklands teacher Helen Tongue, Dorothea travelled to rock art sites in the mountains to the north and east, including those in Basutoland (now Lesotho) and the Orange River Colony (now the Free State province). This series of trips, described in detail in Chapter 2, lasted from late 1905 to 1907. Helen and Dorothea exhibited their rock art copies in Cape Town and London in 1908, and published them the following year in a collaborative book titled *Bushman Paintings*, which presented rock art copies 'mainly copied' by Helen Tongue and accompanied by 'explanations and remarks' by Dorothea Bleek.[52]

Bushman Paintings was a handsome publication containing loose-leaf colour plates and produced in a coffee-table format that was larger in size and more impressive in colour reproduction than any previously published book on rock art. The preface was written by Henry Balfour, at the time curator of the Pitt Rivers Museum at Oxford and president of the Royal Anthropological Institute. In addition, Dorothea and her oldest sister, Edith, contributed an essay based on their memories of the bushmen that had lived in their childhood home.[53] Among other anecdotes, the sisters recounted Wilhelm Bleek's first interlocutor, /A!kungta, making and playing a home-made violin, and his heroic battle, although he was outnumbered, with neighbourhood children at Mowbray. They remembered //Kabbo as a more philosophical and intense prisoner-interlocutor, and also how the men loved to 'come in and hear my mother play' the piano in the sitting room on Sundays. Such romanticised memories reflected the level to which the 'colonial bushmen' became civilised through affirmative contact with the Bleek family.

After the rock art exhibition at the Royal Anthropological Institute in London, Dorothea gave up her teaching position at Rocklands. It was time to return to Cape Town, to her family home, and to the bushman language and folklore she could glean from her aunt's wealth of first-hand experience and knowledge. There is no doubt that Dorothea was in proud attendance when Lucy Lloyd became the first woman to be awarded an honorary doctorate by UCT in 1913. Lucy died just a year later, on 31 August 1914, at the age of 79.

It was during this time of loss that Dorothea began her fieldwork programme. For the next two decades she would travel regularly. Her trips lasted anything from six weeks to six months. Sometimes she travelled alone, at other times with a friend or with other scholars or linguists. Following the death of her mother in 1909, Dorothea set out the next year for the small town of Prieska and the Kenhardt district in the northern Cape. In keeping with the family legacy of research, it is no surprise that Dorothea's first venture into the field was to the region from which her father's 'colonial bushmen' had come, and specifically to areas near Kenhardt, the village closest to the ancestral lands of Wilhelm's main interlocutor //Kabbo.[54] There Dorothea searched for descendants and relatives of the people her father and aunt had interviewed during the 1870s.

The earliest of Dorothea's notebooks in UCT's collection places her, in 1910, with her friends the Lanhams, whose farm Mount Temple was located in the Langeberg district north of Kenhardt in Griqualand West.[55] There, in September, she interviewed the Lanhams' servants. A notebook, inscribed with 'Langeberg Bushmen mostly met on Mr Lanham's farm Mount Temple', records that on 1 September 1910 she interviewed !Kwe /k ke, or Door-ki, as well as others.[56] The following day, Dorothea worked on vocabulary with Sabine, collecting words dealing with body parts (including eye, nose, mouth, cheeks, tooth, foot, leg), before moving on to animals (jackal, lion), family relationships (brother, sister, mother, grandmother), and then items of clothing and adornment (petticoat, *veldschoen*, cap, front apron, bracelet, necklace).[57] More or less following the layout that had been devised by her father and perfected by Lucy, Dorothea used the right-hand pages of her notebook for recordings, keeping the left-hand pages clear for notes and further translations, which in some cases were added years afterwards. Two weeks later, Dorothea began a second notebook, in which she recorded interviews with Dina, beginning on 14 September 1910.[58] Even at this stage, Dorothea's ability to fluently transcribe the languages orthographically is evident in her early notebooks.

Dorothea returned to Prieska the following year for another try at finding descendants of the family's 'colonial bushmen'. The language samples collected at Prieska and Kenhardt would later be included in Dorothea's 'Southern' (/Xam) classification along with the /Xam samples collected by Lucy and Wilhelm. On 11 August 1911, she interviewed Hokan (Janiki), Klaas and others at Prieska Location, reading them pages from *Specimens of Bushman Folklore*, which had been published earlier that year.[59] By good fortune, Dorothea's Prieska trip was extended when the raconteur, adventurer and skeleton-hunter 'Scotty Smith', more formally known as George St Leger Lennox, invited her to accompany him into the Kalahari. On

10 October she set off with Lennox, his daughter Hester, Dorothea's friend and fellow researcher Maria Wilman, and their wagon crew.[60] The trip by ox wagon 'through Gordonia to the lower Nossop' lasted six weeks, through November 1911.[61] It must have been a hot journey as they passed through the sandy desert landscapes north of Upington. Dorothea's research notes suggest they followed the tried and true route still in use by contemporary researchers 'in search of the San'.[62] Dorothea and her party followed the course of the Molopo River until its junction with the Kuruman, passing through Wit Draai close to the Botswana border, on contemporary maps still marked as a police post as it was in Dorothea's day. Here the party was able to post letters and to stock up on water for the remainder of the journey into hot and dry country.[63]

If the fragmented diary notes Dorothea recorded on the journey are anything to go by, the expedition combined research and conviviality with grave digging after dinner. An undated typescript among her papers, perhaps a piece typed up years later for submission to the press or notes for a radio interview, recalled the group spending evenings around the fireside being regaled by Lennox with exotic stories about horse stealing and diamond smuggling.[64] There was also a degree of grave robbing, instigated in all probability by international (and local) 'scientific' interest in the human remains of 'bushman' people.[65] Such skeletons were in great demand in the laboratories of physical anthropologists who believed these were 'living fossils' and primitive relics directly related to the earliest human beings. Lennox and Wilman may either coincidentally or by design have collaborated in a project of proactively acquiring human bones to participate in this trade, which in the opening decades of the twentieth century found rich pickings in the northern Cape. Dorothea participated in these nefarious activities, on some occasions not shying away from identifying the exhumed skeletons by name. The party was barely three days out of Upington when her research notes bluntly recorded 'found skeleton of young married Bushman woman, No.1, Griet, dug her up'. Earlier that very day they had 'sold coffee & tobacco & tea' and 'got bushman skeleton, butter & milk'.[66]

A few days later, on 15 October, the party 'outspanned' on private land identified as belonging to people named 'Van Niekerk'.[67] Dorothea's research notes record a 'digging party' setting out after dinner to graves that yielded a number of skeletons, including 'one very old…skeleton' that had 'fallen to pieces', as well as bones identified as those of a child and a woman.[68] Undeterred by the dust storm that blew up overnight, the grave robbing continued the following day, as Dorothea's research notes for Thursday 16 October 1911 record:

> Dug up 4 graves & found 2 skeletons, one man, one boy – both on Blauw'sland. Man lying flat, boy lying curled on his side in hole off graves. Miss Wilman found lots of stones, eggshell beads & implements in B. werfs. I found a few too in afternoon. We went on in late afternoon & again after supper. Outspanned on stream.[69]

That Dorothea was capable of invasive practices such as the exhumation and collection of human remains is not surprising given the complexities of German approaches to anthropology in which she had been immersed as a student. Part of the discipline of physical anthropology involved anthropometry, the study of the measurements and proportions of the human body. The drive to measure, document and classify the bodies and bones of people deemed 'primitive' and 'ancient' made ready use of emerging scientific technologies of observation, especially the camera. As her father had done previously, and as was common among her colleagues at the time, Dorothea produced photographs of naked human subjects. Her research notes record her efforts to convince unwilling subjects to pose naked for her, and there are instances where she co-opted fellow male travellers to intervene because she thought they would be better at facilitating this. Yet, while taking pictures of naked human subjects was an activity she pursued on later trips, it does not appear that collecting skeletons and human bones was something she repeated on any future occasion. Many of her anthropometric-inspired images remain in the Iziko South African Museum's ethnological collections, where they are classified according to 'ethnic type' and geographic region rather than by the name of the photographer. To my knowledge, none of these invasive photographs can be found in Dorothea's personal albums in UCT's Bleek Collection.[70]

Skeletons and naked bodies aside, it was on this second outing to the Kalahari that Dorothea had her first introduction to the /'Auni, whom she would later describe as living in their 'natural state…entirely without water "on the melon"'.[71] The opportunity to visit the people of the Nossop region could well have appeared heaven-sent. It provided a chance to experience for herself a landscape previously described – in words and by hearsay – by her beloved father. In 1862, in the course of his work as curator of the Cape governor Sir George Grey's book collection, Wilhelm Bleek had drawn up a formal vocabulary based on language samples gathered by the missionary J.G. Krönlein.[72] The samples had come from the very region that Dorothea was able to visit in person decades later – surely a bittersweet moment in which she felt the presence of her father. In his notes attached to the alpha-betised vocabulary, Wilhelm Bleek had made much of the dryness of the landscape, calling the people the 'Dorstveld Bushmen', and mentioning their reliance on the *tsāmā* melon ('tsamma' in English, *Citrullus lanatus*) as their only 'resource against thirst'. Some 50 years later, when she visited a place she called Schilpaddraai, in the vicinity of Tweerivieren in the southern Kalahari, Dorothea found the *tsāmā* in plentiful supply. She tried some and declared it 'very nice with sugar'.[73]

The party continued north along the Molopo River, reaching KyKy on 28 October. Here they stayed until 3 November, before returning via Tweerivieren to Upington on a journey that lasted a further three weeks. The party reached Upington on 22 November, after which Dorothea again visited her friends at Mount Temple. She spent the festive season in Kimberley, perhaps celebrating Christmas and New Year with Maria Wilman, and arrived back in Cape Town in mid-January 1912.

In 1913 Dorothea travelled to southern Botswana, then known as the Bechuanaland Protectorate, with her friend Margarethe Vollmer. As will be seen in Chapter 3, the young women travelled by rail to Lobatsi and thence by ox wagon to Kakia (now Khakhea) in the southern Kalahari, a tiny village situated roughly halfway between the regions now demarcated as the Kgalagadi Transfrontier Park to the north and the Khutse Game Reserve to the south-west. Here, Dorothea interviewed a number of 'Masarwa who were dwelling within walking distance of their Bechuana masters'.[74] The Kakia trip yielded a diary as well as two notebooks containing vocabulary and grammar.[75] It seems likely that World War I interrupted Dorothea's fieldwork programme, but in 1918 she again travelled to Griqualand West, Gordonia and the Langeberg regions.[76] A photograph in one of Dorothea's albums in the Bleek Collection at UCT records that she spent Christmas of 1919 in Bechuanaland.[77] There she interviewed prisoners at the Gaborone jail and travelled as far as Molepolole, where she spent time with Chief Sebele II. Her colleague (later the chair of African languages) at the School of African Life and Languages, G.P. Lestrade, accompanied her on this trip and appears in one of her photographs.[78]

At some point, possibly between the visits to Kakia and Griqualand West, Dorothea visited Lake Chrissie in the then eastern Transvaal, now the province of Mpumalanga, where her friends the Ralstons hosted her. The people of Lake Chrissie, she wrote, had no name for themselves other than 'Batwa', the Zulu and Swazi terms for 'Bushman'. But her research was hampered because she could not get an interpreter, and 'these Bushmen spoke neither English nor the Taal'.[79] Nevertheless, she was able to 'get just sufficient specimens of the language to place it among the others', as well as a founding narrative for the Lake Chrissie bushmen, and a series of folk tales related to the bushmen of the Highveld and their interactions with other groups, including 'white men' and 'Zulus'.[80]

Her next trips were to Sandfontein, east of Gobabis in the territory of South West Africa (now Namibia) in 1920–1922. As described in Chapter 4, Dorothea was invited by the government of the territory to join the South African Museum carrying out anthropological research on the bushmen in the region. For two successive summers, she spent three to four months at Sandfontein, as well as some time in Windhoek, where she interviewed prisoners at the local jail. These trips (from November 1920 to March 1921 and from November 1921 to March 1922) marked a seminal period in Dorothea's career. She was working for the government, in an early instance of the state involving linguists and other academics in their project to 'know' and control 'native' populations. Her notes record that the medical officer of the protectorate, Dr Louis Fourie, an amateur anthropologist who shared her interest in the bushmen of the region, made a disused police station at Sandfontein available to her for use as a research base.[81] Along with her camera, she used a phonograph to make recordings of sounds and songs on wax cylinders.

In 1925, Dorothea visited Angola for six months, travelling by river and overland with the Cambridge-trained botanist Mary Pocock. A sketch map found in one of her notebooks lists all the mission stations at which they stopped along the way. Dorothea's route through Angola may have been inspired by the !Kung children she remembered from her childhood, and by the stories they had told of their violent removal from their 'home countries' near Ngamiland in northern Namibia and southern Angola. The spectres of slavery and kidnapping feature regularly in her research notes here. Soon after this, during the second half of 1928, she set out on a six-week 'cave journey' through the foothills of the Drakensberg to retrace and verify the rock art reproductions made by George Stow. Her edited version of Stow's copies appeared in 1930. Both the cave journey and book are the subject of Chapter 5. Also in 1930, Dorothea went to Tanganyika (now Tanzania) for an unspecified length of time, most probably travelling by air on this occasion.

By 1930, Dorothea was at the height of her career. She had published two book-length studies that drew on her fieldwork up to that point. Her monograph titled *The Naron: A Bushman Tribe of the Central Kalahari* dealt with the Naron people she had studied while at Sandfontein. A second monograph, *Comparative Vocabularies of Bushman Languages*, described all the languages she had by then sampled, classified into three groups and mapped onto the landscape.[82] Her edited collection of George Stow's rock art reproductions would appear that year. Since 1923 she had been Honorary Reader in Bushman Languages at UCT. She had published many journal articles locally and in Germany. Her peers in the linguistic and anthropological fields in South African academies deferred to her on the topic of bushmen. In the acknowledgements to his 1930 book, Isaac Schapera, her younger colleague at the School of African Life and Languages, described her as 'our' foremost authority on 'bushmen' people, and thanked her for sharing her 'unrivalled knowledge' with him.[83] Later, in correspondence related to her bushman dictionary, the Wits linguist L.F. Maingard described her as 'one whom everybody recognises as the greatest authority on Bushman' and congratulated her for the 'mastery which stamps all your work'.[84] In 1932, Dorothea was president of Section E of the South African Association for the Advancement of Science (SAAAS), and in that year she gave as her presidential address a lecture on the current state of rock art in southern Africa.[85]

During the 1930s, the focus of Dorothea's scholarship shifted from rock art verification and language collection in the field to consolidating and publishing from the family legacy. Her background work on the bushman dictionary continued, and she regularly submitted articles to *Bantu Studies*. These submissions were translations, many by Dorothea herself, of notebook texts organised under the general title 'Customs and Beliefs of the /Xam Bushmen'. With editing and interpretation kept to a minimum across the series, the texts were presented in accordance with Dorothea's stated wish that translations from the collection of her father and aunt be 'simply offered to the world, without comments or interpretations in whatsoever form'.[86] Her concern that the scholars of Europe could misinterpret the texts of 'natural' people like the bushmen meant that Dorothea remained insistent that the notebook texts be allowed to speak for themselves.

There would be nine contributions in the series submitted to *Bantu Studies*. All of the contributions, like her 1929 article on folklore in the newly established journal *Africa*, made the point that animals loomed large in the folklore of the /Xam, and that humans were less prominent.[87] The first instalment concerned baboons, and in January 1930 Dorothea wrote to Käthe Woldmann that she was about to publish 'about the customs and superstitions of the Bushman as these relate to the baboon'.[88] It had always been part of her plan to publish as much as she could of the material that her father and aunt had collected.[89]

At the same time, she continued to work on the dictionary. This involved processing into manuscript form the lexicon left by her father and aunt – and adding material gathered during her own fieldwork, as well as language samples that had been recorded by a range of travellers, missionaries and lay linguists in the past, including the early French travellers Thomas Arbousset and François Daumas; the explorer of the south-western parts of southern Africa Siegfried Passarge; and the Rhenish missionary, linguist and historian Heinrich Vedder. After years of writing, editing and production, the dictionary finally appeared in 1956, eight years after Dorothea's death.

By looking at her excursions in retrospect, it is possible to trace a progression beginning with Dorothea's early trips, when she applied her text-based study of bushmen to the field for the first time, through increasingly formalised applications of method and practice in regard to extracting knowledge from the field. From her first field trip in search of rock art with Helen

Tongue, she drew on her familiarity with the notebook texts to interpret some of the pictures she saw on the rocks before her. In so doing, she established a methodology for rock art interpretation that remains an integral facet of the discipline. Dorothea also used her knowledge of George Stow's rock art reproductions (which she had inherited from Lucy) in her interpretations of rain bulls and other imaginary creatures that she saw painted on the rocks, and she identified the figure of the trickster god /Kaggen in at least one recorded instance (Figure 2.2).

Again following Stow, Dorothea argued that the bushmen's previously idyllic lifestyle and their free access to the landscape had made possible their artistic skill. For Dorothea, the art represented the people's vanishing history, and she described the paintings as historical documents left by the bushmen themselves.[90] It was a view that she stuck to and defended throughout her life. In keeping with the salvage paradigm that motivated her work, Dorothea argued that the bushmen's painting tradition was dying out as they were – due to the pressures of 'black' encroachment, the arrival of 'white' settlers, and the violent conflicts engendered by competition over land and water.

Life at home

Two private letters, both addressed to her niece and sometime research assistant Marjorie Bright Scott, provide but a sliver of information about Dorothea's domestic life that encompassed and exceeded her bushman work. From these letters one learns that, in the late 1930s at least, Dorothea led a busy life in Cape Town, one that was perhaps typical of a suburban spinster of independent means during the interwar years. Family memories add the information that she was an active bridge player and loved playing croquet.[91] Dorothea lived at La Rochelle, a Victorian villa on Campground Road in Newlands that she had bought years previously in partnership with her brother-in-law Henry Hepburn Bright. Their joint purchase in 1926 followed the sale of Charlton House, and continued the previous shared ownership. Bright's death just four years later meant the partnership devolved to his widow, Dorothea's youngest sister, Helma.[92] The large property of three acres would remain the Bleek-Bright family home for the next 21 years. La Rochelle turned out to be the site of

Dorothea's most productive years. She lived there with Helma and her two daughters Marjorie and Dorothy until Helma's death on 30 May 1947.[93] At that point, the property was sold at less than market value in order for it to be preserved for cultural and limited social purposes as an Athenaeum, and it remains so to this day.[94]

La Rochelle is still standing, hemmed in now by the Newlands rugby and cricket stadiums as well as office blocks which have taken the place of the large grounds which previously surrounded the house. A sense of its former graciousness remains, but there is no trace of the layout or ambience of the rooms previously inhabited by Dorothea or the members of her extended family. Nothing remains of the study in which she worked, although a sketch plan of the house suggests it was a large bay-windowed room at the front of the house, to the right of the entrance hall, with a superb view of Devil's Peak in the Table Mountain chain.[95] Presumably it was here that Dorothea kept the precious notebooks of her father and aunt ranged on a sturdy shelf, perhaps with portraits of some of the /Xam interlocutors hanging on the walls alongside.[96]

The letter Dorothea wrote in early December 1937 to her niece Marjorie affords a rare moment of insight in a life otherwise defined by its scholarly project, and allows a different register of engagement with Dorothea's biography.[97] Marjorie was married and living in Argentina. She was due to visit Cape Town to deliver her baby.[98] In contrast to Dorothea's correspondence with Käthe Woldmann, here there is not a mention of her bushman work. Instead, the scope is domestic. Dorothea communicates a sense of the social importance of UCT's Graduation Day for Rondebosch families of the time. On 9 December 1937, graduation was held in UCT's Jameson Hall (as is still the case, although now many more students are involved). Dorothea attended the ceremony accompanied by Helma and Dorothy, as well as several friends and relatives, whom Dorothea and her niece transported in their vehicles. The Bleeks knew several of the 210 students who were capped on that day. Dorothea's letter records her irritation at the 'twice too long and very boring address' given by Professor Campbell. He took up so much time with 'stupid statistics' that the vice chancellor and principal J.C. Beattie was able to speak for only a few minutes at the end of the proceedings.

The ceremony ran on until nearly one o'clock, to Dorothea's horror. Then there were further delays going home through traffic caused by the construction of extensions to the geology building, and excavations 'beyond the psychology block for the Bolus Herbarium'.[99]

A second letter, dated 7 September 1939, shows a deliberate intention to avoid the politics of the outside world.[100] Again addressing Marjorie, Dorothea stated that she would steer clear of 'public news'. That Marjorie could read in the paper. Instead, Dorothea would 'confine [herself] to the private little events'. Among these were a disastrous trip to Darling in her car, which developed engine trouble and had to be abandoned, as well as the visit of a young friend with her infant son, whom Dorothea declared to be a 'fine fat big fellow, but very backward'. Recording trips to the 'bioscope', visits of family and friends, and the detail of household furniture relocations geared to accommodating a stream of stay-over guests, the letter offers a view of the mundane transactions of Dorothea's domestic life. The start of World War II on 1 September, just a few days before she sat down to write this letter to Marjorie, was described as the 'momentous Friday 1st'. Yet despite Dorothea's efforts to avoid mentioning it, the world and the war intruded, reaching suburban Rondebosch via friends and relatives. For instance, 'Tom', who had arrived from England on the *Dunvegan Castle* and came to dinner that same evening, was not sure which route would be followed on his return voyage as the outbreak of war could potentially disrupt shipping through the Suez Canal. And 'Jim', 'inspanned to do meteorological survey work' at Simon's Town and 'on loan' from the 'Rhodesian Government', would stay at Newlands until there was more certainty about his immediate future. As it turned out, Dorothea's letter reported that Tom's boat was turned back at East London, with 'Alice and Anson' flying in from Durban to see Tom, necessitating further furniture shuffling at La Rochelle and swelling the numbers at dinner to eight from the 'usual three'.

Dorothea's disastrous road trip to Darling to view the famous spring flowers received as much attention as the disruptions caused by war.[101] Car troubled intervened in the planned journey to Yzerfontein on the West Coast close to Cape Town. Dorothea and her party of friends had to leave the car at a local garage for repairs, and settle for lunch and a walk in the fields at Darling.[102] Then the garage owner, Hein Vollmer, drove them back to Cape Town. (This moment provides an intriguing link with Dorothea's field research – is this Vollmer a relative of the Margarethe Vollmer with whom she travelled to Kakia in 1913? Beyond describing Vollmer as an 'old acquaintance', the letter gives no clue.)

The two letters described here provide a hint of the detail of Dorothea's home life, and they give a sense of the closeness of the relationship between Dorothea and Marjorie.[103] It is this closeness that explains Marjorie and her husband Dick's later determination to see 'Aunt D's' dictionary through its excruciating last years of production.

As this biography and history of ideas will show, Dorothea's interest in rock art continued throughout her career, interspersed with longer excursions centred on the collection of language samples. Informing all, however, was the sense of loyalty to her father and aunt, and to the intellectual project which had become a family legacy by the time the dictionary was published, posthumously, just short of 100 years after Wilhelm's bushman work had begun in the 1860s. The chapters that follow show that Dorothea's contribution to rock art research during the early years of the twentieth century was substantial, but that this contribution is often diminished in favour of a narrative that seeks to tell a more heroic story of the history of rock art research in southern Africa.

2 | Tracing rock art in the field with Helen Tongue, 1905–1907

The walls of this long cave are covered with paintings. Here have been dances, processions, weird dressed-up figures, pictures with ornamented background, hunts; in short, a whole panorama of scenes from Bushman life.[1]

Dorothea Bleek and fellow teacher Helen Tongue made this observation, probably in the summer of 1905–1906, during a trip through the mountains of south-eastern southern Africa. The young women were on a rock art copying expedition that had brought them to this cave in the Malotis. They followed, in some instances, in the footsteps of George Stow, who had trod nearby ground with a similar mission in mind some 40 years earlier. What they saw on the rock walls before them underlined the urgency of their task. In the co-published book published just four years later, Dorothea wrote of the damage that had been done to the painting, commenting that 'native herd boys have chipped at these paintings with stones, wherever they could reach them, and spoilt them, as no mere rubbing of sheep or cattle could do. Most are so effaced that to trace them was out of the question. We could only make out just enough to regret most bitterly the impossibility of restoring the whole.'[2]

Helen and Dorothea had travelled 'five hours' from Maseru (passing Roma, the 'chief station of the Roman Catholic missionaries in Basutoland') to reach this rock shelter, where they worked through an afternoon thunderstorm. 'The rain poured down in torrents, but not a drop touched us in the cave,' Dorothea wrote later.[3] The researchers had to pile up stones in order to reach paintings that had not been damaged. They carried out their copying work watched by a crowd of curious local people, described later as 'an attentive audience of four Basuto men, two youths and ten pickaninnies' who had followed them from the village.[4] The site was on the slopes of a peak known as 'Mochacha', one of the highest in the foothills of the Malotis, 'close to the village of Theko'. It was located on a well-traversed route that was known to other copyists, including the French artist and Protestant missionary Frédéric Christol, who had left in the cave 'the mangled remains of a drawing of archers' he had copied and published several years previously.[5] Now, sadly, Dorothea and Helen found the group 'past tracing'.[6]

This was the second of two sites the young women visited in the then Basutoland (now Lesotho). The other was much easier to reach, being 'past Teyateyaneng, near the ruins of Advance Post' (Figures 2.1 and 2.2). Dorothea wrote of a smooth slab of rock inside a cave 'which has been used over and over again by succeeding generations of artists'.[7] The artwork was now only faintly discernible to the naked eye – Dorothea recorded that the 'oldest paintings [were] quite impossible to trace'. Yet they formed 'a sort of iridescent background' to the two uppermost layers that were still visible. It was here that Dorothea was able to draw on her intellectual legacy to interpret some of the painted scenes she saw before her. At Advance Post, Helen and Dorothea saw what they described as a 'frog transformation picture'. The 'figure in the middle' was 'like a frog, but with horns; the side figures, stooping and kneeling', were 'more human'.[8] In the same shelter Dorothea copied a small group of figures that she thought illustrated the final scene in her father's tale of the mantis and the dead hartebeest:

> To frighten some children, the Mantis assumes the appearance of a dead hartebeest, which is found and cut up by the children – they attempt to carry it home in pieces – the parts move – the head speaks – the different members are dropped by the alarmed children and form again into a whole; the Mantis, who has now resumed his own shape, chases the children – they escape.[9]

Dorothea believed the painted group was a representation of the children escaping from the trickster deity (Figure 2.2). 'This jaunty figure has just the harmless and vain air one associates with /Kaggen, the hero of so many Bushman tales. The way in which the children cling to one another shows their fright plainly enough.'[10] Unfortunately, given that they were in the midst of a region so rich in rock art, the weather constrained further research: 'Any further exploration of the country-side for more caves was out of the question, as it was summer time and thunder-storms came up almost every afternoon. The Little Caledon, which was not low when we crossed, was reported to be steadily rising, so we dared not wait for further storms to make it impassable. As it was, we had some difficulty in getting back to Maseru.'[11]

Besides marking one of the earliest occasions when tales from the /Xam collection of folklore were invoked to explain rock paintings, these excursions with Helen were noteworthy because they gave Dorothea her first opportunity to fulfil a crucial part of her family legacy. At last she was able to act on one of her father's final wishes – to learn more about bushman art. Moreover, she would be able to apply her familiarity with George Stow's extensive collection of watercolour reproductions to what she saw in the field. Dorothea doubtless knew about her father's engagement with and comments on the rock art specimens collected in the Malotis by Joseph Orpen.[12] Via Lucy, she knew that Wilhelm had posited the possibility of a link between the scenes Orpen had copied and the mythology or 'legendary lore' of the bushmen.[13] She knew that her father and Lucy had shown rock art copies to Dia!kwain and /Han≠kass'o, reasoning that they might be able to throw light on the meaning of the painted scenes.[14] She knew also that Wilhelm had been aware of Stow's copying work, and she re-membered seeing the watercolours in her aunt's flat in Charlottenburg, near Berlin, when she had visited as a schoolgirl.[15] She would have remembered Lu-cy's efforts to publish Stow's *The Native Races of South Africa*, in which was in-cluded a tiny selection of Stow's 'pictures'. She knew that in 1882 Lucy had pur-chased Stow's entire collection from his widow, Fanny, and taken all the material with her to Europe.[16] So there is no doubt that Dorothea took a copy of Stow's book with her to Cradock, and that it became an important resource in the field.

Helen visited at least one of Stow's sites, at Buffelsfontein in the Upper Stormberg near Wodehouse, during her initial solo travels 'through the north-eastern parts of the Cape Colony'.[17] It is no surprise that Helen iden-tified a preponderance of eland in the paintings, which suggested to her that these large antelope were the 'favourite' game animals of the bushmen. In-spired by Stow, the young women noticed 'purely imaginary animals, often accompanied by fish, snakes, a tortoise', as well as 'rain-bulls' that were 'spot-ted or variegated in some way'. As we have seen, they identified the figure of the trickster god /Kaggen in more than one instance.[18]

Along with using Stow's book to assist in finding sites, Dorothea brought into the field his ideas about the antiquity of the 'bushmen' and their threatened future in the wake of encroachment by 'stronger black tribes'. Dorothea's understanding of the South African past as a record of encroachment on indigenous 'bushmen' by stronger 'black races' from the north and 'white settlers' from the south was a view she held onto throughout her life. Following Stow, Dorothea argued that the bushmen's previously idyllic lifestyle and their free access to the landscape had made possible their artistic skill. For Dorothea, the art represented the people's vanishing history, and she described the paintings as historical documents left by the bushmen themselves.[19] In line with the salvage paradigm that motivated her work, Dorothea argued that the painting tradition had died out as the people had. Their inevitable demise – in Dorothea's opinion the result of pressures of 'black' encroachment, the arrival of 'white' settlers, and conflicts over land and water – was linked to a larger understanding about natural laws of human evolution in which weaker, 'primitive' people were fated to 'extinction'. The same fate, she would argue just a few years later, had met their rich tradition of storytelling.

This chapter describes Dorothea's first research trip on South African soil, and locates her fieldwork methods, practices and ideas within the broader context of rock art reproduction methods then employed, and the general thinking of the time about the meaning of the art. It describes Dorothea's (and Helen's) early understandings and interpretations of bushmen and their rock art, which up to this point had been based entirely on her family inheritance and mentorship with Aunt Lucy, as well as her tertiary education at universities and colleges in Berlin and London.

Available literature suggests that the documentation of rock art was a haphazard and *ad hoc* endeavour in the early years of the twentieth century, with few pretensions in regard to science. The story begins with Stow's work in the 1860s, after which copying continued irregularly through the 1870s and 1880s. In the Natal Drakensberg region, copying was most often carried out by figures of colonial authority.[20] The copies recorded in the Malotis by Joseph Orpen in 1873 mark a watershed moment in rock art scholarship because of the comments Orpen recorded from his 'bushman' guide Qing.[21] The French copyist Frédéric Christol, whose crumpled copy work Dorothea and Helen found at a shelter in the Malotis, was one of several missionaries who indulged in rock art copying, as did amateurs such as H. Charles Schunke.[22] An early guidebook to Natal provides a record of the earliest rock art photography, produced in 1894–1895 by the Trappist missionary Brother Otto Mäeder in the Underberg region near Marianhill. Brother Otto would later record rock art in the Kei River area, and Dorothea cited his research in her books and scholarly articles.[23]

So it was a rather unruly field that Dorothea and Helen entered when they joined forces sometime after Dorothea's arrival at Rocklands Girls' High School in 1905. Dorothea's collected papers remain silent about whether the shared interest in rock art was a subject of earlier correspondence between the two young women, or whether it was simply coincidence that led to them teaming up at Rocklands. Staff photographs preserved in the school archive suggest a mutually supportive and companionable environment that combined productively with the two women's individual and independent spirits (Figure 2.3). One can imagine a general interest and encouragement from their colleagues. Perhaps they enlisted the aid of their pupils on rock art copying trips near the school. Their co-authored book tells us that Helen had already done some copying at sites north of Cradock by the time Dorothea joined in for their travels to the Orange River Colony and Basutoland.[24]

Cradock provided a convenient base from which the women were well placed to journey to rock art sites that had been recorded earlier by Stow, as well as to carry out their own field research. The small Karoo town located on the banks of the Great Fish River had been the centre of a bustling and prosperous sheep farming region that was devastated during the Second South African War, which ended in 1902. No doubt the ostrich-feather boom of the early 1900s brought a welcomed rush of prosperity. Dorothea may have taught some of the daughters of feather barons. And while Cradock may have been far removed from the long-established centres of colonial government and learning at the Cape, the rich presence of rock art in the region suggests that the area had been of central importance to earlier art-making inhabitants of the landscape. The terrain that Dorothea and Helen were about to survey had been the site of contact between indigenous and immigrant groups of people for thousands of years previously. As has been documented, the seventeenth and eighteenth centuries had marked the Karoo and surrounding landscapes as sites of conflict and interaction resulting from frontier struggles between settlers, pastoralists, and farming and foraging groups in the region.[25] For Dorothea, it was a landscape in which she applied her text-based knowledge of bushmen to the field for the first time.

Dorothea's sustained contribution to rock art research features only peripherally in accounts of the development of rock art research in the South African academy. That history is more generally framed by reference to the late-nineteenth-century contributions of Wilhelm Bleek, Joseph Orpen and George Stow, with the occasional copying work of the missionaries mentioned previously adding to the mix.[26] As the field grew increasingly crowded during the 1930s to 1950s, aficionados such as Bert Woodhouse, Alexander Willcox and Harald Pager, among others, concentrated their research and publishing on the rock art of the Drakensberg/Lesotho regions.[27] In these decades the country's first formally trained archaeologist, A.J.H. Goodwin, based at UCT, could still regard rock art as 'a rich field for the amateur' since stone tools, bones, stratification and excavation were the focus of attention among prehistorians and emerging archaeologists.[28]

It is worth noting that neither Pager nor Willcox was trained as an archaeologist. The Austrian-born Pager was a photographer and designer, while Willcox was a quantity surveyor.[29] Similarly, the Wits professor of archaeology Clarence van Riet Lowe, appointed by Jan Smuts in 1935, had developed his interest in prehistory and rock art while working as a civil engineer overseeing bridge building in the Orange Free State. Still, early archaeology was a dynamic and contested field of inquiry bolstered by the encouragement of Smuts, whose interest in prehistory and human origins has been widely documented. Smuts encouraged the visits of scholars from abroad, including Abbé Henri Breuil, Miles Burkitt and Leo Frobenius, all of whom made contact with Dorothea as they passed through Cape Town. But, as Siyakha Mguni has argued, at this time research tended to be quantitative rather than qualitative, and speculations about meaning tended to circulate around the simple 'narrative of bushman life' or 'art for art's sake' ideas.[30]

By the 1970s the discipline was attempting to become more systematic and scientific. Patricia Vinnicombe's 1976 publication, *People of the Eland: Rock Paintings of the Drakensberg Bushmen as a Reflection of Their Life and Thought*, advanced a first suggestion of the possibility of symbolic

49

meaning being encoded in the rock paintings. Basing her work on research begun in the 1950s, Vinnicombe pioneered the use of computer-aided quantitative methods of rock art recording. Her research aimed to record every single painting (regardless of content or state of preservation) in a demarcated area of the Drakensberg, and to generate statistics for quanti-fying and describing faunal and human types using methods designed to mirror those of 'dirt' (or field) archaeology.[31] Yet Vinnicombe also ground-ed her findings in a fine-grained historical understanding of the region and in archive- and field-based ethnographies of the bushmen. In the course of her work, she produced thousands of field copies, tracings and a wealth of associated documents that are now preserved at the Rock Art Research Institute at Wits University, constituting an archive of immeas-urable value and importance.

Rock art and knowledge making

The US archaeologist Lynn Meskell has described Vinnicombe's *People of the Eland* as a 'social archaeology' in which 'textual sources are used to de-velop a dialogue with the artistic record, the archaeological findings and the work of social anthropologists'.[32] In her contribution to a collection of essays published in memory of Vinnicombe after her death in 2003, Meskell suggests that *People of the Eland* diverged from the 'culture his-torical or positivist traditions' that were typical of other writings of the time. Instead of presenting 'flat accounts of prehistoric economies…or sterile cross-cultural analogies of such communities', Vinnicombe's work attempted 'actively to people the past' and to 'include historical subjects and moments through the progressive interplay of evidential sources'.[33] Vinnicombe's sensitive and intuitive attention to issues such as gender, the body, social life, ritual and spirituality, and politics allowed a weaving together of multiple strands of evidence to produce a representation of the people through a nuanced and complex reading of their art that remains inspirational for current scholarship.[34]

Just five years later, in 1981, the influential work of David Lewis-Williams appeared. Drawing in many respects on Vinnicombe's theories regarding the symbolic significance of the eland, Lewis-Williams's seminal *Believing and Seeing: Symbolic Meanings in Southern San Rock Paintings* went a step

further in detailing the eland's (and other animals') central place in the belief systems of the bushmen. The work ushered in a new framework of interpretation in which altered states of consciousness, ritual specialists and shamanism replaced the earlier, prosaic linkages of the art to everyday scenes
including hunting, raiding parties and social events, or art for art's sake. It
was a breathtaking new thesis that eclipsed the tentative symbolic readings
that Vinnicombe had suggested.

In his introduction, Lewis-Williams commented on the haphazard nature of the work of early copyists, including Stow, Tongue and Bleek.[35] For
Lewis-Williams, these 'highly selective' and 'eclectic sampling' and recording practices were based on the assumption that the paintings were 'scale
models of San life as it was lived by the now-extinct southern groups' – a
view that in his opinion limited and distorted interpretations of the rock
art.[36] Lewis-Williams offered, in contrast, an examination of rock art based
on rigorous and scientific sampling methods. His interpretative study
was based on systematic sampling of all the paintings found within clearly demarcated areas in the Barkly East and Giant's Castle regions of the
Drakensberg.[37] Both Lewis-Williams and Vinnicombe drew on the Bleek-
Lloyd notebooks of bushman folk tales and ethnography, as well as on Orp-
en's notes on his interactions with Qing, for clues to the interpretation of the
rock art of the south-eastern mountains of the Drakensberg and the Malotis
of Basutoland. In addition, Lewis-Williams accompanied the anthropologist
Megan Biesele on fieldwork among the Kalahari Ju/'hoansi (!Kung), where,
through interviews and observation of rituals still practised by the group, he
found support for the existence of a 'pan-San' belief system shared across all
bushman groups, certain aspects of which could be judiciously employed
in the interpretation of rock art.[38] At the same time, cognitive archaeology
introduced theoretical approaches that focused on the material expression
of human ways of thinking, leading to increasingly complex interpretations
of rock art that branched into neuropsychology to explain some of the geometric patterns and images included in certain paintings.[39]

In the context of this paradigm-shifting scholarship, Dorothea's early
contribution to the documentation of rock art was often dismissed with a
rehearsal of her oft-quoted view of the art as a literal representation of the
bushman's history and everyday life, and her conceptualisation of the artists

as members of a 'child' race.⁴⁰ It was suggested that she had 'missed the import of the art' and did not share her father's perception of the paintings as being filled with 'religious feeling'.⁴¹ Despite the importance of her published work and research, it was argued that Dorothea's thinking on rock art had ushered in an era during which the art was trivialised as an art of illustration which, although acknowledged for being aesthetically competent and pleasing, merely recorded daily life.⁴² Yet Dorothea's views had not been exceptional for the time. The artist Walter Battiss, while acknowledging – indeed acclaiming – the art for its technical proficiency and exceptional aesthetics, nevertheless dismissed the artists and subject matter as primitive and naive, an attitude that found ready acceptance in the 1930s and 1940s, a time of hardening racial prejudice and continued political focus on the 'native question'.⁴³

Viewed in the context of disciplinary history and the intellectual trajectory of rock art studies, Dorothea's opinions became part of a competing paradigm of thought that could not be accommodated within the dominant theories that took hold after the 1970s. Dorothea's interpretation of the art as an illustration of everyday life, social contact and historical events, and occasionally about myth, was regarded as part of a mistaken and even ignorant set of ideas inherited from George Stow. Many scholars of the 1970s and beyond saw these ideas as out of keeping with sophisticated views of the art as symbolic and related to shamanism and altered states of consciousness. Dorothea's rock art scholarship, as well as her staunch defence of bushman authorship, was therefore largely written out of rock art's historical narrative. However, recent scholarship appears to be striving for a detailed, contextualised rereading of rock art that, while understandably theoretically more sophisticated and nuanced than scholarship of the early twentieth century ever could be, takes social mobility and interaction into consideration. Such approaches bring nuance to interpretations of the art that frame it as essentially shamanistic.

Contemporary rock art scholarship offers particular interpretations of specific painted images or sequences of images in locally defined geographical areas. The Rock Art Research Institute at Wits, for instance, views its study of rock art as an avenue through which can be understood 'how people in Africa perceived and responded to social changes during the last ten thousand years and through the colonial process'.⁴⁴ The Institute's framing of the 'complex symbolism of African image-making' found at rock art sites across the continent as 'a history...based on African perceptions rather than just colonial records' echoes Dorothea Bleek's description of rock art as 'among our most important historical documents left us by the early inhabitants of the country'.[45] From the 1990s, South African scholars have deployed rock art as evidence in the writing of histories of contact between particular groups of people living in defined geographical regions of the country. The painted images are shown to draw meaning from their specific and general locations together with their content to provide an interpretation that is cognisant of broader historical trajectories and the dynamics of social contact and identity making among groups in different landscapes.[46] This line of interpretation signals a treatment of rock art as intertwined in historical change rather than an expression of an underlying 'essence' of belief and cosmology characteristic of all bushman groups across space and time. It also returns the discussion to earlier interpretations by Dorothea of the art being a record, authored by the people themselves, of early habitation in southern Africa.

This story of Dorothea's rock art research explores fieldwork as a complex activity involving social and emotional networks and associations rather than a cold and unfeeling 'science' of accurate recording combined with a 'theory' of reflection on collected data. How exactly were the rock art copies collected by Dorothea (and her companions) actually rendered as free-standing watercolours on loose-leafed sheets of paper? What materials did she and her research assistants use in the practice of their task, and how did they regard their work and process? What was their attitude to the art itself, and to its interpretation and meaning?

Selectivity and subject matter

Vinnicombe's research shows that nearly 50 years after Helen and Dorothea's first expeditions, methodologies of rock art recording were not much more sophisticated. Vinnicombe's copies were traced onto 'transparent polythene sheeting' which had been fixed to the rock with masking tape. The copying was done *in situ* with 'a fine brush dipped in Indian ink or water-colour paint mixed with a wetting agent'.[47] Colours were confirmed later with recourse to a specially composed colour chart. Vinnicombe took photographs to accompany her reproductions, a method that Dorothea had employed on later trips.

As far as selectivity was concerned, Vinnicombe was sensitive to the limits of her methods. Her intention had been to make a 'thorough survey' of a specified area, 'to record all the paintings within it, avoiding any element of personal preference or selection'.[48] She also undertook to 'plot the sites as accurately as possible on available maps, and to record every recognisable painting by both tracing and photography'. But her field experiences clearly demarcated the limits she encountered. She wrote: 'It is obvious...that the objectives of the survey were not fully realised. It proved impossible to investigate thoroughly the whole of the terrain within the limited period of time, and the unprecedented number of sites located were more than could be adequately recorded by one person.' Of the 308 sites located in her survey area, '150 were fully recorded, seventy-nine partly recorded, fifty not recorded at all, and twenty had deteriorated to such an extent that no meaningful observations could be made'.[49]

In 1905 or thereabouts, Helen and Dorothea were venturing into a field that was methodologically unreflective. Orpen, Stow and the other early copyists gave little thought to making known the specifics of their task beyond committing themselves to the making of 'accurate' copies. It is not clear how they dealt with the many difficulties enumerated by Henry Balfour in his preface to *Bushman Paintings*. These included access to awkwardly positioned paintings, lighting and degree of preservation, and the effects of these on reproduction.[50] Other difficulties, such as mapping the exact geographical location of sites in such a way that they could be revisited, or the need to make a complete copy of every single painting at each and every site, were apparently not even considered. We have gained an inkling of Dorothea's and Helen's dedication and vulnerability to the elements from learning how their research in Lesotho was limited by the rising Little Caledon River. But apart from occasional references to railway lines, postcarts and the use of borrowed cottages, they gave no record of how they travelled from place to place, nor of what arrangements they made for staying overnight in out-of-the-way locations.[51] Neither is it clear how much time they were able to devote to a particular site, although at Mochacha the site notes do give a clue that the two women may have spent more than one day at work, with Dorothea making reference to 'the *first* afternoon that we worked there'.[52]

Like earlier copyists, Helen and Dorothea were cryptic when it came to describing their actual activities in the field. It is not clear exactly how they made their copies or who helped them, although hints may occasionally be gleaned from a close reading of their notes published in *Bushman Paintings*. The terminology employed for copying varies from page to page in the book and, in line with their quest to salvage the final vestiges of a vanishing people, hints at underlying notions of collecting or taking ownership of each image. The words imply that the tracing process involved physical contact with the rock and with the painted image itself, and suggests that tracing paper was fixed to the rock surface. At the farm Zandfontein in the Molteno district, for instance, Helen alluded to her method: 'Here I got the *tracing* shown on Plate IV, No. 6, of a hippopotamus charging into a cage (a trap) ...' For another example at the same site, she wrote: 'Besides this I *traced* a rhino, a small dark-red elephant ...'[53] Elsewhere she wrote that she '*took*' the clearest specimens and that she '*copied* the curious frog transformation picture'.[54] The title page of *Bushmen Paintings* tells us that Helen did most of the copying work, while Dorothea provided contextual notes and interpretation.[55] The Iziko South African Museum's collection of Helen Tongue's reproductions includes eight watercolour reproductions made by Dorothea, who would also produce a small number of charcoal rubbings of rock engravings in the vicinity of Sandfontein in South West Africa while doing language research there in 1920.

Dorothea's attitudes towards her techniques of field research and the processes of tracing and copying became more acute during her career. Years later, she would reflect on earlier methodologies. She was aware of the consequences of reproduction making in respect of the accompanying loss of physical context: 'From the nature of the background the paintings seem to melt into the rock in a manner that cannot be reproduced on paper, which invariably gives the figures too sharp an outline.'[56] Elsewhere in that introduction to her 1930 edited publication of Stow's copies, she commented perceptively on the perspective of many of the painted animals and figures, noting that the paintings of animals were 'too long and narrow', just as the human figures were: 'It has been noticed by many visitors to rock-shelters that cattle passing at a distance had just that long-drawn-out appearance given to animals by Bushmen, so one concludes they painted what they saw.'[57] Only much later did Dorothea's personal correspondence offer an occasional glimpse of her views in this regard, which suggest that the problem of selectivity was something she thought about later. About 20 years after this first research outing, Dorothea would express her concern about the selectivity that was characteristic of Stow's copied work: 'Stow did not copy a hundredth, not a thousandth, of existing paintings. While searching for the paintings we came upon magnificent caves, which he never knew, and in the caves where he did some copying, he left quite a lot unrecorded.'[58] At time of writing that particular letter, Dorothea was engaged in revisiting as many Stow sites as she could in preparation for publication of the first batch of Stow's copies.[59] Writing in 1928 from Winburg in the Orange Free State, she would bemoan the inadequacy of Stow's directions and the fragility of so many of the paintings she came across: 'I have found the originals of about half of Stow's paintings. Of the others, some are destroyed, but most of them could not be found because of inadequate directions.'[60]

However, for her first trip with Helen there is no record in the archive of any discussion between the two young women about which pictures should be traced and which not. In the absence of preserved documents, what can be said must be deduced from what appears in the published outcome of the trip. Based on the images included in *Bushman Paintings*, one can see that they copied the unusual, such as rain-bulls or other creatures of the imagination, along with run-of-the-mill representations of animals.[61] We have seen that Helen noticed that eland were by far the most common animal appearing in the paintings, describing these as the 'favourite' game animal of the 'bushmen'.[62] She noted too the presence of Stow's 'imaginary' animals accompanied by fish, snakes or tortoises, and 'rain-bulls'.[63] Dorothea and Helen also favoured images which to them represented 'bushman history' and the presence of different groups of people in the landscape. They elected to copy group scenes where different 'tribes' could be discerned by type of weapon (bow and arrow or spear, for example), or shape of shield, or where cultural adornments such as beadwork or type of dress could be seen.[64] They also copied and included painted scenes that illustrated their view of the past as a narrative of conflict between different 'tribes'. At Modderpoort near Ladybrand, where Dorothea joined Helen, they visited three caves located behind the mission house of the St Augustine Brotherhood (Figure 2.4).[65]

Here, among paintings 'much faded and rubbed out', they were able to copy 'the gem of the place, a large battle-piece or raid', presumably preserved because of its position in 'an inaccessible place in the curve of the overhanging roof'.[66] Dorothea's notes reveal her judgement about the value of this particular painted scene, and an aspect of their field practice related to reaching paintings in out-of-the-way places. This involved constructing, probably with assistance, a 'high tower of stones', in this case 'against a fallen boulder', in order to reach the scene they had chosen to copy.[67] Dorothea's description of this scene gives a sense of the nuance of her observations and her incorporation of ethnographic knowledge:

> Of the thirty-five men, the front ones are kneeling down, apparently defending themselves behind shields, others brandishing sticks, those behind rushing down to the fray. The two or three quiet figures seem to be the men driving the cattle. One woman is also there. The up-turned ox is dead, the head has been rubbed out. The two blotches of red colour are probably accidental.
>
> This picture looks like one side of a battle scene, of which the rest with the enemy has been washed away.
>
> The men have karosses, that is skins hanging downward from the shoulders, and the little bags Bushmen used to wear suspended from the waist, in which they often carried their poison. The weapons are knobkerries [clubs] and short spears.[68]

Based on evidence provided by Father Norton of the St Augustine Mission and from her own observations, Dorothea thought the painting represented a cattle raid involving two opposing 'bushman tribes' rather than between different groups of people.[69] 'Their dress makes it seem possible that the men in the battle-piece are Bushmen,' she wrote. At Orange Spring, 'Mr Adrian Deneys's pretty farm' near Modderpoort, the two women used a ladder to reach a painting 'high up at one end of the cave' to copy a 'procession of men'.[70] The figures seemed to be bleeding from the nose, prompting a mention of what Stow liked to call a 'blood-dance'.[71] Dorothea disagreed. Her notes recorded her opinion that it looked 'more like men on a march than dancers'. She thought the crude style was a result of the difficult spot in which the painted scene was located, reasoning that the 'Bushman artist probably stood on a comrade's back'.[72] In the same rock shelter they recorded another dance scene. This one involved a group of men with sticks 'wearing heads of antelopes', with 'women on either side and some of the seated men' in the scene 'beating time by clapping their hands'. To explain this, Dorothea drew on what she had read in the notebooks and learnt from Lucy. 'Bushmen were very fond of dressing up as animals. The leader in a dance, and sometimes others, put on the head of a bird or beast and imitated its cry and movements,' she noted. She also saw in the painting what looked like the 'bushman' musical instrument termed a *!goin !goin.*[73]

Earlier, at Glengyle farm (Barkly East district), Helen copied a ceiling painting where the cave was so choked with earth and dung that 'we had to dig a hole under the painting in order to trace it'.[74] The drawing copied is one of the two collotypes that appear in the book.[75] These were printed using a special reproduction process in order to show the beautiful shading.[76] At some sites, an understanding of the African past in terms of encroachment influenced their decision to copy certain scenes. At Greenvale, near Clark Siding in the Wodehouse district, for instance, they copied a scene which Dorothea thought could be a representation by 'bushmen' witnesses to an 'encounter or parley between soldiers and natives':[77]

> Behind what appears to be a barricade are redcoats in busbies [fur hats]; one is waving a sword; the natives on the nearer side of the barricade are dressed in karosses or skin cloaks. Portions of the bodies and especially the white karosses have disappeared in the figures to the left-hand side of the picture, figures that appear to be supplicating.[78]

We have seen how Dorothea turned to the folklore gathered by her father and aunt in order to understand some of the stranger images and scenes she saw on the rocks, even at this early stage of her career. At Advance Post, she saw what she thought was an illustration of the final scene from her father's tale of the mantis and the dead hartebeest. At the same site, she and Helen identified what they thought was a frog-transformation scene, and again, at Mount Victory near Wodehouse, they copied another 'curious frog transformation picture in which is represented in rough semi-circle of figures a man being changed into a frog'. The scene reminded Dorothea of 'Bushman folk-lore', where she had read tales of 'people who have displeased the rain being changed into frogs'.[79] Along with battles, raids and myth illustration, they copied paintings that showed some superpositioning or layers of paintings, although printing constraints probably meant only two levels could be represented. Dorothea's notes bear witness to several examples of many more levels of superpositioning on the rocks.[80] And, along with all of these, they included many pictures of animals simply because they found them beautiful and/or technically proficient in the use of unusual and difficult techniques of perspective, foreshortening and shading (Figure 2.5).[81]

Invisible assistants

In retrospect, one can see how the field practices of Dorothea and Helen contributed to the inexorable process of erasing local knowledge from these early attempts at a systematic engagement with rock art. Both women would have interacted regularly and closely with local people, not only when locating sites, but also for their day-to-day living and travelling support. But any knowledge the young women may have learned from conversations with local people or 'field assistants' is not acknowledged in the published record. It is possible that Helen and Dorothea may have come across first-hand instances of art making in certain of the landscapes they explored. There is some evidence that painting may have continued, at least in the south-eastern mountains, until the early 1900s.[82] In a few instances indigenous voices do slip into focus amid the more routine and systematic practices of describing, documenting and constructing the painted images as objects of contemplation (either scientific or aesthetic) for an audience far removed in time and space from the art's originators. Helen's decision to record a particular image at Burley Cave in the Barkly East district, for example, may inadvertently have preserved a fragment of local knowledge. Here, in a cave filled with well-preserved paintings positioned above a rocky ledge and out of damaging contact with the sheep that sheltered there, she copied a snake with a dassie's head. A faint trace of engagement with local people is discernible in her published notes. It was, she wrote, a 'common superstition in these parts among the natives that such a snake exists'.[83]

On another occasion, Helen made a direct reference to the presence of a field companion. In the notes accompanying paintings copied at the farm Montague Hill near Magdala in the Wodehouse district, she wrote that she explored the rock shelters 'in the company of a Basuto girl', adding that it 'was a pleasure to see her jump from rock to rock on her big bare feet'.[84] That comment speaks of a measure of sympathy and connection between researcher and assistant, and it is intriguing to speculate that some level of (albeit unrecorded) knowledge sharing about the paintings may have taken place. We read earlier about the interested presence of local people who watched the research activity in the big shelter on the slopes of Mochacha, but any contribution they may have made remained unattributed.[85] At Glengyle farm near Barkly East, the ghostly presence of a companion is suggested in Helen's reference to receiving a gift of a digging-stick stone.[86] The identity of the giver remains unknown.

Archaeologists Nathan Schlanger and Nick Shepherd and historian Andrew Bank have described the ambivalent and ambiguous nature of the relationships that characterised fieldwork from the early 1900s into the present. These scholars provide fine-grained descriptions of relationships, ranging from indifferent to intimate, that built up between pioneering researchers in varied areas of inquiry and their assistants.[87]

Apart from the fleeting presence of anonymous field companions, Dorothea and Helen drew in a haphazard manner on the support of missionaries and landowners to facilitate their research. At Modderpoort, the young women based themselves in a cottage lent by 'Miss Chandler of Bloemfontein'.[88] Father Norton of the St Augustine Mission conducted them to three caves located behind the mission house, where they found paintings much faded and rubbed out, and others 'improved' by the 'Black Watch, who…kindly left their autograph'.[89] Father Norton provided certain interpretations of the paintings which he was said to have 'collected from the natives'. As described earlier, Dorothea thought the painting represented a cattle raid. She disputed the missionary's suggestion that certain of the painted figures were African, arguing that bushmen too wore jackal-skin caps, bracelets and anklets.[90]

At other locations, farmers featured through exercising a proprietary attitude towards the painted sites on their land, and by claiming authority of knowledge about the bushmen artists. At Buffelsfontein, for instance, the farmer Henry Stretton showed Helen those paintings he thought were the best in the cave, and found her bits of red ochre paint on the cave floor and along the bed of the stream.[91] At Zandfontein, Helen copied paintings in a cave now used as a sheep pen. She was accompanied by a 'young' farmer, 'Mr Kruger', who piled up stones to enable her to reach that which she considered to be the best portion of paintings situated above – the ones lower down being 'much rubbed' by the animals.[92] Jan Nel, of the farm Montagu Hill, shared information about fire making using 'two bits of wood' observed from his servants, about 'dacha' smoking using pipes made from hollow bones, and about paints obtained from 'hollow stones with a coloured powder inside'.[93] Stories about bushmen using extra-long bows steadied by the foot, wearing arrows in a band around the head (Dorothea observed both these habits in painted scenes), and methods of making and applying poison to arrows were part of this exchange.[94] On a bloodier note, Nel related his and his father's experiences of participating in a 'bushman hunt' in the district in 1855. From this exchange, Dorothea took note of Nel's assertion that bushmen raiders would choose to kill all the cattle they had captured rather than take only what they could eat. This fitted with Dorothea's inherited understanding of bushman ways, and she repeated the idea in her notes in *Bushman Paintings* and in the essay co-written with Edith.[95]

Dorothea's and Helen's final field trip took them to a different part of the Orange River Colony, where they recorded chippings and engravings at three sites. It must have been a long, hot journey. Travelling by rail from Cradock, the women most probably changed trains at Springfontein and took the branch line to Fauresmith, after which they travelled a further six hours by wagon to the little town of Luckhoff on the edge of the Great Karoo. According to Dorothea's notes, this was hot, dry country, completely flat save for the 'tiniest kopjes' which broke the bare plains and with only 'bare, brown boulders' instead of the 'smooth and sheltered' surfaces on which bushmen elsewhere chose to paint.[96] On the neighbouring farms Baviaan's Krantz and Roodekop, the women viewed engravings displaying a variety of techniques: animal pictures with scraped or chipped outlines, sometimes filled in with chipped-in detail. The third location they visited also lay close to the Orange River, but was three hours from Luckhoff in a different direction. On this farm, Jonasfontein, they found three chippings, one of these

61

an 'indecipherable' symbol which Dorothea linked to similar paintings or chippings of 'signs' found by Stow on the banks of the Great Riet River, and by George McCall Theal near the Keiskamma River.[97]

Helen and Dorothea reproduced 13 engravings which were dealt with in a separate section in their book under the heading 'Chippings'.[98] In line with German ethnology and *Volksgeist* thinking, Dorothea viewed the engravings as evidence of a local adaptation by the people to their particular environment. The bushmen in that region, she argued, had 'no smooth and sheltered surface to work on' and so 'made a picture on the rock itself with a stone'.[99] In her 1932 lecture, she would describe the engravings she had seen as 'very perfect'.[100] She argued that many of the engravings were 'proved by their weathering to be of a very great age', while others were 'comparatively recent'. In terms of form, the 'exaggerated length of the animals in comparison with their height' reminded her of the paintings. Likewise, symbols chipped onto the rocks were similar to those found in some painted areas.

Learning in the field

In notes written to explain the rock art copies published in Helen's book, Dorothea declared that the bushmen were the artists who 'covered' the walls of their 'cave homes' with pictures of animals and people. Although exact paint-making methods had 'apparently never been disclosed by Bushmen', she knew that their pigments were derived from natural ochres mixed with animal fat – resulting in paints that were extremely durable and resistant to weathering and even rubbing by animals.[101] On the dating of paintings, her reasoning was based on the degree to which certain colours had faded. She argued that some colours were less durable, and that lighter colours wore off more quickly. In paintings she had seen in the open at Lillihoek near Ladybrand, she deduced that what remained of an eland's body meant the painting was 'at the lowest estimate of time' at least 50 years old.[102] All the lighter colours in the painting had faded. Following Stow, she dated paintings also in relation to local memory of bushman habitation in a particular area, arguing that the painting tradition continued until the people were either driven out of their ancestral land or 'exterminated'.[103] Again following Stow, she was convinced that the arrival of 'stronger black tribes' in southern Africa brought with it competition over resources and ended the painting tradition. Variations on this sentiment are expressed again and again in her writings:

> In this manner a most primitive race of hunters, the little Bushmen of
> South Africa, have left their record on the rocks of the land that long was
> theirs, but that knows them no more. Some seventy years ago the last
> Bushman artist perished in battle, his paint pots still strapped to his belt.
> Fifty years earlier many artists of the race must still have been busy, as the
> pictures showing the last fights of the hunters with invading Zulus, Basu-
> tos and Europeans testify. The dress, weapons and physiognomy of the
> different peoples are so characteristically depicted, as to leave no doubt as
> to their identity. Nor is there any question as to what they are doing, even
> feeling, so great was the skill of the artists in portraying action in few but
> telling lines.[104]

The comments made in this undated typescript were based on rock art
research in the field, in contrast to the statements in the co-written essay
of 1909 that recycled opinions expressed by her father and aunt. The essay
described the bushmen as a people with a 'vivid imagination' expressed in
their 'rich and varied folklore' and their complex tradition of music and
song. Their rituals and beliefs were expressed as 'dressing up' and 'acting'
the part of animals for simple amusement.[105] Perhaps her lack of hands-on
ethnographic material at that point caused Dorothea to rely on the memories of Edith for the main content of the essay they co-wrote for Helen's
book. Without field experience, Dorothea's essay, except for the first two
pages, amounted to a series of Edith's nostalgic memories of the bushman
interlocutors at the Bleek family home. Edith and Dorothea told the family
anecdotes in a way that emphasised bushman loyalty and honesty, their respect as servants, their independence of spirit and resourcefulness, and their
bravery in battle, all traits Dorothea may well have inferred from conversations with Aunt Lucy, or from her reading of Stow's book.[106]

Dorothea returned to Cape Town in early 1908. She had left her teaching
post at Rocklands. It was going to be a busy year, with exhibitions of rock art
reproductions planned for the South African Public Library in Cape Town
and, later that year, at the Royal Anthropological Institute (RAI) library in
London. It is certain that these exhibitions were visited by large numbers

of the intelligentsia in both cities. Aunt Lucy was living in Berlin at that time and may have travelled to London for the event.[107] Fuelled by discoveries in Europe, interest in South African rock art would have been high.[108] Dorothea's family-wide project aimed at documenting and preserving the stories and pictures of a group of 'primitive' peoples perceived as 'dying out' would have been received with empathy. Just two years later, Roger Fry's exhibition Manet and the Post-Impressionists opened at the Grafton Gallery in London, setting the British art world agog at the suggestion of parallels between post-impressionism and primitive art making.[109]

The interaction with the RAI proved fortuitous. The young researchers found a useful patron in the person of Henry Balfour, archaeologist and founding curator of the Pitt Rivers Museum at Oxford, whose interest in South Africa had led him to make four visits to the country.[110] Balfour's interest in decorative arts no doubt disposed him kindly to Helen's rock art reproductions. In his preface to *Bushman Paintings*, Balfour made an impassioned plea for the systematic documentation and protection of South Africa's rock art. He compared bushman art to that of the prehistoric cave dwellers of southern France, echoing Dorothea's and Helen's opinion of the art as reflecting the bushman past, and a means of illustrating and supplementing descriptions written by European travellers who had come into contact with them.[111] His call for government protection to preserve the fragile paintings *in situ* may have contributed to the colonial government passing the Bushman Relics Act of 1911.[112] Like Dorothea, Balfour argued that as many accurate copies as possible should be collected so that they would be available for comparative study in the future.[113]

Towards a systematic study

Although it was early in her career, it is clear that by 1909 Dorothea had thought a good deal more seriously and deeply about rock art than she has been given credit for in the history of the discipline. Her visits to rock art sites in the south-eastern Orange River Colony and in the foothills of the Drakensberg and Malotis, and the interpretations she produced afterwards, indicate that her view of rock art was based on several fieldwork trips. At this point in her research, Dorothea was able to express with certainty her opinion that bushmen were responsible for both the paintings and the engravings which seemed so widely scattered throughout the country. She drew a distinction between paintings and engravings while insisting on affinities in style, but arriving at different relative ages for the respective forms of art. She outlined the beginnings of her later, more settled position on the use of colour preservation (as opposed to characteristics of style) to arrive at a relatively recent date for most paintings. All of these were positions she would need to defend in later years. As the 1909 book *Bushman Paintings* suggests, Dorothea did not simply regard the paintings as 'scale-drawings' of bushman life. Rather, she read in them a changing record of daily life, social interaction and historical events. She was interested in the methods used by the painters, and was careful to site the paintings in the context of their surrounding landscapes. Finally, her familiarity with her intellectual legacy contained in the notebooks allowed Dorothea to suggest the possibility that mythical tales were in some instances illustrated on the rocks, and she drew a connection between the art and the folklore recorded by her father and aunt. Following a proposition suggested in the *Cape Monthly Magazine* years earlier by her father, she pioneered this line of interpretation long before it became a key method for the discipline.[114]

3 | Return to the Kalahari, July–August 1913

Sunday 6th July
Fine clear morning. Trekked from early till breakfast. Ouspanned in pretty park-
like ground. The whole way from Legombe has been very pretty so far – with very
fine trees. Long trek in morning – encamped in lovely spot – watered oxen. Still
longer trek in afternoon. Reached Kakia long after dark. Stopped near village under
fine Kamelthorn trees. Old Masarwa greeted us on entry – gave me tobacco and
sugar. Hot day.[1]

Now that she had shown her rock art research to an international audience, it was time for Dorothea to return to the field. It must have been a bittersweet period for her, with the prospect of finding descendants of her father's interlocutors and doing her own language fieldwork shadowed by the death of her mother in October 1909.[2] Dorothea managed two trips in the months following her mother's death: a short visit to the northern Cape in 1910, followed by a longer trip in 1911.[3] She returned to Cape Town early in 1912, in time to welcome Lucy back from Germany to Charlton House, which her mother had bequeathed to the surviving Bleek daughters.[4] Having completed the long process of readying a collection of notebook texts for publication in *Specimens of Bushman Folklore*, Lucy had left Charlottenburg and returned to Cape Town to set up home near her nieces.

Dorothea could now pay serious attention to the notebooks and related material Lucy had brought back with her from Europe, and hone the language skills she would need to support her research plans.[5] But this interlude of a warm sharing of knowledge was short-lived. Lloyd died at Charlton House on 31 August 1914. Dorothea was now alone in the Cape save for her sister Helma Bright and her family who lived at Somerset West, these days a mere thirty minutes by car from Cape Town.[6] But the Brights shortly returned to live with Dorothea at Charlton House. In 1926, the family – including Dorothea, Helma, her husband and their two young daughters Marjorie and Dorothy – moved to La Rochelle, Newlands, an arrangement that was to last until Helma's death in 1947.[7]

In the years following the move, Dorothea chose to concentrate on field expeditions aimed at language research. She may have decided to consolidate what she had learnt from Lucy. The La Rochelle years would prove to be a time of great productivity during which Dorothea would undertake extensive travel and language fieldwork among the Naron in South West Africa and travel as far as Angola, where she found 'remnants of Bushman tribes'. She went to Tanganyika, where she was puzzled by the presence of a 'tribe' whose language and customs resembled that of the bushmen but who did not resemble the bushmen physically.[8] She made several shorter visits to her friends the Ralstons, who farmed at Mount Temple in the Langeberg, a range of mountains in the northern Cape angling through regions in those years known as Gordonia, Griqualand West and Bushmanland. She also made her first trips to the Kalahari, which, as we have been, involved the collection of human remains, often from newly consecrated but also from older burial sites.

Dorothea's early language research in southern Africa can be understood in reference to her educational roots in Europe. Her schooling and tertiary education took place in the milieu of classical German philology, the formalisation of *Ethnologie* and anthropology, and interest in the *Volksgeist* tradition of Johann Gottfried Herder. While studying in London, she might have been interested in Charles Darwin's theories of natural selection and evolution, in the cultural evolutionary theories of Edward Burnett Tylor, and in the comparative studies of religion and myth of the prolific folklorist Andrew Lang. These strands were intertwined with her later scholarship and institutional attachments within the emerging South African academy.

A close reading of Dorothea's research notes suggests that her fieldwork was flavoured by Adolf Bastian's ideas about *Elementargedanke* (elementary ideas), the theory that all human beings shared the same species-specific mental make-up and therefore the same 'mind'. Bastian argued that elementary ideas were influenced by geographic location and historical background, and these local variations he called *Völkergedanken*, or 'folk ideas'. Bastian's mission was to find 'elementary ideas' of all the world's people and, through analysis of differences among 'natural' people, to reveal a set of seminal ideas from which every civilisation had grown.[9] These observations of the objective and 'natural' would provide evidence for the formulation of empirical laws regarding the effects of physiological, psychological and social conditions on the human mind. Thus it is likely that Dorothea's quest to identify 'elemental' characteristics of 'natural' people may have been couched in classical philological terms within a notion of universalised humanity. But when translated onto southern African soil, her endeavour encompassed also the classification of groups of people in terms of their presumed racial type, and their projection within a hierarchy based on potential for civilisation, or educability.[10] Both the notion of racial types and the concept of stages of civilisation were elements of evolutionary theory underpinning the study of human societies, cultures (or races and tribes) and psychology that were emerging as separate disciplines within the academies being established in colonial South Africa at the time.[11] The earlier classical tradition of comparative philology and linguistic studies provided the larger intellectual environment in which newer studies such as *Ethnologie* took root in Germany. We have seen that comparative philology was a mode of thought that figured large in Dorothea's intellectual inheritance from her father. The link between philology, biblical exegesis or interpretation, language studies and the spread of German missionary activity through Africa has been well established in relation to Wilhelm Bleek's scholarly interests as well as his ongoing interaction with missionaries who would send him language and folklore samples from the field.[12]

Taming the landscape

As has been well documented, Christian evangelical activity and its 'civilising' mission was in full swing across southern Africa in 1904 when Dorothea returned to Cape Town. The effects of mission work were embedded across the spectrum of society, not least in the designation of tribal groups and their corresponding languages, and more subtly in the gradual emergence of formal academic disciplines devoted to the study of these.

Patrick Harries's detailed study of Swiss missionary activity in southern Mozambique and neighbouring regions in South Africa at the end of the nineteenth century elaborates on the codification of language – the standardisation of oral languages and the production of dictionaries and grammars – as part of a process by which missionaries sought to tame and control an unruly and strange environment using the 'tools' of science.[13] The missionaries 'used aneroid barometers to measure atmospheric pressure and altitude and gauges and thermometers to establish mean variables of rainfall, temperature and wind velocity'. They 'drew up charts' and 'erected a range of probability and an element of cognitive control on the vagaries of climate'. As far as the land was concerned, they 'invested long hours in cartographic work through which they condensed the otherwise engulfing landscape into the manageable proportions of a simple representation on paper'. At the same time, they 'reduced the chaos of nature by collecting insects, animals and plants'. These environmental and spatial markers were sent to Europe to be classified and placed in herbaria, botanical gardens, hothouses, natural history museums and zoos. Harries notes that '[t]hrough this categorisation and conservation of nature the missionaries imposed on Africa the familiar practices and perspectives through which they had made sense of the Alpine wilderness'.[14]

Harries argues that similar 'scientific' processes were applied to the task of rendering languages intelligible. He describes how missionaries classified the languages and communities they found in southern Mozambique, and in the northern and eastern parts of the Lowveld and KwaZulu-Natal, in terms of their knowledge of early European divisions of people into 'tribes', a political term derived from the classics that was applied to a linguistically defined community. They further divided the 'tribe', again on linguistic grounds, into 'clans', a word drawn from kinship terminology.[15]

In her detailed study of the development of *Afrikanistik*, or African language studies, in Germany between 1814 and 1945, the US historian Sara Pugach has followed scholars such as Patrick Harries, Diana Jeater, and John and Jean Comaroff in describing the long-term consequences for local cultures and identities of the intensive missionary activity that took place in Africa from the beginning of the nineteenth century.[16] Pugach explores how the early decades of the nineteenth century saw deeply devout German Christian (mostly Protestant) missionaries translating Bibles into various African languages in their efforts to bring African converts to Christianity.[17] The missionaries' early involvement in language codification through the production of grammars, dictionaries, primers and translations arose out of their belief that 'a native language, not a foreign one', was the only suitable tongue for expressing the gospel to Africans.[18] In Europe, meanwhile, new theories about the relationship between Sanskrit and the languages of Europe had 'transformed the field of language studies and...biblical criticism' – ushering in the golden age of philology – and in the process had reignited ideas about the 'significance of a distinctly German culture embodied in its heritage and its language'.[19] Thus, there were close parallels between nineteenth-century German pietism and its associated missionary projects in southern Africa, and in the early-nineteenth-century German interest in comparative philology and the philosophical legacies of Johann Gottfried Herder (1744–1803), Wilhelm von Humboldt (1767–1835) and Johann Gottlieb Fichte (1762–1814).[20] While Herder is credited with laying the foundations of comparative philology in late-eighteenth-century German thought, all three scholars are associated with the forging of German nationalism through their theorising of a deep-seated relationship between language and national spirit. Fichte is often perceived to be one of the founding figures of German idealism and nationalism, while Humboldt's legacy can be measured in his contributions to the philosophy of language as well as to the theory and practice of education and state educational systems in Germany and the US.

Pugach tracks how German interest in Africans and their languages, initially aimed at converting (and thereby 'saving') African souls, evolved into a field of scientific research motivated by a desire to control, order and domesticate populations perceived as unruly and chaotic. What began as a spiritual quest to bring Christian truths to African peoples in their native languages set in motion an association between language and culture that grew increasingly intertwined as the century progressed. A growing association between language and race was an intrinsic part of this process, as was an increasingly objectified view of Africa and its people, particularly during the brief period of German colonisation in Africa.[21] As Pugach notes: 'German scholars imagined that Africans spoke and acted in a certain manner and were unlikely to deviate from a specific set of behaviours. The Africa of their [German] imagination did not correlate with what they encountered on the ground, but that was of little consequence;

colonisers...believed in the exotic, primitive Africa of their invention.' While German images of Africans and their languages were not stable, the effect of language codification and ordering was an attempt to clarify what was perceived to be a 'murky ethnic situation in Africa' by devising hierarchical linguistic models which were then mapped onto the landscape.[22] Thus were produced distinct ethnic groups or 'tribes' where these had sometimes not previously existed.

Pugach suggests that the establishment of the *Seminar für Oriental-ische Sprachen* (School for Oriental Languages) in Berlin in 1887 and the Colonial Institute at Hamburg in 1908 marked a shift in the location of African language study from the field to the metropolitan centre. At this point, intellectual contacts between Germany and South Africa, which had been informally established through the early missionaries including F.W. Kolbe and J.G. Krönlein, as well as through philologists such as Wilhelm Bleek, were now formalised. This establishment of formal institutions for the study of African languages in Germany cemented ties between the two countries as South Africans of German descent later travelled to Germany to further their knowledge of African languages. From these entanglements flowed a 'complicated' connection between German and South African thought on the nature of language, race and nationalism.[23] Pugach argues that aspects of German religious and philological traditions struck a chord in South Africa, especially among twentieth-century Afrikaans linguists wrestling with the 'native question' in the 1920s and 1930s.[24] Decades later, the German missionary tradition that 'emphasised the significance of language to ethnicity and cultural particularism' provided some of the rationale for segregation in a country whose white population 'feared urbanisation' and wanted Africans 'kept at a distance'.[25]

In many respects, Diana Jeater's study of language and literacy instruction in colonised southern Zimbabwe echoes what Pugach has argued in relation to the emergence of African language studies in Germany.[26] Both scholars highlight how language standardisation in grammars and dictionaries limited the unruly nature of orality and rendered the language available to underwrite a particular conception of social order. Jeater's study of grammar primers and Shona–English dictionaries produced for schools and missions in the early twentieth century suggests that the phrases selected for translation and the vocabulary used reflected and reinforced settler and missionary ideology, but offered 'little that would be useful in everyday conversation between Africans and whites'.[27] Educational materials were 'not so much concerned with talking *to* Africans as with talking *about* them'.[28] Missionaries and early settlers in southern Zimbabwe produced vocabularies and grammars designed for giving orders rather than for listening to what people had to say. Jeater contends that only words and concepts important to white communities were translated into the vernacular. In keeping with the notion of communication as control, Jeater argues that early primers were designed 'for those who [wished] to communicate a thought or order to a listener, rather than for those who [wanted] to listen and learn from someone else'.[29]

It is within this tradition of missionary and settler colonial language instruction, comparative linguistics and the German study of African languages, as well as the broader intellectual humanism, cosmopolitanism and anti-humanist thinking of the times, that Dorothea's fieldwork can be located. An uneasy fusion of the humanist tradition of classical German philology, an emerging 'anti-humanist' and determinist strain in German anthropology that tended to deny human agency, and hierarchical Victorian notions of civilisation and progress coexisted in Dorothea's research and scholarship, contributing to the complicated and contradictory interpretation of her life story and archive.[30] Inconsistencies of thought and action are an inevitable part of daily life in the field and evidence of the unstable and negotiated nature of the activity that rarely finds its way into the text written up and produced as 'scientific' research in publications afterwards. As this story of Dorothea's trip to Kakia shows, it is a futile exercise to attempt to trace coherence of thought through a life course or set of experiences. Similarly, intellectual histories cannot be reduced to neat and straightforward stories with beginning, middle and end. Rather, they are marked by the untidiness and inconsistency that characterises daily thought and experience.[31]

We have seen in the previous chapter the extent to which Dorothea and her co-researcher Helen Tongue relied on missionary assistance in their rock art excursions through the Orange River Colony and Basutoland in 1905–1907. When Dorothea set out for the Kalahari in 1913, she would rely on a different set of networks, some of them personal and others official. From June through August 1913, Dorothea travelled to southern Bechuanaland (now Botswana) and spent two weeks gathering language samples at the small village of Kakia (now Khakhea).[32] Investigated retrospectively, that trip signals an interesting juncture in her scholarship, a point where her research practice in the field combined both social and scientific purposes. Unusually, she wrote a daily diary. Both trip and diary are the subject of this chapter.

Travelling to Kakia

The record of Dorothea's 1913 trip to Bechuanaland uncharacteristically includes a day-by-day diary which she kept along with her research notes.[33] In addition to the limited private correspondence preserved in her collection, this diary presents a glimpse of rare personal narrative in an archive containing a greater proportion of general and official material (Figure 3.1). The diary of Dorothea's Kakia trip stands alongside two notebooks of language samples, measurements and other research material recorded at the same time.[34] Read together with the personal narrative recorded in the diary, one is able to piece together a more complete record of her fieldwork than can be gleaned from what remains available of her later trips. What can a detailed reading of this field trip tell us about the texture of Dorothea's field encounters and the process of her early linguistic research?

The official version of this trip appeared 15 years later, in the introduction to her *Comparative Vocabularies of Bushman Languages*. There we read that Dorothea travelled by rail to Lobatsi in Bechuanaland, and then by ox wagon to Kakia in the Kalahari. She spent two weeks among people she described as 'Masarwa' who were 'dwelling within walking distance of their Bechuana masters'.[35] Her representation of time here is limited to the hands-on research time, and leaves out the weeks of travelling before and after during which she continued to collect language samples and take photographs. In total, the entire trip lasted just short of six weeks, from 23 June to 1 August 1913, as her diary entries show.[36] On this trip she had the use of an interpreter but, as described below, she also made use of the language skills of others when convenient. Dorothea noted that the 'Masarwa' people had no 'Bushman name' for themselves, but used a 'Sechuana word denoting any kind of Bushman'. 'The fact that these people had forgotten their own tribal name and called themselves by a name given by their masters, showed how long they had been in subjection,' she wrote.[37]

Dorothea's bland one-paragraph summary in her published book excluded the arduous realities of ox-wagon trekking through the desert; the drama of water shortages, icy weather and illness; and the vagaries of human relationships and interactions. Left out of the sanitised account were the people who assisted her, the enormous scale of the landscape through which they passed compared to the confines and sociability of the journey and camp contexts, and the degree of technical and human development that already marked the country through which they travelled. Brief daily entries in the diary reveal a wealth of information regarding the banalities of scientific research, and the relations of conquest and domination that were by that time well entrenched in the region. On Monday 23 June, Dorothea's first diary entry noted that she travelled in 'a small wagon with full tent drawn by sixteen oxen' with 'three men & a boy ... in attendance'.[38] Both notes and diary make clear that Dorothea's research process centred on the giving of 'presents' (*doeke*, or head coverings, and knives for the men; blouses and printed cloth for the women; tobacco and food for everyone), and on the purchasing of material items such as skins, needle cases, charms and karosses.[39] But more than the daily detail, the diary provides a sense of Dorothea's varied levels of engagement with the country she passed through and the people she met. At that time, Dorothea's travel by ox wagon had a precedent in the person of her colleague the anthropologist Winifred Hoernlé (*née* Tucker), who travelled to the Kalahari to study the Nama in 1912–1913.[40] In her diary, Hoernlé detailed her personal feelings of distress and depression while travelling, and expressed frustration and irritation at what she perceived as the non-cooperation of her field interviewees. Like Dorothea, and indeed like most scholars across all disciplines in both the sciences and the humanities, Hoernlé excluded this kind of personal detail from the public lecture she delivered later.[41]

In Dorothea's Kakia diary, each entry begins with a record of the weather, which ranged from icy cold to hot. Most entries featured a description of the landscape through which the party journeyed. Dorothea portrayed her surroundings in terms that revealed an underlying familiarity with the imperialist discourses that have been associated with modern British landscape painting.[42] She used language to further domesticate and order a physical environment that had already been conquered by colonial authority, as in her use of phrases such as 'park-like', 'pretty copse of bushes' and 'grassy country with graceful trees and bushes' to describe the different camps and stopover sites (or 'halts') on the journey. In line with the tradition of travel writing established during the Age of Imperialism, Dorothea hid her complicity with colonial power behind a language of painterly aesthetics invoked to naturalise and domesticate the landscape as she scanned the panorama for future prospects and resources – in this case, the presence of suitable people to interview and/or photograph.[43]

Dorothea travelled to Kakia with her friend Margarethe Vollmer. Along with written material, a collection of 50 or so photographs recording groups, individuals and scenes from the journey survives from the trip.[44] And, drawn from Iziko South African Museum's (SAM) large collection of ethnographic photographs, one intriguing image in particular survives to document the unusual, perhaps incommensurable interactions that were a feature of this excursion. This remarkable photograph features Dorothea and Margarethe sitting at the opening of their wagon with three of their wagon crew ranged around them (Figure 3.2). An entry in Dorothea's diary confirms that this photograph was taken by her guide and interpreter Ompilletsi. Her exact words were: 'Photos taken by Omp of us in wagon.' This entry dates the image-making occasion to the second-to-last day of the trip, 31 July, just before they left 'Lottakan' and began the long trek 'all afternoon & most of the night' back to Kanye.[45]

In the photograph, the men, whose full-length figures seem to crowd out the two women sitting on the wagon above, face the camera assuredly. All three wear hats. The women appear slightly windswept by comparison. Dorothea, wearing a striped blouse with a high collar, squints into the sun. Margarethe wears a cardigan and a silk bow at her throat. The image speaks to intriguing levels of intimacy among the group, offering a visual and intimate avenue into the study of language and linguistics and its practice in southern Africa which is different from that offered in the texts that Dorothea produced through formal methods of research.[46]

75

The nature of Dorothea's interactions with Ompilletsi, ostensibly her guide but also called on to translate and interpret Masarwa and other languages, is intriguing. She allowed him to use her camera, and the image produced speaks to the possibility of complex interactions which are not written about in or corroborated by any documents or texts preserved in the colonial archive. In her first diary entry, Dorothea notes that her field crew included a 'transport man' and '4 natives – three men & a boy'. Which of the three men appear in the photograph cannot be confirmed. Dorothea's support staff remain nameless except for Ompilletsi, whom we first read about in the entry for 26 June. There he is referred to as 'our real guide' who 'appeared on horseback in the evening having come by a more northerly road...[with]...another man to go into desert with us'.[47] Elsewhere, we read of him being laid up with toothache – so much so that travelling was delayed for a day or two.[48] Ompilletsi apparently had a 'cousin' who was 'master' of a number of Masarwa men. We learn too that his father had a cattle post near 'Uolise, a little pan on Lecha'.[49] It seems that Dorothea found his presence heavy going at times, for she was relieved when he left the expedition for a day or two.[50] 'Ompilletsi & keiner off to Kakory – much nicer without them,' she wrote in her diary on 15 July.

Another image offers an alternative view of the researcher set against her field of study. The photo is from the SAM's collection of images from the Bechuanaland Protectorate, and carries the inscription 'Miss Bleek (?)'. It features a woman in sun hat and scarf with face so shaded as to be unrecognisable. But it is likely to be Dorothea, who is pictured wearing sunglasses and sitting on a rock ledge with cattle being herded across a 'pan' (dry shallow waterhole) in the middle distance behind her. No record of its making survives.

The presence of Margarethe Vollmer on the trip to Kakia was in keeping with Dorothea's preference to travel and work with other women. In this instance, there is no evidence to suggest that Margarethe was along for anything other than companionship. Aside from developing a 'tiresome' cold and searching for doves to photograph, Margarethe – or Ete, as Dorothea referred to her – spent most of her time reading, sewing or doing 'fancy work'. Sewing seemed a rather incongruous pastime for a woman who was trekking, often through the night, and camping in 'a small ox wagon with full tent drawn by sixteen oxen'.[51] Dorothea, when not taking down language, measuring people, taking photographs or purchasing 'curios', busied herself with reading, packing and repacking the wagon, organising supplies, and walking.[52] Walking, apparently alone, was something she seemed to need to do each day. Her diary entries share the information that she 'walked across pan' or 'down to the water pits' or 'ahead of wagon in evening'.[53] These moments hint at Dorothea's need to escape the cramped confines of the wagon and camp, and suggest that fieldwork provided the freedom for a more intense and passionate way of engaging with her environment than was possible in the constrained suburban milieu of her home in Newlands.[54]

On 4 July, Dorothea's leisure time involved practising 'with pistol on tree in evening', marking another moment in which the field permitted her to step outside of traditional domesticity. Collective family memory suggests the Bleek women were no strangers to guns. Both Jemima and Lucy had apparently carried guns for protection while travelling and living in Natal during the 1860s (as had Wilhelm Bleek).[55] It seems that Dorothea continued this tradition, judging by the memories of her great-niece Patricia Scott Deetz: 'It was said in the family that when Aunt D was preparing for her expedition to Angola, her brother-in-law Henry (Harry) Hepburn Bright asked if she was taking a gun with her for protection. When she said no, he insisted that she at least take a pistol which she then packed at the bottom of her haversack and never removed! Well, having read Mamie [Pocock]'s description of their buck hunt, Dorothea not only took the gun but was quite able to use it if needed. But typically she probably never mentioned the hunt and it was assumed by the family that Harry's pistol had remained at the bottom of her luggage for the duration of the expedition!'[56]

On the same day of her target-practice session at Legombe, Dorothea's diary records that 'natives sent by a chief' were digging a well 'with the help of gunpowder'.[57] Insertions such as these were commonplace in the diary, where the regular comings and goings of government officials and private individuals were recorded, marking the extent to which scientific and technological intrusions were reshaping the land. On 2 July, for instance, the party passed a policeman who was en route 'to fetch the Dutchman wanted by Govt to dig wells', while on 26 July a 'policeman going to Lehusiter brought us letters from Mr Drury'.[58] The road Dorothea followed was well travelled, and they met others who readily involved themselves in Dorothea's research activities. At Kakia, the young women shared meals with fellow travellers in settings that attempted to reproduce life in suburbia. It is not clear why the Openshaw family were at Kakia, but they provided polite society as well as assistance with translations and the delicate question of taking photographs of naked male subjects.[59] The diary confirmed also that Dorothea remained in contact with James Drury, the 'modeller' and taxidermist from the South African Museum whom she had helped on her earlier trips to the northern Cape by identifying for him 'pure bushman types' to be used in his body-casting project. At the time, Drury was at the beginning of a project that would occupy him for nearly 20 years. Working under the direction of Louis Péringuey, director of the South African Museum, Drury was tasked to produce 'exact' physical reproductions modelled from the 'living flesh' of human beings deemed to be 'survivors' of 'nearly extinguished races'.[60] Drury's casting efforts resulted in a collection of 88 casts, some of which were painted and displayed in the museum in 1911, and others that were not used until the 1980s.[61] In the 1950s, casts from the collection were used to create the museum's infamous bushman diorama that remained open to public view until 2001, when it was 'archived' amid great controversy.[62] Such institutional connections to the museum, and the moments at Kakia when Dorothea was on the lookout for subjects to photograph naked, provide a reminder of the scientific aims of her trip, and complicate the otherwise chatty, social tone of her diary entries.

From the vocabulary and grammar samples collected in the notebooks and recorded on days corresponding to diary entries, we learn that Dorothea was addressed as 'missis'.[63] There is a sense of the intimate scale and performative nature of moments in the research process. It is quite possible that Dorothea found herself needing to act out and bring to life words and phrases in order to obtain language samples. Following methods inaugurated by Wilhelm and Lucy decades ago in their Mowbray sitting room, Dorothea used objects available in her immediate environment to extract words and phrases. Where her father and aunt had relied on picture books and domestic fittings, Dorothea turned to nature, as in the descriptive phrase 'smaller black beetle with stripes on back'.[64] One can imagine the closeness of this interaction, presumably requiring both parties to look closely together at the tiny insect.[65] The active and demonstrative nature of the work becomes apparent in such phrases as 'we lie down, we sleep'; 'the axe chops it down'; 'the stone, I pound with it'; 'I am taking my jacket off'; 'I am putting my jacket on the ground'.[66]

Interspersed with these exchanges are notes related to other orders of research practice (oral and physical) that record biographical and genealogical snippets and lists of measurements in feet and inches written next to lists of names.[67] For instance, the diary entry for 29 June records that Dorothea 'unpacked measuring instruments'.[68] The notebooks include lists of body measurements and Dorothea's comments on the state of people's teeth. The measurements point to an intimate space of measuring. For example, she recorded 'breadth of thigh', as well as depth of chest at inspiration and depth of chest at expiration.[69] Another series of measurements focused on the head, recording 'nasal height', 'nasal breadth' and 'breadth of eyehole'. At times, Dorothea recorded the person's name; at other times a Roman numeral at the top of the list distinguished one individual from another.

Such lists of measurements provide examples of objective research outcomes in which the researcher is essentially absent from the text. However, there are instances where diary and notebooks seem to offer a degree of insight into Dorothea's personal involvement with her research. Brief and fleeting as these are, they reveal the closeness of some of her field encounters, and communicate a visceral sense of the sweat, blood and suffering she encountered, as well as moments in which there may have been recognition of a common humanity between Dorothea and her research subjects.

Scarcity of water, a continuing motif throughout the Kakia trip, provoked one of these instances. On 3 July, Dorothea's diary noted there was 'trouble with oxen half the night who got wild with thirst'.[70] But the real drama of the situation and its emotional effect on the travelling party became apparent only weeks later in Dorothea's language notebook in an entry dated 30 July:

we are very glad, our oxen have got water
we thought they would die
we are very glad, because they shall be able to take Missis home[71]

Arising as these comments do in the midst of vocabulary and phrase lists, the lines are striking in their power. Perhaps their force derives from the presence of shared humanity that can be glimpsed in the short transcription. Read in a particular way, such texts reveal moments of chaos and unpredictability in which an experiential connection may be forged between the researcher and the (human) objects of her attention. A similar instance of shared experience surfaces on 24 July:

> we yesterday saw a baboon
> we this morning saw a flock of ostrich
> …
> we saw a secretary bird
> S. tried to go to it, it flew away
> he wanted to shoot it, it flew away
> it is beautiful[72]

Again, these phrases seem replete with shared experience and suggest a moment of genuine reciprocal communication, rather than an interaction singularly focused on the extraction of language for scientific study.[73] They suggest the possibility that even though Dorothea's project was to map, in the most objective and scientifically correct way, the traces of a 'dying' language and its speakers onto the landscape of southern Africa, the actualities and messiness of human interactions occasionally broke through her screen of scientific objectivity.

Making subjects

Dorothea's Kakia diary and notebooks reveal a tentative process of identity formation that draws not only on the presence of the 'bushman' other, but also on the role of landscape and place. Nupur Chaudhuri and Margaret Strobel have succinctly described the many and varied ways in which imperialism impacted on women's identities and the changing roles they could inhabit when travelling away from metropolitan centres.[74] As has been shown in feminist analyses of women travel writers of the colonial period, the notion of travel and of freedom of movement between home and away provided space for the formation of more fluid senses of self that women travellers could express through descriptions not only of landscapes, but also of the people they encountered on their travels.[75] That Dorothea found the fieldwork environment empowering, affirming and emancipatory is certainly suggested in her frequent references to her solo walks beyond the confines of the wagon and camp, and in the interlude when she indulges in target shooting with her pistol.

At that early stage in her career, Dorothea's journey to Kakia set the tone for her future commitment to gathering knowledge in the field. Her materials produced on that occasion reflect her faith in the processes of observing, recording and documenting as critical to the making of scientific knowledge. In line with the German ethnologists whose thinking she most likely came into contact with during her education in Europe, Dorothea believed that analysis could come later, particularly in the case of the bushmen, whose cultural survival was in her opinion threatened by modernity and civilisation.[76] Typically, as noted on several occasions in her correspondence, she deferred deskwork (her ongoing translations of the /Xam and !Kung notebooks) in favour of research in the field.

Through all of her research notes and subsequent publications, Dorothea's strategy of classifying people according to their language, and of mapping languages and their speakers onto the landscape, become noticeable. Notebooks recorded earlier (at Prieska and with Helen Tongue) and later (at Sandfontein in 1920–1921) show how Dorothea framed her questions in order to extract a set of cultural markers to support her language classification. She carried books by George Stow and the Prussian geographer Siegfried Passarge together with *Specimens of Bushman Folklore* into the field to assist in this process, although she did not refer specifically to them during her journey to Kakia. The diary and notes recorded there reflect her developing practices and field methods around the systematic collection of language, a full 10 years before she would be accorded the institutional status of 'Honorary Reader in Bushman Languages' at UCT in 1923. At Kakia, her research notes show how she began to develop methodologies or, perhaps more accurately, took the methods developed in her father's and aunt's project in Mowbray and adapted them to the field.

Dorothea's notebooks show the concern with breaking language into observable, measurable components for the purposes of empirical

81

modelling and comparison. This was typical of linguistic practice developed in the comparative tradition of philology and applied to ancient, biblical and Sanskrit texts in the academies of Enlightenment Europe.[77] It was a method that would be transferred into the colonial and modernist discipline of linguistics and find its way to the dusty semi-deserts of southern Africa, where it would receive new vitality through its use in the classification and categorisation of oral languages spoken by people considered to be the relics from a prehistoric past or the 'ancient races' of the region.[78] Dorothea's method derived its logic from classificatory scientific disciplines such as botany and entomology that were being adapted for the study of humans by European and British scholars of the day. As her work intensified, Dorothea would apply an analytical model that was typical at the time, breaking culture into constituent parts (method of arrow making, type of dwelling, type of musical instrument, and so on) for comparison across groups.

Dorothea's field notebooks reveal a structure and purpose underlying what on the surface could be seen as a haphazard collection of material. Her surviving 32 field notebooks offer a fragmentary mix of vocabulary, phrases and grammar in one or other of the languages she was researching, along with translations in English. Her research records include biographical notes and details of genealogy and family history about the particular person being interviewed, or about the person's immediate family and/or 'tribe'. Ethnographic entries were common and concerned such topics as food preparation, beer making, initiation rites, and so on. Whenever she could, Dorothea recorded folk tales. But the day-to-day diary she recorded on the Kakia trip turned out to be an isolated mode of writing that she did not repeat.

Fig 1.1: This regularly reproduced studio portrait of Dorothea is dated to 1929, the year she travelled to London to arrange the publishing of her edited book of Stow rock art copies. It was taken by the London photographer Navana of Oxford Street, Kensington.
(Courtesy of the University of Cape Town Libraries' Bleek Collection)

Fig 1.2: A *carte de visite* portrait of Dorothea Bleek taken in Charlottenburg, Berlin, in 1899, from the family's Oakleaf Album compiled by Dorothea's niece Marjorie Scott in the 1980s. The reverse of the *carte de visite* reveals that the portrait was taken by Theodor Penz Atelier of Tauenzienstr.
(Courtesy of the University of Cape Town Libraries' Bleek Collection)

Fig 1.3: Tamme's drawing of an animal drinking water and a tree from his home country was annotated by Lucy Lloyd on 18 June 1881.
(Courtesy of Iziko South African Museum.)

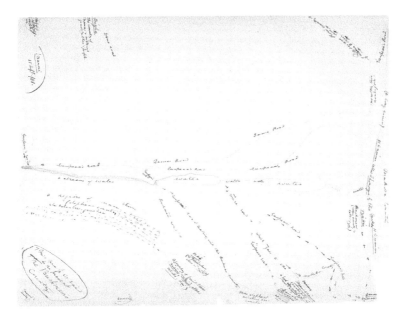

Fig 1.4: A sketch of !Nanni's home 'country' produced by the teenage boy during research with Lucy Lloyd at Mowbray, 15 September 1881.
(Courtesy of Iziko South African Museum.)

Fig 1.5: A studio portrait of Jemima Bleek and her daughters taken in Bonn in 1886 by the photographer Emil Koch of Hofgartenstrasse. Pictured, from left, are Edith (seated), Dorothea, Jemima (seated), Margie, May (seated) and Helma.
(Courtesy of the University of Cape Town Libraries' Bleek Collection)

Fig 1.6: An undated photograph from the Oakleaf Album shows Dorothea seated amidst a group of gentlemen. An annotation made by Majorie Scott in the 1980s suggests it was taken at an anthropological or linguistics conference in Berlin.
(Courtesy of the University of Cape Town Libraries' Bleek Collection)

Fig 2.1: Dorothea copied this unusual painting of a leaping lion seemingly in pursuit of a person at a site near Advance Post, Basutholand.
(Courtesy of Iziko South African Museum.)

Fig 2.2: At Advance Post, Dorothea copied a painting that she thought illustrated the final scene in her father's tale of the mantis and the dead hartebeest. The 'jaunty figure has just the harmless and vain air one associates with /Kaggen, the hero of so many Bushman tales. The way in which the children cling to one another shows their fright plainly enough', she wrote.
(Courtesy of Iziko South African Museum.)

Fig 2.3: This photograph from the archives of Cradock High School is inscribed 'Miss Hockley and Staff, 1906'. It shows the teachers of Rocklands Girls' School with Miss Bleek standing on the left and Miss Tongue seated, second from left.
(Courtesy of Cradock High School.)

Fig 2.4: Another of the eight copies that Dorothea produced with Helen Tongue. The inscription on this watercolour records that Dorothea copied it at Modderpoort near Ladybrand in the Orange Free State. She thought that some of the paintings she saw there represented a cattle raid between two bushman groups rather than a battle between different tribes.
(Courtesy of Iziko South African Museum.)

Fig 2.5: Helen Tongue copied this painting in a cave near Cradock, most likely to show its beautiful shading and technical proficiency.
(Courtesy of Iziko South African Museum.)

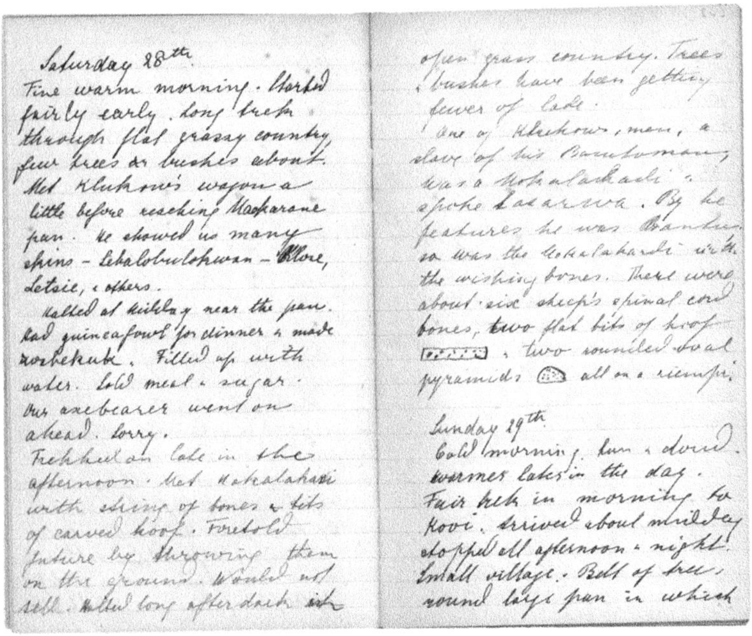
Saturday 28th.
Fine warm morning. Started
fairly early. Long trek
through flat grassy country,
few trees or bushes about.
Met Kluckow's wagon a
little before reaching Maakarane
pan. He showed us many
skins – Lebalobulokwan – Klore,
Letsie, & others.
Halted at midday near the pan.
Had guineafowl for dinner & made
roosterkoek. Filled up with
water. Sold meal & sugar.
Our axebearer went on
ahead. Lorry.
Trekked on late in the
afternoon. Met Kgalagadi
with string of bones & bits
of carved hoof. Foretold
future by throwing them
on the ground. Would not
sell. Halted long after dark with

open grass country. Trees
& bushes have been getting
fewer of late.
One of Kluckow's men, a
slave of his Bamangwato,
was a Kgalagadi &
spoke Sesarwa. By his
features he was Bantu,
so was the Kgalagadi with
the wishing bones. There were
about six sheep's spinal cord
bones, two flat bits of hoof
[drawing], two rounded oval
pyramids [drawing] all on a riempie.

Sunday 29th.
Cold morning, sun & cloud.
Warmer later in the day.
Fair trek in morning to
Kooi. Arrived about midday
stopped all afternoon & night.
Small village. Belt of trees
round large pan in which

Fig 3.1: A page from the diary that Dorothea recorded on each day of her journey to Kakia. She noted details such as the weather, the day's activities, her interviews, the photographs she took, and the progress of her language sampling.
(Courtesy of the University of Cape Town Libraries' Bleek Collection)

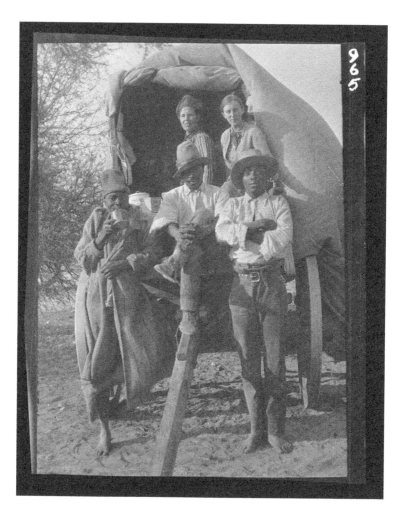

Fig 3.2: Dorothea's guide and interpreter Omplilletsi took this photograph on 31 July 1913, two days before their return to Kanye in the Bechuanaland Protectorate. (Courtesy of Iziko South African Museum.)

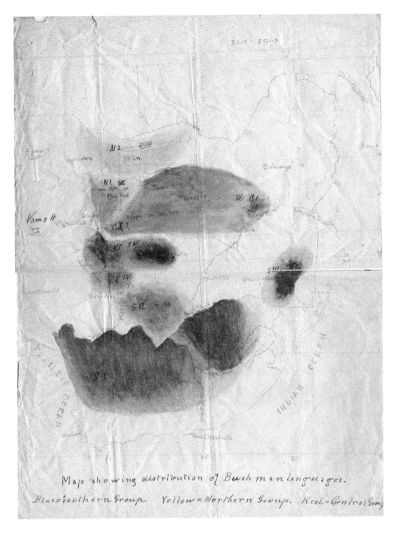

Fig 4.1: Dorothea coloured this map to show her model of the distribution of bushman people across southern Africa. She used it to illustrate her lecture to UCT's Vacation School in January 1924.
(Courtesy of the University of Cape Town Libraries' Bleek Collection)

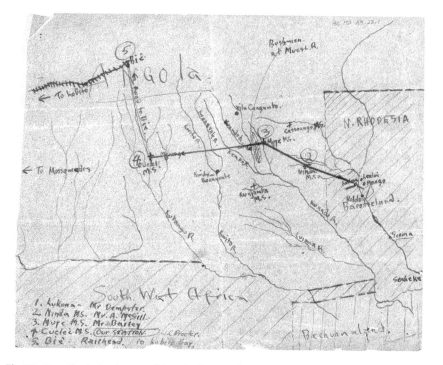

Fig 4.2: Dorothea's sketch map of Angola shows major rivers and the mission stations at which she and Mary Pocock stopped during their journey overland.
(Courtesy of the University of Cape Town Libraries' Bleek Collection)

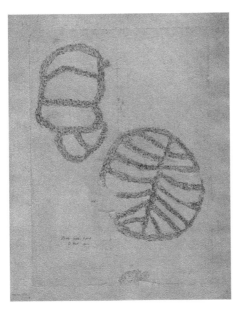

Fig 5.1: This charcoal rubbing of geometric rock art was made sometime during Dorothea's research at Sandfontein in 1921.
(Courtesy of Iziko South African Museum.)

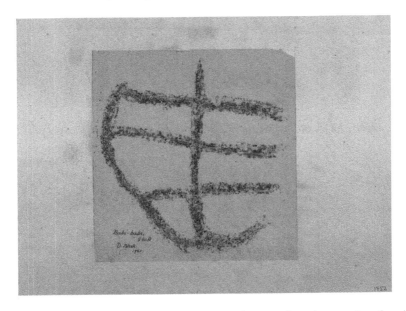

Fig 5.2: Another of Dorothea's charcoal rubbings of geometric rock engravings found at BabiBabi close to Sandtontein.
(Courtesy of Iziko South African Museum.)

Fig 6.1: Mollie van der Riet copying paintings at Boesman's Kloof, Oudtshoorn
(Courtesy of the University of Cape Town Libraries' Bleek Collection)

Fig 6.2: An undated photograph showing Dorothea possibly giving a rock art lecture is taken from the family album compiled by her niece Marjorie in the 1980s. (Courtesy of the University of Cape Town Libraries' Bleek Collection)

Fig 7.1: This photograph of a meeting of the South African Association for the Advancement of Science shows Dorothea seated in the centre of the front row with the palaeontologist Robert Broom on her left. Her niece Marjorie is four rows behind, in a white beret. The photograph was taken in Durban in 1932 when Dorothea delivered her survey on the rock art of southern Africa.

(Courtesy of the University of Cape Town Libraries' Bleek Collection)

4 | Ambiguities of Interaction: South West Africa, Angola and Tanganyika, 1920–1930

the white man covered me...
the white man covered my legs (thighs)
the white man covered my lower legs

...

the white man covered my body
the white man covered my chest
... [further parts of body specified]
I'm very cold[1]

This reference to body casting arises unexpectedly in Dorothea's field notebook amid exchanges about extracting poison from worms for use in hunting, and a discussion about the role of 'old' and 'young' women 'doktors' [sic] in healing. It was December 1920, and Dorothea was at the start of a five-month-long, government-initiated research sojourn in which the aim was to document the 'bushman types' of the territory that Dorothea mistakenly referred to as the South West Protectorate (SWP), more commonly known as South West Africa (now Namibia). It was also the beginning of what was arguably the most active decade in Dorothea's career, in terms of both fieldwork and publications. This chapter deals with Dorothea's research trips to South West Africa (November 1920 to March 1921, and again from November 1921 to March 1922), Angola (1925) and Tanganyika (1930), and describes the day-to-day practice and texture of her work in the field, locating these in relation to Dorothea's intellectual progression and the development of her research process and methodology. It suggests too what these ideas and practices have brought to understandings of the term 'bushman' in popular and academic contexts in southern Africa and the world.

In South West Africa, first at the Windhoek prison and later at Sandfontein, Dorothea was working alongside 'two gentlemen' from the South African Museum whom she did not identify. Collectively, their task was to undertake 'anthropological research among the Bushmen of the Protectorate'.[2] The men, one of whom was identified in later correspondence as James Drury, were assigned 'the physical research work, such as taking casts, measurements, etc., and I, though unconnected with the Museum, was asked to undertake the philological research', she wrote later in her monograph *The Naron*.[3]

The reference to casting confirms Dorothea's continued albeit peripheral involvement in this intrusive form of body sampling. It was not the first time that Dorothea had worked alongside Drury. Their association went back to her 1910 and 1911 trips to the northern Cape, where she had helped to identify 'pure bushman' types as suitable specimens for life casting. We have seen too that she participated in collecting human remains for 'scientific' study while in the Kalahari with Maria Wilman and George Lennox in 1911. Such practices highlight scholarly alignments between language and 'race' that underpinned linguistic research and physical anthropology at the time.[4] Now, nearly 10 years later, Drury's project was still under way, fuelled by museum director Louis Péringuey's enthusiastic desire to collect anthropometric data from exact 'models' produced from the 'living flesh' of people he insisted were doomed to extinction.[5] British art historian Annie Coombes argues that Péringuey's interest in bushman bodies amounted to a 'virtual obsession' that influenced the direction of the museum's research for the next two decades, and contributed to the elevation of physical anthropology (a branch of anthropology that in the late nineteenth and early twentieth centuries used physical data to determine the intellectual, moral and evolutionary status of people, but that in contemporary times concerns itself with the study of the origin, evolution and diversity of human groups) as a 'dominating intellectual force' in South African prehistory.[6] Péringuey's legacy at the museum continued well into the early 2000s through the presentation of 'ethnic' displays including the notorious bushman diorama which was constructed in the 1950s using body casts that had been made by Drury.

The museum researchers' trip to South West Africa was in some respects modelled on British colonial projects of research aimed at understanding and controlling native populations. Dorothea's research, admittedly on a smaller scale, took place in the decades during which anthropology was transforming from a generalised, 'survey' approach to fieldwork exemplified by the Torres Strait expedition of 1898 to the 'intensive' method of fieldwork inspired by Bronislaw Malinowski and published in 1922 as *Argonauts of the Western Pacific*. But while the Torres Strait expedition led by the zoologist-turned-anthropologist A.C. Haddon has been described as a 'watershed event in British anthropology' that ushered in a modern school of systematic and scientific fieldwork incorporating multidisciplinary teams of researchers,[7] it remained steeped in evolutionary thinking and motivated by a desire to salvage what was left of people and cultures perceived to be threatened with extinction. Just 15 years later, Malinowski's prolonged stay among the Trobriand Islanders during World War I again revolutionised anthropological fieldwork by encouraging the researcher to move from a 'comfortable position on the veranda into the village' to spend extended periods of time living 'among' the people who were the objects of his (*sic*) research,[8] thereby inaugurating an early version of participant observation. Another 10 years later, in the early 1930s, the young Monica Hunter (Wilson) would embark on ethnographic fieldwork at a series of sites in Pondoland and elsewhere in the eastern Cape, following in the footsteps of Malinowski and gathering the research that would later appear as the landmark South African monograph in the social anthropology tradition, *Reaction to Conquest: Effects of Contact with Europeans on the Pondo of South Africa*.[9]

But while Hunter's emphasis throughout her long career lay on cultural contact and historical change, Dorothea kept within the narrow range of sampling, collection and salvage.[10] For Dorothea, change was a consequence of modernity, with negative impacts on the life ways, languages, and rich storytelling and artistic traditions of the bushmen. Her passion was to record what traditions and materials she could recover from a vanishing 'race' and to continue to publish her father's and aunt's research. She made her approach clear on several occasions in her private correspondence, as in a letter to Käthe Woldmann in 1929: 'My goal is to write up as many Bushman languages and literatures as possible, before it is too late. The comparative work others can do later.'[11]

Windhoek and Sandfontein, 1920–1921

Dorothea arrived in Windhoek ahead of her companions from the South African Museum, and began work at the prison immediately. She recorded her first language session on 20 November 1920 on page 1 of the notebook she had labelled '!Kun and Naron'.[12] Her letter of 25 November to museum director Louis Péringuey indicated that she was ensconced at the Hotel Röhlig despite its expense, and that Drury had arrived that morning.[13] In keeping with the official status of the expedition, Dorothea and Drury made contact with government networks in the territory. They met the medical officer of health, Dr Louis Fourie, on the morning of 25 November, and through him made transport and equipment arrangements for their Sandfontein expedition.[14] Dorothea and her colleagues were assigned an 'empty police station of Sandfontein on the border of the Bechuanaland Protectorate' for use as a research station.[15]

Dorothea's correspondence with Péringuey suggests that his interests may have added structure to her own research agenda. The letters add context and detail to the information contained in her notebooks regarding conditions at the Windhoek prison. She reported regularly to Péringuey, noting that there were 18 individuals identified as 'bushmen' being held in the prison. At times, Péringuey's research agenda called for more than what Dorothea was comfortable with:

> I will note the particular information you wish obtained. Some of it is not obtainable under the circumstances of my prison investigations. The men are evidently afraid of admitting anything the white man might disapprove – such as putting people to death as a punishment, etc. I must wait for free Bushmen for that.[16]

In the same letter, it becomes apparent that Péringuey had gender-specific research requirements. Dorothea had evidently promised to attempt to interview women. But she only found 'one Hei //um woman' in the prison, and being forced to 'see' her 'before half a dozen men' did not make the interview conducive to fulfilling Péringuey's 'wishes'.[17] It seems possible to discern a moment of awareness on Dorothea's part of the gender and power relations inherent in the prison situation that was analogous to an earlier passage in her Kakia diary, where she deferred the task of taking photographs of naked men to her travelling companion the 'elder Openshaw'.[18] As much as they affirm the generalised and objective context of science, Dorothea's letters and notes from Windhoek contain points of difference that disturb the prevailing norms that then underpinned the making of scientific knowledge, and allow for the expression of personal interest in and intimate engagement with her 'subjects', as in this excerpt from a letter to Péringuey written soon after she began work:

> Seven of these are !Kung Bushmen. They speak much the same language as the four boys from Lake Ngami *that my Aunt had*, who also called themselves !Kung. They all have the cut between the eyebrows that the older three boys had. One is a very interesting man from far north, a big game hunter. But all are worth seeing. I fancy two have been in Mr Drury's hands, but not all of them.[19]

The extract gives a sense of a genuine human connection and implied violence. Connection seems to be encapsulated in the passing reference to other possibilities of engagement with the 'interesting man' who exceeded his prisoner identity and for a moment reverted to an earlier identity as a 'big game hunter'. Dorothea's descriptive phrases tie the individual into larger networks than were typically allowed for in her notion of 'bushman', and suggest a possibility of shared rapport. At the same time, there is the possibility of uncertainty, as well as the potential for force or violence, encapsulated in the phrase that 'two have been in Mr Drury's hands' – no doubt a reference to the traumatic life-casting process. Perhaps the most that can be said about such enigmatic moments is that they complicate and undermine the writing of a seamless account of Dorothea's fieldwork and scholarly project, and remind us of the unknowability at its core.

In the same sense, Dorothea's reference to the !Kung boys from her childhood raises intriguing questions about the blurring of boundaries between biography and scholarship.[20] Notebook texts recorded by Lucy Lloyd report that the youngsters had been 'raided' by enemy groups and separated from their families. Perhaps Dorothea had their tales of abduction in mind when she came upon !Kung speakers at the Windhoek prison. But her 1920 notebook is silent about the coincidence that one of her first !Kung-speaking interviewees at the prison shared the same name (!Nanni) as one of the boys left in Lucy's care when Dorothea was six years old. Perhaps Dorothea's encounters with the children and the illustrations they produced informed her research agenda not quite 40 years later. Her prior knowledge of !Nanni's sketch map of his home country (Figure 1.4), either from her childhood or later, when she helped Lucy edit *Specimens of Bushman Folklore*, could have informed her interactions with people in South West Africa and from southern Angola, and influenced the conclusions she drew.

Mapping language, trade, genealogies and boundaries

Many exchanges recorded in Dorothea's notes suggest the extent to which bushmen people lived cooperatively and interacted with 'Ovambos' and 'Hereros', terminology of the day for early agricultural and herding societies historically occupying the far northern and central parts respectively of what is now Namibia. Apart from passing acknowledgement of the presence of Germans in the landscape, Dorothea made no reference to the traumatic recent colonial past nor to the pre-World War I atrocities and wars of dispossession that would have remained in the memory of at least some of her interlocutors.[21] She was interested in different histories. Notebooks recorded at the Windhoek prison, at Sandfontein and elsewhere contain references to bushmen trading ostrich-eggshell beads, skins, honey and *veldkos* with others, including 'Ovambo' and 'Herero', in exchange for clay pots, metal knives, spears and arrowheads.[22] But Dorothea's method was to reduce this record of integration in line with her notions (inherited from her father and George Stow) of encroachment, disintegration and extinction. As she had done more tentatively at Kakia, she now made a point of recording details of what she saw as a threatened way of life, focusing on gathering as opposed to cultivating, the use of particular kinds of shelters, eating veldkos and certain kinds of insects, and, most importantly, physical features as a means of identifying people as bushmen.[23] Her interviewees provided information that Dorothea could interpret as evidence of an ideal past with plentiful resources for foraging and hunting:

[There] was always water in the spring. They always have had enough to eat – they got so much *veldkos* that they borrow a cart from the Boers to fetch it. There is always plenty.[24]

The record of interaction resonates with themes in the notebooks of Wilhelm Bleek and Lucy Lloyd that reflect /Xam networks of ostrich-feather trading and other forms of interaction with the Boers and early settlers, particularly in the case of Dia!kwain, who lived closest to the colonial frontier.[25] In addition, Dorothea built on information she had drawn from earlier writers, including the Rhenish missionary, linguist and historian Heinrich Vedder and the Prussian geographer and traveller Siegfried Passarge, both of whom focused on South West Africa and the Kalahari, and, less frequently, the German explorer-turned-physical-anthropologist Gustav Fritsch. Fritsch had published several books about *Eingeborenen* or 'native inhabitants' based on his journey through southern Africa between 1863 and 1865, and these had become celebrated handbooks for the study of physical anthropology.[26] Dorothea's notebooks indicate that in the field she regularly referred to George Stow's *The Native Races of South Africa* as well as Lucy's *Specimens of Bushman Folklore*. She used the illustrations in both these publications in discussions with interlocutors about the design and making of arrows, and the construction and use of musical instruments.[27] She also referred to Passarge in discussions about hunting and bows and arrows, and about types of shelters used by her interviewees.[28]

Dorothea's research papers include copies of typed word lists that were used to collect vocabulary in the field.[29] From the lists, typed in many carbon copies, it can be seen that she extracted the same vocabulary from all the different language speakers she came across. She grouped her words under categories such as body parts, landscape and environment, animals and domestic implements, among others. It was important to be able to compare the various translations of words such as 'lung', 'stomach', 'tongue' and 'lip', as well as words for 'ashes', 'embers', 'hut', 'doorway' and 'iron pot'. Dorothea also collected words for abstract concepts, such as colours ('white', 'black', 'yellow', 'red', 'green', 'purple', 'orange' – on one list she marked each colour next to the word) and 'good', 'bad', 'rich' and 'poor'.[30]

Dorothea was sensitive to the possibility of misunderstanding that could arise during the translation of concepts between what she regarded as fundamentally different categories of people. As she wrote in a letter to Käthe Woldmann in 1930: 'Among the Bushman one finds the word "good" or "bad" mostly used or applied as when we use the expression "good butter". The same word is often used for lovely, pleasing, young.'[31] Her view was inflected by a particular notion drawn from German *Ethnologie* in the tradition of Adolf Bastian that placed 'natural' and 'cultured' peoples in an opposing relation to each other in the world at large. Thus she warned about applying the concepts and thought systems of the cultured people of the world to those of the natural and immature. First-hand observation and experience were the means by which an accurate understanding of all the peoples of the earth could be fully grasped. Dorothea was adamant that the stories (and culture) of the bushmen could not be interpreted by those who were not thoroughly familiar with bushman ways of life and landscapes. The people of Europe who had no personal experience of 'natural' people in their environment would not correctly or appropriately interpret the meanings of their stories, but would be influenced by the ideas of their own (European) culture. The ability to interpret bushmen and their languages adequately could be achieved only through detailed observation in the field:

> The interpretation of ideas about bad and good gods, bad and good heroes in your [Woldmann's, i.e. European] legends is a matter related to the Europeans, and the less a researcher has to do with the little people (Völkchen) [i.e. bushmen], the more he interprets their stories according to the way he sees it, and the further he is removed from their childlike position, in which nothing is absolutely good or bad. For example, the sun can bring good things, but can also cause destruction, the rain makes everything grow and prosper, but can also, in the form of a storm, destroy them and their huts.[32]

After a month's work at the Windhoek prison, Dorothea and her colleagues travelled to Sandfontein and began work there early in January 1921.[33] Now she found herself in daily contact with a number of //K'au//en ('or Auen as they are generally called by Europeans who cannot pronounce the clicks') and Naron families who lived near the police station.[34] She would later classify these in her Northern and Central bushman language groups respectively. Her decision to concentrate on the Naron was made in the interests of building up a complete scientific picture of the peoples of South West Africa. The Naron were under-researched because a 'fair amount of literature [had] already been published about the !Kung and the Auen'.[35] She cited Lucy's translations of !Kung texts in *Specimens of Bushman Folklore*, as well as work in German by the missionary Vedder, and the language scholars Hans Kaufmann and Franz Seiner.

Photography

Dorothea was no stranger to the use of the camera in the field. Photography was, after all, an accepted method of visual documentation in anthropological research and had been since her father's time.[36] Her photographic output was haphazard. It included a large number of anthropometric-style photographs of men and women whom she had succeeded in persuading to remove their clothing. These images can be found among the Iziko South African Museum's ethnographic collections, where they are categorised by 'ethnicity' and geographic region. A less invasive kind of field photography can be found in Dorothea's personal collection arranged in a green photograph album inscribed with 'Post-cards' in italicised lettering. This album, donated by Dorothea to UCT just before her death, features 300 or so photographs taken on her trips to the northern Cape and the Kalahari, to the Langeberg, to Lake Chrissie in the then eastern Transvaal, to Sandfontein and to Angola.[37] But apart from photographs taken on the 1911 trip to Prieska, and four from Angola that appeared in *Bantu Studies*, none of these images have been published.[38] Only 24 of a total of 158 photographs taken on the expedition to Prieska were published in the journal *Bantu Studies* in 1936.

In his fine-detailed reading of Dorothea's expedition from Prieska in the northern Cape to Kyky in the Kalahari, Andrew Bank has explained this omission by suggesting that Dorothea 'packaged' the Prieska photographs to present evidence of 'a fragmented community whose traditions and culture had been irrevocably lost', in keeping with her sense that modernity had destroyed and impoverished a society that had once possessed the rich oral tradition that Wilhelm and Lucy had recovered for posterity.[39] Given the timing of her expeditions in the early decades of the twentieth century, Bank argues that Dorothea's field photography straddled 'two eras of anthropology and anthropological photography', coinciding with the ending of the 'era of officially archived comparative photography', of which the evolutionary biologist Thomas Henry Huxley's quest to produce a visual record of all the races of the British Empire was an example, and the beginning of a new era in which photographs taken in the course of fieldwork were kept as a private record to visually augment notes taken in the field.[40] The separation between the anthropometric photography at the South African Museum and the domestic-themed images in her album at UCT suggests that some of Dorothea's photography was intended for private rather than public use – as a visual record of a particular field trip intended to be read alongside notes recorded at the time, rather than for official submission or publishing.

Sound

Along with making a visual record, Dorothea sought to record the songs and speech of the bushmen. At Sandfontein she recorded songs and languages onto wax cylinders using an Edison Bell phonograph or, in her words, 'an Ediphone'. It was the second time she had used a phonograph in the field, but she was not impressed by its efficacy and found it frustrating to use. She complained bitterly that the gramophone did not record the clicks, and therefore her interviewees struggled to hear and confirm what they had just spoken into the recorder. Because they were unable to understand what they had said, they could not repeat it word for word, thus rendering her language-transcription work impossible.[41]

In a typescript written after leaving the field, Dorothea prefaced her text with a warning: 'I say, intentionally with regard to Saul's speech, that he is supposed to have said so. But neither he nor any of the Bushmen could understand their own sentences when reproduced by the phonograph, because the instrument omits nearly all the clicks. They therefore told me the gist of what they had said. It is not accurate sentence for sentence.'[42] The phonograph was useful for recording the incantation of songs, she told Käthe Woldmann later. But as far as the language was concerned, without the click sounds Dorothea was guessing what had been said.[43]

Years later, Dorothea went to the trouble of having her phonograph repaired in order to assist the Wits musicologist Percival Kirby with his query about /Xam music.[44] Other correspondence reveals that the sound recordings in the South African Museum collections were from the Kanye neighbourhood on the eastern (Bechuanaland) side of the Kalahari – perhaps recordings that had been taken on her trip to Kakia in 1913. The recordings made in South West Africa, together with a cinematograph camera and films, had been 'commandeered by the authorities at Windhoek and never came back [to the museum] at all'.[45]

Objects

In keeping with her aim to salvage what remained of bushman culture, Dorothea collected objects as she proceeded through the field. The Iziko South African Museum, the Kirby Collection of Ethno-Musicology at UCT and the McGregor Museum in Kimberley continue to hold material that Dorothea collected. At the South African Museum, objects requisitioned by Dorothea remain on display to this day.[46]

At the end of her first stay at Sandfontein in March 1921, Dorothea dispatched by post from Gobabis to Maria Wilman at the McGregor Museum a selection of 'curios', including a 'bushman mortar made by //K'au //en (Auen) & sold to Naron', 'dancing rattles worn by //K'au //en (Auen) & Naron', a 'sinew bag made & used by both to carry ostrich eggshells', 'dollas [sic] (2 male & 2 female) bought from Naron', a 'buchu necklace worn by girls', an 'ostrich eggshell hair ornament', a 'half-finished eggshell chain with implements, horn, polishing stone & fibre for twisting in between', 'roots worn & nibbled at by girls & women', a 'young man's [?] pipe' and, most fascinating, 'poison grubs from which poisons for arrows is extracted'.[47] These were objects that remained in her possession after James Drury had taken 'all he wanted first for Cape Town'.[48] Dorothea chose not to be reimbursed for what she sent to Kimberley – the collection did not represent much in terms of financial outlay. 'You don't owe me anything for the things I sent,' she wrote to Wilman. 'As you know one gets them for a trifle in the wilds.'[49]

Some of Dorothea's sampling and salvage efforts were frustrated, however. She was unable to collect any examples of pottery, as she found such items had been 'quite supplanted by the white man's jam & paint tins at Sandfontein'. And her attempts to collect items of clothing were stymied by her lack of suitable exchange: 'As you know, Bushmen only give clothes for clothes or material,' she wrote to Wilman on her return to Cape Town early in May.[50]

On her way home from Sandfontein, Dorothea took a 'detour to the south'. She spent time among the /Nu//en (or Nusan) at Tsachas, Uichenas, and Amenius, and also with a 'branch of the /Nu //en living at Nausanab-itz', people whom she later described as 'famous for making ostrich eggshell beads' and who were known locally as the !Ko: or '!Koon'.[51] From the rail hub at De Aar, she sent items 'too long' for posting with a 'fellow passenger Miss Irving'. These were a spear 'used by the Naron…for despatching game that has been wounded', and a bow with arrows.[52]

Dorothea's first trip to South West Africa was extremely productive, particularly as it drew to a close: 'I stayed at Sandfontein till March, the last six weeks alone with the Bushmen and my interpreter. During that time the Bushmen became more confidential, and as I began to understand and speak their language, I obtained a good deal of information.'[53] Her guide and interpreter known as 'Saul', who held the rank of 'constable', had grown up near Sandfontein. He was fluent in Naron and 'could understand the //K'au//en tongue fairly'. He would also play the role of interlocutor, providing material for Dorothea's phonograph. Dorothea was thrilled to be able to return to Sandfontein for a second research session following an invitation from the government of the territory. She returned at the beginning of November 1921 and stayed until mid-March 1922. This time she worked entirely without an interpreter.[54]

By January 1924, just a year after her appointment as Honorary Reader in Bushman Languages at UCT, Dorothea had drawn up her model of the distribution of bushman people across southern Africa 'as far as we can fix it by their language' (Figure 4.1).[55] Her classification of the languages into three groups was based on her fieldwork to date and on the notebooks of her father and aunt. She unveiled her mapping of the three categories (Southern, Central and Northern) and their subfields onto the landscape of southern Africa at a lecture titled 'Bushman Life' at the UCT Vacation School (Map C).[56] The public lecture series was held under the auspices of Alfred Radcliffe-Brown's newly established Centre for African Life and Languages, and followed one given by Winifred Hoernlé on 'Hottentot' (a term coined by the first Dutch settlers for early pastoralists at the Cape, now used pejoratively) customs and beliefs.[57]

Angola, 1925

> From Livingstone we went by boat up the Zambesi to about the 15° S. latitude (opposite Lialui), then by carriers into and across Angola keeping between the 14° and 15° S. latitude till we reached the Cuelei river near the 16° East longitude. Thence we struck north to the railway, which we reached at Vila Silva Porta, better known as Bie. There we took train for Lobito Bay.[58]

Dorothea's written description of her six-and-a-half-month journey through Angola truncates what must have been a gruelling physical exercise into a few concise sentences abstracted from any sense of personal experience. This and further practical details of the 1925 trip can be drawn from the first couple of paragraphs of her journal article that appeared in *Bantu Studies* in 1928.[59] In that article she confirmed that her trip began at Livingstone (near Victoria Falls), and that she travelled with 'Miss M. A. Pocock', who would pursue 'botanical studies'.[60]

Details about the physical challenges of the trip can be read in the newspaper articles that Mary Pocock published.[61] There we learn that the women were conveyed first in dugout canoes for 17 days, and thereafter in *machilas*. These were covered, hammock-like conveyances that were carried by two or three porters.[62] Like travellers in Africa 50 or 100 years before, their excursion was noteworthy for the size of its support team, the amount of equipment it entailed, and its impact on local environments and people. From Pocock's reports, we know that the trip involved a harrowing 'truck' journey on terrible roads on day one, several boats and oarsmen thereafter, and cooks and porters throughout. Johannes Fabian has unearthed amusing details describing the enormous logistical requirements of German explorers travelling in Africa in the 1880s, attending also to the idiosyncratic and outlandish Western artefacts (including clockwork toys) that the travellers brought along to win over the 'natives'.[63] It is unlikely that Dorothea relied on quite that level of logistical support, or that she employed such marvels of Imperial German and Victorian toy making in her interactions with the local people. Her tactic was to hand out food items, tobacco, knives and occasionally clothing, as we have seen. Pocock's reports indicated that in Angola commodities such as calico and salt were in great demand, and give a sense of the economic power the researchers wielded in the region.[64]

Dorothea and Mary were able to stay with 'missionary friends' and made 'lengthy stays' at various points along the way.[65] But they spent a fair amount of time camping in the bush as well, and Pocock's newspaper reports describe special fire and sleeping arrangements that were made in areas where lions or hyenas were said to roam. Dorothea's sketch map shows the major rivers in the region, including the Kwito and Kuando, and locates the succession of mission stations where they stopped along the way (Figure 4.2). Most likely the researchers were based at Cuelei Mission Station on the Kubango River, marked 'Our Station' on the map. Pocock's reports make Muye, a small mission station in the centre of Angola, their destination. A note at the end of Dorothea's published paper thanks the 'members of the South African General Mission for much hospitality, help and advice'.[66] As Dorothea's map records, central Angola was well served with mission stations in the mid-1920s.[67] En route, Dorothea's party stopped at Ninde Mission, 'two days march from the Portuguese border', where they 'saw and talked to three Bushmen'. After 'five days march further on', they 'camped on the Kutsi river' near the 'homes of a group of Bushmen' who were amenable to being 'visited'. But 'ten days march' southwest to the Kunzumbia River, Dorothea's research agenda ran afoul of the consequences of indirect rule being set up by the Portuguese colonial authorities in the region:

Here we played hide-and-seek with [the bushmen] for several weeks, finding many recently occupied encampments, but only twice getting speech with the people themselves. The Kangali chiefs were evidently keeping them away. I think the local officials had been trying to make the chiefs responsible for the Bushmen paying hut tax and had beaten the chiefs when the payment was not forthcoming. Naturally they denied the presence of the little people, and tried to prevent any Europeans from seeing them.[68]

Dorothea did not shy away from making note of cultural contact and the impact of civilisation in her journal article. She recorded instances of trade and bartering between groups, and made a faithful record of changes in lifestyle in response to new forces impinging on the landscape. She recorded the presence of guns, and also of the Portuguese traders at 'Menonge' who, in exchange for honey and beeswax, traded powder and shot to 'one or two middle-aged men' who kept 'old muzzle loaders ... tucked away in the roofs of [their] huts'.[69] She recorded the presence of a metal forge in a 'bushman' village near Caiongo, describing it as 'an exact replica of those seen in many Bantu villages'. Pocock's newspaper report of January 1926 made much more of this, billing it as an 'immensely surprising' discovery of 'the only record of metal work by Bushmen' ever seen. Dorothea's feelings about the effects of colonialism on the landscape can be measured from a personal perspective, as illustrated by her comment in a letter to Käthe Woldmann: 'I have travelled in Angola. Under Portuguese leadership, it is not a country for white settlers. If it were controlled by others it could become the home of Europeans, with that I mean, the central high-lying area.'[70]

Apart from language sampling, Dorothea's research in Angola involved taking physical measurements of individuals.[71] As has been discussed by a range of scholars, forms of empirical investigation, often under the guise of 'science', have been deployed in physical anthropology to underpin the notion of 'race' or 'type' with acute ramifications into the present with regard to constructions of 'bushman' as a distinct physical type.[72] In keeping with the methodologies of the day, Dorothea was diligent in defining her research subjects in terms of their physical appearance. As she had done many times previously when selecting 'pure' types for Drury's casting activities, she confidently made pronouncements on degrees of 'purity' or its lack in relation to gradations of skin colour, height and stature, size of feet, and so on.[73] She made similar pronouncements about language purity, generally marking sharing between languages as a sign of disintegration and decline, rather than a marker of interaction over a long period of time. Dorothea noted, for example, that in the west of the country in particular, young people spoke the Nyemba language as well as their own and would 'interlard their conversation with Nyemba words'. They were 'beginning to drop clicks at the beginning of many words', even though their elders did not.[74]

For physical appearance as for language, she interpreted interaction as a threat to the bushmen and as a playing out of inevitable forces impacting on the *Völkegedanke*, or 'folk ideas' or 'collective mind' of natural peoples. In keeping with evolutionary thinking in which those people perceived to be 'primitive' or 'ancient' (such as the bushmen) would disappear or be swamped by other groups who were stronger and more populous (such as black Africans), Dorothea concluded in her article that 'the end' was in sight for the bushmen of central Angola. They were 'steadily adopting more and more Bantu customs, and mixing more with the black race in every generation'. This was especially so in the populous west, but was also a feature of the east. 'The more permanent homes, the use of garden produce for food, the practical state of servitude this entails, distinguish these !Ko from all others. That polygamy, fetish worship, and Bantu modes of dancing should also creep in is natural', she wrote.[75]

Tanganyika, 1930

Dorothea spent six weeks in northern Tanganyika Territory in 1930, living among a group of people inhabiting land spread around Lake Eyasi, a shallow, salty lake on a plateau within the Great Rift Valley. She was 57 at the time.[76] The trip was sandwiched between several years of intensive work, including a trip to London in 1928 to arrange for the publishing of her edited book of Stow's rock art reproductions.

The Tanganyika expedition would be the last that took her a meaningful distance away from Cape Town.[77] It yielded two notebooks, and just a few pages of handwritten notes that formed the basis of her article in the journal *Africa* the following year.[78] As usual, details about the physical cost of travel are elusive, save that she contracted malaria at some point on this trip.[79] Aside from that, Dorothea mentioned the Tanganyika trip in passing two or three times in her correspondence with Käthe Woldmann.[80] She was extremely busy at the time, she wrote, but was reluctant to pass up on an opportunity to investigate a 'tribe' so far north. While doubtful of finding 'pure bushmen', Dorothea was tantalised enough by the possibility to make the trip. Before she left, she speculated to Käthe Woldmann that the people under discussion were most likely related to the 'Sandawe', whom Dorothea described as 'half Hottentot mixed with Bantu blood'.[81]

Contrary to her expectations, she found the trip worth her while. She found 'similar customs', and a language which resembled those she classified 'bushman' even though many words were 'borrowed' from neighbouring tribes. Much more exciting were the rock paintings found in the vicinity – 'three beautiful giraffes in red', to be exact – all this despite only slight physical resemblance to bushmen! 'The situation is puzzling, therefore most interesting,' she wrote to Woldmann.

Aside from snippets of correspondence, there is very little surviving in the archive that would allow one to reconstruct the practical details of this trip. But one can draw a sense of what her travel might have been like by dipping into the experience of Anne Louise (Hay) Dundas, who began her honeymoon en route to Tanganyika Territory in the immediate post-World War I period.[82] Travelling in 1921 as wife of a new district commissioner to the region meant Dundas was part of Britain's hasty post-war division of German East Africa into administrative units for the new colony. Dundas's impressionistic narrative of her life at the foot of Mount Kilimanjaro in 1921 emphasised physical discomfort on one hand, and the opportunity for meaningful interaction with fellow sojourners on the other. She warned: 'Equatorial Africa is not a white man's country in its broadest sense, for no country can be such where the menacing sun compels the wearing of a heavy helmet throughout the hours of daylight.' But, among colonial settlers at least, she experienced a 'camaraderie in a new country' that broke down the 'walls of self-centredness and let in a flood of warm, humanising influences'. While political and administrative adjustments were no doubt more settled, the heat and mosquitoes remained unchanged when Dorothea arrived in Tanganyika just nine years later.

In her paper published in *Africa*, Dorothea stated that she spent 'six weeks' in an area 'some twelve miles north of Mkalama' among 'one family and others [who had] moved up from the east, some from near Kondoa'.[83] The article located Hadzapi territory in the 'northern part of the Central Province of Tanganyika Territory, near the swamp or lake marked on maps as Lake Eyasi'. It identified the Hadzapi as 'a tribe of hunters speaking a clicking language which is related to the Bushman and Hottentot tongues'. Dorothea compared the Hadzapi against her list of 'bushman' attributes, including life ways (hunters using bow and arrows), the making of rudimentary shelters from branches, their speech ('clicking language'), and physically, in terms of skin colour, height and size:

> Judging by looks I should deny them any relationship to the Bushmen of South Africa, yet a sojourn in their midst with daily study of their language, habits, and thoughts has convinced me that there must have been some connexion between this black, ape-like tribe and the small, delicately built yellow men who used to dwell in all the wilder parts of South Africa, and who are still to be found in the Kalahari.[84]

Her approach to skin colour and the elevation of lighter-skinned bushmen above what she elsewhere described as 'invading black tribes' resonated with similar opinions expressed years earlier by her father.[85] Yet Dorothea's 1930 vocabulary and findings are not much different from the ideas contained in a contemporary *National Geographic* photo-essay on the Hadza, in which they are portrayed as people living a threatened 'hunter-gatherer existence…little changed from 10 000 years ago' and who are of great interest to anthropologists because they offer 'a glimpse of what life may have been like before the birth of agriculture'.[86]

As in previous publications, Dorothea noted the presence of 'European materials' (calico) that some of the men had recently begun to use as clothing, in preference to being otherwise entirely without clothing.[87] She noted her favourite ritual – tattooing or scarification, in this case to cure illness – again a resonance with her father's great interest in finger-cutting rituals, related by //Kabbo in particular. As she had done at Sandfontein and Angola, she recorded trading or bartering and interactions with neighbours or other groups in terms of cultural disintegration, as in the use of beads of 'European or Indian make' in place of the more authentic ostrich-eggshell beads.[88] She reported on the use of clay pots and calabashes, and on the presence of 'meal' and tobacco obtained from the Isanzu (the neighbouring 'Bantu' group):

> Besides tobacco they buy iron, pots, calabashes, beads, copper rings, and stuffs from their neighbours, giving in exchange meat, skins, honey, and beeswax. The latter they sometimes take to the Indian stores and sell for money.[89]

As in her Naron and !Kung writings, Dorothea did not hide the effects of her research on the local people. She reported on her own involvement in the local economy, noting that the boxes of matches she gave to her interviewees became currency with which to gamble.[90]

Maturing science and making 'bushmen'

Scholars have pointed to the 1920s and 1930s as being crucial decades for consolidating the 'native question' as part of the making of the South African state and its politics, and as an important area for intellectual inquiry in the academy and institutions of scientific research.[91] This was the epistemic context or overarching body of ideas that influenced research in anthropology and the study of language, and shaped the kinds of knowledge that Dorothea and her fellow scholars produced. Dorothea's research took place amid the formalising of state and academic apparatuses focused on producing notions of 'native', 'bushman' or 'Bantu' studies for official, scholarly and public consumption. Academic departments aimed at studying, understanding and controlling 'native' populations were emerging at universities around the country. A centre of ethnology aimed at studying 'the native' following in the English (functionalist or social anthropology) tradition appeared at Wits and UCT, while Stellenbosch and the other Afrikaans universities took a different tack in following the German *Völkerkunde* tradition of study focused on clearly defined 'folk', 'ethnic' or 'tribal' groups.[92] The anthropologist Isaac Schapera, who was Dorothea's colleague at UCT, framed his 1930 publication explicitly in these terms. Schapera argued that the 'results of scientific research should be…of service not only to the theoretical anthropologist', but also to 'the administrator, the missionary, the economist, and the educationist, each in his own way now moulding the life of the Native into conformity with the standards of European civilisation'.[93] For such professionals, Schapera continued, 'a thorough knowledge and understanding of the people with whom he is concerned is an indispensable preliminary to the successful execution of his task'.[94]

By 1930, through her institutional connections and via her publications and lectures, Dorothea had made a significant contribution to a scientific grid for the classification of 'bushman' peoples in terms of their languages. During a productive decade, she published a book and several journal articles dealing with folklore, a monograph on the Naron, and several articles on language in local and European journals. Her affiliation to UCT had been formalised through her designation in 1923 as Honorary Reader in Bushman Languages within the newly established School of African Life and Languages. It was also the year in which her first edited publication of stories from Wilhelm's and Lucy's notebooks had appeared. That edited collection, with the full title *The Mantis and His Friends: Bushman Folklore Collected by the Late Dr. W.H.I. Bleek and the Late Dr. Lucy C. Lloyd*, contained English translations of a small sample of notebook tales dealing, as its title suggests, with the figure of /Kaggen, a character that Dorothea likened to the character Puck from Shakespeare's play *A Midsummer Night's Dream*.[95]

Dorothea mid-career research trips show a formalising research style developing with the use of systematic and scientific methods, and participation in projects underwritten by the state. She filtered what she saw in the field through her intellectual antecedents in nineteenth-century German *Ethnologie*. Her view of bushmen was informed by ideas about *Naturvölker*, the view that 'natural' peoples displayed specific sets of habits, abilities and life ways that could be threatened by modernity and the advance of 'stronger' peoples in the landscape. Nevertheless, she maintained that what remained of these 'natural' people should be evaluated on their own terms, and should not be contaminated by the ideas or expectations of the cultured. This kind of thinking contributed to the establishment of bushman studies as a discrete field of academic inquiry which persists into the present. Through her classification of languages, Dorothea drew on and enabled a structure that continues to allow people identified as 'bushmen' to be regarded as 'ethnically', linguistically and physically distinct.[96]

5 | Testimony of the rocks: A 'cave journey', 1928–1932

The caves are so crowded with pictures that the student or copyist does not know where to begin. Superpositions are innumerable, five or six layers can be deciphered in places…Not one or two generations only have worked here, but many generations have used these spots for artistic purposes.[1]

It was not until the late 1920s that Dorothea once again turned her full attention to rock art. Sandwiched between the trips to Angola in 1925 and Tanganyika in 1930 was the three-month 'cave journey' she took to sites recorded years earlier by Stow. The expedition, which culminated in her 1930 edited book of Stow's copies as well as a lecture delivered to the South African Association for the Advancement of Science (SAAAS) in 1932, provided evidence to confirm views she had already expressed in her 1909 collaborative book with Helen Tongue.

This chapter discusses continuities in Dorothea's thinking about rock art and locates her arguments within broader intellectual currents of the time. It suggests that her negative feelings about modernity may have influenced how she structured her research of sites, and the ways in which she responded to debates about the authorship and meaning of rock art. It draws on her introduction and notes in *Rock Paintings in South Africa from Parts of the Eastern Province and Orange Free State*, and on the published version of her presidential address to the SAAAS meeting in 1932. Titled 'A Survey of Our Present Knowledge of Rockpaintings in South Africa', the lecture presented a synthesis of Dorothea's rock art scholarship up to that point, and delivered her findings regarding authorship, age and meaning of the art, assertions that were sometimes at odds with the ideas of other specialists of the day. These two public texts are analysed alongside her field notebooks, her private correspondence and other writings dealing with rock art. All are situated within the wider thinking around archaeology and prehistory, and provide a texture of Dorothea's interactions with the internationally known prehistorians who passed through Cape Town during the 1920s. Dorothea's renewed interest in rock art late in the 1920s was no mere coincidence, but a response to the intellectual climate.

The Abbé Henri Breuil, Miles Burkitt and Leo Frobenius were the prehistorians who travelled with their expeditions through Cape Town. At the time, Dorothea was immersed in integrating the results of her fieldwork with her collection of Stow's copies, and preparing these for publication.[2] She located her research in a context in which 'new finds' of rock art sites were being reported every year, asserting that rock paintings, while not evenly distributed through the country, were nevertheless located 'wherever suitable caves and rock shelters occur in South Africa'.[3] As with bushman language and culture, Dorothea's aim was to produce a comprehensive record of the country's rock art, which she thought was 'fading before our eyes'.[4] A yellowed and fragile clipping from *The Friend* of Bloemfontein, with the date 28 September 1920 noted in Dorothea's black ink at the top, records that she staged an exhibition of Stow's rock art copies at the Bloemfontein Museum that year.[5] According to the clipping, this 'remarkable collection of copies of Bushman paintings' had never been displayed before, and it drew a record number of visitors to the museum. Dorothea, or 'Doris', as she is referred to in the report, delivered an accompanying lecture that *The Friend* carried in full in two instalments on 28 and 29 September 1920.[6] These reports reveal how Dorothea, as she had in the notes co-written for Helen's book, again relied on nostalgic recollections about the 'colonial' bushmen from her childhood. This situation would change substantially just a few years later. By the end of 1928 she had completed extensive research of rock art sites and would draw on this fieldwork to back up the statements she made thereafter.

By late 1928, following on her language work at Sandfontein (where tracings in the Iziko South African Museum collection show that she visited and recorded several engravings at BabiBabi; see Figures 5.1 and 5.2), Angola and Tanganyika, she had completed what she could of the demanding task of tracking down as many as possible of the rock art sites visited by Stow at least 60 years earlier.[7] The trip would be followed closely by the appearance of Dorothea's edited version of Stow's reproductions, finally making good on Lucy's undertaking to Fanny Stow that she would try to have the 'pictures' published.[8] Bearing the lengthy title *Rock Paintings in South Africa from Parts of the Eastern Province and Orange Free State*, the substantial volume was illustrated with full-colour reproductions.[9] Its appearance in 1930 coincided with several other firsts in Dorothea's scholarship and publishing career and added to her status as the country's leading authority on the bushman. Dorothea's project of retracing and verifying the Stow sites at that time established her as the first in a line of scholars who would in subsequent years return to Stow sites to probe his accuracy (or otherwise) and methods of copying.[10]

The edited book

When Dorothea's edited book of Stow's copies appeared, many of the foundational views it expressed had become contested, particularly in regard to the authorship and age of the paintings. The opinion that an earlier, ancient civilisation had influenced African prehistory was widely held.[11] In her introduction, Dorothea set out her belief that the paintings recorded 'bushman history', that they were of bushman authorship and that most of them were hundreds rather than thousands of years old. Based on the style, form and detail of the hundreds of painted scenes and figures she had seen on her trip, she argued that this provided proof that bushmen initially had the country to themselves, and then were impacted by the arrival of 'black' groups from the north.

These new social contacts and interactions had produced a change in the style and content of the art that could be seen on the rocks. While the range and abundance of animals in the landscape and their critical role in bushman lives meant these had always required detailed illustration, 'so long as only one race of men dwelt in the land, any caricature of a human would represent it'. Animals, she explained, were worked out in great detail because it had always been important to bushman artists to clearly distinguish between different species of buck, birds and other animals.[12] Here Dorothea's background knowledge of folklore developed through years of working closely on the notebooks with Lucy Lloyd was crucial to her understanding of the importance of animals in bushman cosmology, a point she made in her 1929 journal article on folklore.[13] In contrast, she argued, human figures drawn at an earlier time needed less detail than those drawn after herding and farming groups had arrived on the scene. Then 'more care had to be given to the human figure to distinguish between Bushman and Bantu, and the advent of the white man also led to greater detail in portraying human beings', she argued in her introduction.[14]

As she had done earlier, Dorothea drew on her knowledge of /Xam folklore to understand some of what she saw painted on the rock walls before her. Years before, in the field with Helen Tongue, she had established a connection between the notebook tales and some rock art scenes, and she built on this link in her Stow book. Her knowledge of the notebooks allowed her to recognise painted scenes illustrating transformations (from human beings into frogs, for instance), and 'wonderful animals' that she knew were representations of rain animals, often depicted together with frogs, fish, snakes and tortoises.[15] Her knowledge of bushman ideas about the rain, rain making and rain animals, their interactions with the mantis figure and their connection to the 'Early Race', or mythical ancestors who lived at a time when the boundaries between bushmen and animals were blurred, were all beliefs she had come across in the notebooks, and they enriched her engagement with the art. She knew that animals rather than people played the leading part in bushman thought and therefore she understood why animals were so widely illustrated in the art. 'I think their life in small family groups scattered over very wide spaces has tended to make the surrounding animal world and the bodies loom large in their sight, the human hero small,' she wrote in her 1929 folklore article.[16] She argued that the hunting and foraging lifestyle of the bushmen and the leisure time this afforded was the source of their storytelling and painting traditions.

Dorothea's formulation (inherited from Stow) of the African past as a narrative told in terms of a 'bushman idyll' that was destroyed by an influx of stronger 'races' from the north and the 'white man' from Europe provided her with a framework in which to interpret some of the painted scenes she came across. She dismissed speculation that the paintings were made for magical purposes directed at securing success in the hunt, or for decoration. Rather, she suggested, the paintings stemmed from the 'large part pleasure, and the search for pleasure, [played] in the life of primitive people'.[17] She bolstered her argument by referring to her many years of research among the bushmen of southern Africa, both of those 'in servitude, others living their natural life'. Modernity and the forces of civilisation had impacted negatively on bushman life ways. '[F]rom what I have seen, as well as from the picture of themselves given in their folk-lore, I am sure they lived a care-free, idle life, as long as they were unmolested by invaders of their land.'[18] Their 'idle' lifestyle, she argued, left much time for talking, and contributed to their developing excellent powers of observation, which in turn had contributed to the 'growth of their art'.[19] 'Those who know the people and have seen the great quantities of artistic work they have left, cannot help feeling that only from love of painting would they ever have painted so much, only from a spirit of emulation would they have covered the same rock-surface over and over again.'[20]

Reasoning on the basis of colour, layering and preservation, Dorothea arrived at a 'recent' rather than ancient date for many of the paintings. But she warned that dates were relative rather than absolute. Her view was that while the painting tradition could date back to prehistoric times, what remained on the rocks was likely to be hundreds rather than thousands of years old.[21] She argued that the red ochre paint was the longest-lasting, while the lighter pinks, yellows and whites showed evidence of fading quickly. Thus, paintings in which those lighter colours could still be seen were more recent than those in which red ochre remained while other colours had faded.[22] She noted that painting materials were derived from locally available ochres, oxides and clays, with dark red and orange being most frequently found at the 'lowest [earliest] levels' of painting, and also the 'most lasting'.[23] White, while in use throughout, had generally faded from the oldest paintings, leaving the stereotypical renderings of the bichrome eland, which at lower levels was often seen with only the dark parts remaining.

Dorothea noted that all colours were found at all levels of superpositioning, 'except that blue, pink and violet are only in the upper layers: perhaps they are colours that fade rapidly'. In many paintings, the same colour could be found in the lowest and in the topmost layer: 'red is on black here, black on red there'.[24] The preponderance of certain colours at lower levels could be ascribed to different rates of weathering. 'I have only seen shaded elands and those with clearly marked horns, hoofs and eyes in upper layers, but that may be because these parts disappear first. Monochromes in all colours but pink, blue and violet are found in all layers; red and orange, the two most lasting paints, preponderate in the lower ones. Sometimes where black is on red, the black wears away and the red shows through; where red is on black, there is no such effect.'[25] She dismissed attempts to date work according to superpositioning of style and aesthetic quality, arguing that 'the testimony of the rocks' did not support suggestions that the 'early people' made the 'good work' while the 'later Bushmen were a decadent race'.

Dorothea's dating method based on observations of the preservation of pigments and colours on the rock walls found her disagreeing with some of the thinking of the time – for instance, with Miles Burkitt's suggestion that an analysis of the various colours found in successive layers of super-positioning could be used to calculate relative dates for the art.[26] In his 1928 book, Burkitt had called for the four methods of archaeological investigation of stone-tool-making 'industries' to be applied with minor adaptions to the study of rock art located across South Africa and the then Southern Rhodesia.[27] As with stone tools and other artefacts excavated from soil layers, the methods of stratigraphy and typology were important in the investigation of rock art and were mirrored in the superimposed layers of paint. Different styles or typologies could be linked to each of the different layers. The 'law of superposition', Burkitt wrote, was that 'any drawing below must be older than one which is made above it'.[28] The other two methods, preservation and association, could be applied with slight adjustments. In stone-tool archaeology, associations were drawn with faunal remains found adjacent to objects. In rock art, associations were made with the species of animal depicted. Following the model he had applied to the various stone-tool-making 'industries' of South Africa, Burkitt devised a chronological table assigning a particular pigment and style to a particular epoch of rock art production.[29] As we have seen, Dorothea did not agree with this method. However, she was in agreement with Burkitt's use of archaeological finds to assist in dating the art. Burkitt reported that his excavations had found tools belonging to the 'Upper Smithfield culture' associated with painted caves. This led to his conclusion that 'the Bushman art of this region is not very ancient in time, perhaps indeed it is only a few hundred years old'.[30]

Burkitt, along with Leo Frobenius and the artist Walter Battiss, tried to formulate a hierarchical model of different stylistic stages in the art ranging from crude to excellent to decadent, following the three-tier scheme mapped out by Henry Balfour in his preface to Helen Tongue's book.[31] In contrast, Dorothea argued that there was 'good and bad workmanship in old layers as well as new ones'.[32] She referenced her father's and Lloyd's use of Stow's copies in sessions with their 'colonial Bushmen' at Mowbray in 1874 to support her claims of bushman authorship. Her father and aunt were 'careful observers and made it a rule not to ask leading questions'. 'Their' bushmen not only 'recognised the pictures as copies of the work of their people, but could often explain puzzling figures and scenes, and in doing so gave information about many curious customs and beliefs and related some new folk-lore. On the other hand they did not hesitate to say, "I do not know this," when shown some of the copies of symbols, particularly the graven ones', she insisted.[33] For Dorothea, the question of authorship had been answered by the testimony of her father's and aunt's interlocutors. 'To the end of their independent life the Colonial and Free State Bushmen were painting and chipping pictures in stone. Does that look as if they were new-comers?' she wrote in 1926 in an article in the *Cape Times*.[34]

As with meaning, the dating of paintings was – and remains – a thorny issue.[35] Dorothea warned that the state of preservation of a painting could not be used as means to judge the age of the painting. She argued that age could only be speculated upon with any accuracy in regard to the 'topmost layers of pictures'.[36] She drew on Stow to suggest that the historical record of bushman habitation in a particular area could be used as a starting point for calculating the age of paintings. 'We know approximately when the Bushmen were killed off in each district,' she wrote, 'hence we know that the paintings were not made later than that period.'[37] She was adamant that all of the art had been created by the same group of people, perhaps distinguished by their different languages, but all bushmen who had inhabited the country before the arrival of white settlers from the south and 'black tribes' from the north. She cited 'early travellers' such as John Barrow, Anders Sparrman and Carl Lichtenstein as her sources. These early travellers had narrated their own experiences of a rock art tradition continuing among some of the people they came across. Dorothea's estimations, based on Stow's assumptions, suggested that a period of 90 years had elapsed since bushmen last inhabited the country around Queenstown, 80 years for the Barkly East region, and 60 years for the Free State territory on the Basutoland border. She was careful to qualify her data, however, and pointed out that her estimations needed to be understood in relative rather than absolute terms: 'But that is, of course, a negative proof; it does not tell us whether the Bushmen painted up to the time of their destruction or dispersal, or not.'[38]

Neither could style and characteristic be used to assign art to particular parts of the country. Again, her opinion was based on her recent trip. While she was 'hunting for the originals of these copies', her observations suggested there were regions with 'slight characteristics of [their] own'. Her field investigations had not warranted the allocation of 'particular features to any special part of the country, for the characteristics of a group in the south are sometimes repeated in a group further north'. There were differences in terms of superpositioning, shading, colour, line and artistic proficiency, but the basic style of the paintings was the same across most of the country. 'The large caves in the mountainous regions have more polychromes, more shaded animals and more grouping of figures than the paintings found farther out in the low country, as those near Tarkastad [eastern Cape], and somewhat similar ones I saw near Grahamstown, but polychromes are not entirely absent in these districts or in others much farther away from the country represented in this volume,' she wrote.[39]

Dorothea drew on her language research to support her contention that bushman groups had in the past been spread across southern and central Africa, lodged between 'the pastoral Hottentots in the west, and in the east and north fighting for their existence against large Bantu tribes who both kept cattle and practised hoe-culture'.[40] But while all bushman groups shared a hunter-gatherer lifestyle, they did not necessarily share the same language, beliefs and customs. As far as the painting tradition was concerned, she ventured to assert only what direct observation allowed: 'The two tribes who are known to have been painters up to the time of their destruction as a race are the Bushmen of the old Cape Colony, inhabiting the whole northern part of the land south of the Orange River, and the tribe occupying the country between the Vaal and Orange Rivers, the present Free State and Basutoland. Paintings have been found in territory inhabited by other Bushman tribes, but proof that these were painted latterly is still lacking, which may be of course an accidental circumstance.'[41]

She disputed the labelling of 'bushman tribes' as nomads. Drawing on //Kabbo's narrations about his home territory in the Bleek and Lloyd notebooks and on her own research, she argued that large tracts of land were needed to support hunting and gathering, and that land arrangements were based on ancestral links to waterholes.[42] Dorothea's own record of the dying-out of folklore in her Kenhardt and Prieska fieldwork in 1910 and 1911 had provided personal experience to back her argument that the painting tradition could die out as quickly.[43] But as with all Dorothea's arguments about rock art, caution was her watchword. She was careful to avoid generalisations, offering instead close readings of specific paintings, with detailed attention paid to site, location, style and content. Through this approach, Dorothea established the importance of the particular in rock art studies decades ahead of contemporary scholarship's return to localised historical readings of the art that are now being offered alongside interpretations linked to the widespread practice of shamanism in trance and healing dances, and an expression of spiritual potency, that have predominated since the 1980s.

Commenting on Stow's reproductions in her edited book, Dorothea's opinion was that his field methods, while not exhaustive, reached an acceptable standard. Despite 'small slips' and his 'difficulties in obtaining suitable paper', he had 'usually given a very truthful reproduction of the Bushman touch and spirit', she wrote in her introduction.[44] While Stow was necessarily selective due to lack of paper, and forced to copy figures randomly without accurately recording the distances between them, Dorothea felt that Stow's reproduction of colour and form was acceptable. 'Apparently Stow copied the figures on any rough paper available as accurately as he could, took specimens of the colours often in the actual paint then obtainable in some caves, and later traced through the rough copy on to a large sheet and coloured it, this work probably being done in his tent. As a background he washed the paper over with the tone most prevalent on the rock.'[45] At the same time, Stow had collected information about the paintings from bushmen he came across in the field, which gave the explanations he provided alongside his paintings an authenticity not available to later arrivals to the field.[46] But she was critical of Stow's (and Joseph Orpen's) use of

111

interpreters. Stow in particular, she wrote to Käthe Woldmann, 'most probably made a number of mistakes' through not speaking the language. One of these was his reference to bushman 'headmen', even though there was no such word in their vocabulary.[47]

In the field

As was the case for her earlier trips, archival traces are scanty in relation to questions of companionship, means of travel and sustenance during Dorothea's 'cave journey'. It must have been a gruelling trip. Dorothea, then aged 56, travelled alone, and felt the strain of travel. 'I apologise for my bad handwriting. My hands are tired from the long journey – as I myself am the coachman,' she wrote to Käthe from Winburg in the Orange Free State.[48] She visited more than 100 sites in the Drakensberg foothills of the eastern Cape and the Orange Free State areas she would describe in her survey as exhibiting 'by far' the greatest number of sites and paintings featuring 'innumerable, incalculable' superpositionings, and surpassing in 'grouping, movement and shading' all of the work found elsewhere.[49]

Dorothea deliberately chose not to make tracings or reproductions at any of the many rock art sites she visited on that trip. The opportunity of copying presented to Stow was no longer available.[50] Stow's reproductions had been made between 1867 and 1882, some 60 years earlier. Since then time and modernity had taken their toll. Many paintings could not be copied due to weathering, flaking, soot and dirt from human habitation and the rubbing of animals. And worse than the rockfalls that had damaged some panels, others had been 'cut out and removed, possibly for museums'.[51] Having studied Stow's watercolours of the 'cattle raid' scene at Ventershoek farm near Wepener in the south-eastern Free State, Dorothea must have been shocked at the devastation she found when she reached the shelter. A previous owner had given 'leave to a French missionary to cut out one of the painted cattle to send to France as a sample of Bushman art', she wrote in her notes alongside the two plates she included in the book.[52] Dorothea thought it was a recent painting dating from the 'Zulu invasion of about 1821'. She was impressed by what was left behind. It was 'one of the best group paintings, a sign that the artists belonged to no decadent race', she wrote. 'Here for once we see an attempt to reproduce the real colours of the objects depicted...the markings of the cattle may be seen in native herds today.'[53]

An entry in one of Dorothea's field notebooks tells us that she visited a second shelter where a panel had been removed. Mrs Bulwer, wife of the 'present missionary' at St Marks Mission Station on the White Kei River (eastern Cape), told Dorothea that most of the best paintings in the area had been 'chipped out and sent to museums or sold'.[54] Dorothea was unable to find the paintings Stow had copied in this area, among them a white rhino that Mrs Bulwer remembered seeing as a girl. Dorothea concluded her field notes at this particular site with the comment that 'Stow copied the best pictures and the men who cut them away looked out for the same. Let us hope some are in museums'.[55]

Painted panels collected by landowners, archaeologists and amateur enthusiasts arrived at museums across the country during the early decades of the twentieth century.[56] Some remain in contemporary displays, of which the Linton panel in the Iziko South African Museum's exhibition /Qe – The Power of Rock Art is a striking example.[57] But for Dorothea, the aim now was observation. Her book tells us that she managed to track down 60 of 74 Stow 'cartoons' for publishing.[58] From a letter to Käthe Woldmann, we learn that Dorothea's three-month trip found her at Winburg on 6 June. She had made 'a brief detour' to that northern Free State town to visit a 'living Bushman…[who] apparently still [spoke] the language of the Bushmen of the Freestate'.[59]

The field notebooks

The rough details of Dorothea's 1928 trip are recorded in three of her 32 field notebooks.[60] Site visits are numbered haphazardly rather than in numerical order, in this way reflecting the ability of the field to resist sequential order. Of the three notebooks, one is more than half filled with empty pages.[61] This 200-page reporter's notebook with red cover contains some notes related to Dorothea's visits to Stow sites interrupted by pages of language and vocabulary samples, as well as more mundane items, including what is perhaps a shopping or to-do list.[62] As in the other two notebooks, in this one Dorothea filled only one side of the page. She did not write her name in any of them, nor did she number the pages. She plunged straight into her subject, beginning with the geographical location of the site and/or its number (derived from Stow's copy) – for example, 'Groendraai', or 'Cave on left bank by Klipplaas river', or 'Lower Imvani 24.25'.[63] One notebook carries the heading 'O.F.S.'[64]

Her notes are written in pencil, and judging from certain scrawled pages, these are *in situ* recordings. Here and there a rudimentary sketch or graphic is included to flesh out her verbal description. Her notes show that, where possible, she checked the accuracy of Stow's copies with regard to the size and detail of individual paintings, as well as to the composition of groups. She paid particular attention to the way in which individual animals and/ or figures related to each other on the rock wall, and to the presence of discrepancies in Stow's record. She had a camera with her, as some of the pages carry a reference to 'Film III No 1' in the top right-hand corner.[65] Other entries are accompanied by numbered headings such as 'No 27 – 33', which may be a reference to a numbered Stow copy and/or to Dorothea's photographic record of it.

The most extensive continuous piece of writing from this trip was recorded in a notebook now labelled A3.26. Like its twin A3.25, this reporter's notebook carries the inscription 'Dee Bee Bazaar, Parliament Street, Cape Town' on its grey cover, presumably the name and address of the stationers where it was purchased. Dorothea's at times illegible, expansive scrawl covers all of the pages running from front to back of the notebook, then turning and continuing from the back of the notebook. Halfway through, however, her notes peter out. To an extent, the notebook conveys a record of visits to sites located in the eastern Cape roughly between the 'Swartz' (Black) and 'Wit' (White) Kei River region. Directions to particular sites are rudimentary, beginning most often with the name of the farm and the farmer. For example: 'Ewan's Hope (formerly Rietfontein owned by Mr Barend Buys at time of Kafir [*sic*] wars) now owned by Mr McEwan. Spruit which runs into Elands river, called Buys rivier. Small shelter on right about ¼ hrs walk above house. – one very good yellow & white eland – head missing, sup [superpositioned] on old red', and so on.[66] Often she listed animals or figures by number, including identifying features if any, and colour. She tended to describe scenes and panels from left to right, noting additional figures above or below. She always made notes of the presence of superpositioning.

Sometimes she started her description with what was probably Stow's number. At one site, presumably Stow's number 46, her description reads thus: 'Large cave on Diepspruit on Queensborne farm 5 minutes' walk from Mr O.S. Liddy's house …' The description goes on for three pages, even though Dorothea found the lower paintings 'rubbed out' by the cattle that the farmer penned in the cave. Her closing comment was that there were 'not many' paintings for the size of the cave.[67] Elsewhere, what appears to be a self-contained notebook entry runs as follows: '73. Mr Karels' farm Tygerkrantz 2 miles from Barkly East. Wittekrans spruit about 3–4 miles from house – difficult to reach. Not found paintings.'[68] Towards the end of her notes, at the bottom of a page, she seems to have recorded randomly 'Mr Beswick, Queenstown'. Yet, in a record framed by references to farmers and landownership, the following entry hints that at times she consulted with ordinary people in her search for paintings. It appears five pages into this section of her fieldwork record, bracketed off as transcribed below:

(Bushmans painting on commonage at Nousa [not sure of transcription] location other side of Hankey Road to Hex plantation then Whittlesea side of Hankey then footpath to [indecipherable] plantation. Headman Jameson Utombeni will show the way. Large cave take 200–300 sheep.

John Chandow of Whittlesea knows about it. 2–3 hours on foot. Little stream Nousa by it)

?[69]

Science, society and visiting prehistorians

Compared with her work in 1905, Dorothea's ideas and methods were now circulating in a more crowded intellectual context, and she was working in a landscape that had become a disciplined target of archaeological research.[70] In the country as a whole, interest in science, research and education had shifted into high gear.[71] Globally, southern Africa was an important research destination for those interested in unearthing material evidence in support of one or other narrative related to prehistory and the origin of the human species. Rock art was beginning to feature in the flurry of research around the dating of stone tools, the racial typing of skeletons, and the classification of South African prehistory according to a schedule that was separate from Europe's. The late 1920s saw the visits of celebrated prehistorians from Europe and Britain to southern Africa. As noted earlier, Dorothea met the

Abbé Henri Breuil and Leo Frobenius as they passed through Cape Town *en route* to meetings and sites further afield.[72] She met Miles Burkitt when he visited in 1927, and showed him her 'collection', presumably of rock art copies.[73] The last years of the decade saw the publication of the first two major works on South African prehistory and archaeology: Miles Burkitt's *South Africa's Past in Stone and Paint* in 1928, and A. Goodwin and C. van Riet Lowe's *The Stone Age Cultures of South Africa* in 1929.[74] The decade ended with the triumphant staging of the SAAAS meeting in 1929.[75]

Thus Dorothea's two rock art excursions bracket trajectories of development and change in her own life and scholarship as much as they parallel trends in the intellectual life of the colony and then member of the British Commonwealth. Dorothea's 1905 trip was made in the era of antiquarian collecting activities framed as gentlemanly pursuit. Her 1928 rock art tour took place during a time of maturing scholarship, wider recognition and personal productivity, when activity in the field carried formal expectations of gathering and presenting scientific data.

In 1929, Dorothea stopped in Johannesburg for the SAAAS meeting. She was on her way home from meeting with her publishers in London. She surely heard Jan Smuts speak – his celebration of the 'social and intellectual transformation' that had taken place in South Africa, with references to the 'reconstruction of the country', 'the achievement of political unity and the yet-to-be-achieved ideal of united nationhood'.[76] She would have heard Jan Hofmeyr's keynote address on 'Africa and science', in which he famously referred to the 'South Africanisation' of science.[77] She doubtless attended with interest the presentations by international luminaries in the field of prehistory: Leo Frobenius, Henri Breuil, Gertrude Caton-Thompson and Henry Balfour.[78]

Dorothea would certainly have disagreed with the expansive ideas of Frobenius and his suggestion that an earlier, ancient civilisation, described as 'Sumerian-Babylonian', had influenced the establishment of Great Zimbabwe and the different styles of rock art in the region.[79] On the other hand, she admired his rock art reproductions that she saw on public display.[80] She would publicly disagree with Frobenius in her own lecture given in the same forum just three years later.[81] In 1929, Frobenius's talk had been extensively publicised in the press as he was expected 'to offer startling evidence for the existence of a great and civilised race which had apparently lived for over 7 000 years in the area between Great Zimbabwe and Lake Malawi, worshipping the stars and the moon'.[82] Dorothea challenged this view in her cautious, empirical way. Her opinion was that the rock art spread through-out the country confirmed the prior presence of bushmen in the landscape.

For Dorothea, bushman authorship of the 'many thousands of paintings in caves and on the rocks' had been 'irrefutably proven', both on the basis of historical documents produced by travellers such as Stow and Lichtenstein, and by the style of the paintings.[83] She dismissed Frobenius's speculation that the oldest paintings could be linked to the 'ancestors of the Bushman, or to an earlier race'. 'This has not been proven,' she wrote privately to Wold-mann.[84] She remained firm that the art was hundreds rather than thousands of years old. Dorothea would have listened with interest to the acrimonious exchange between Gertrude Caton-Thompson and Raymond Dart over the origins of Great Zimbabwe.[85] Dart had attacked Caton-Thompson's pres-entation of the Zimbabwe civilisation as an indigenous African endeav-our, arguing from the floor that the ruins were evidence of contact with an ancient and exotic superior civilisation.[86] In private, Dorothea reiterated her characteristic insistence on evidence and observation as a basis for theory. Frobenius's assumption about Zimbabwe was not worthy of comment at this early stage, she declared. 'When I have read the proofs, I shall let you know whether they convince me or not,' she wrote to Woldmann.[87]

Dorothea had met the Abbé Breuil when he stopped in Cape Town *en route* on his '1 200 mile archaeological tour' of the country as part of an expedition organised by Wits University.[88] His route took in many of the rock art sites she had visited the previous year, and probably some she had seen 20 years ago with Helen Tongue.[89] Years later, Breuil would claim to have been influential in 'inducing' Miss Bleek to have Stow's copies pub-lished.[90] But Dorothea's correspondence proves her publishing plans were well under way by the time she met him. Her private correspondence has her meeting with her publishers in London by early May 1929.[91]

Breuil, who occupied a chair at Wits from 1944 to 1951, believed that Palaeolithic art in southern European caves had been painted for mag-ical purposes related to fertility, hunting and survival during the Ice Age.[92] This was a view that Dorothea could only partly agree with. While acknowledging that some of the art may have had a magical purpose

117

and that some scenes may have illustrated bushman folklore and beliefs, Dorothea's view was that most of the art was a record of the daily life of the artists drawn for the love of painting.[93] She argued:

> In a huge cave full of paintings Stow would leave unnoticed hundreds of figures of animals and men engaged in ordinary pursuits – walking, running, jumping, fighting, hunting, eating – to copy some little bit that seemed to portray a ceremony or rite, possibly a magic one…Had it been possible to publish copies of whole caves, it would have been clear to the public that the majority of the paintings could hardly have served a magic purpose.[94]

In her lecture to the SAAAS in 1932, Dorothea questioned Breuil's classification of rock paintings into 'earlier' and 'later' periods each of which he subdivided into sequential phases based on use of colour and style.[95] She argued that his research was based on 'observations in a few caves' which could not be applied to 'the majority of sites'.[96] Her own fieldwork had allowed her to gather data from 'over a hundred sites', 88 of which had shown clear superpositioning.[97] Her data suggested the possibility that the earliest work may have been in one colour, but there was, she believed, insufficient evidence to support the 'idea of a sequence of colours, each being used by a different generation'.[98] Dorothea's observations ruled out any uniformity of colour at particular levels, and showed that polychromes could be found both at early levels as well as 'at the very top', where they could include depictions of cattle. She had observed that 'good drawing and bad' was visible in old layers and new. 'To me,' she said in her lecture, 'there does not seem to be evidence of any change greater than would be natural in an art practised through centuries.'[99]

Leo Frobenius's visit had more impact on Dorothea. She remembered meeting him in her youth when he had visited Aunt Lucy at Charlottenburg to look at the Stow copies.[100] By the late 1920s, when they renewed contact, he was a leading ethnologist in Germany, teaching at the University of Frankfurt, and a veteran of several trips to Africa, beginning with a visit to the Congo in 1905.[101] His support for a 'creative' rather than dry, empirical approach to the study of others, Africans in particular, inevitably launched him on a collision course with Dorothea.

From 1928 to 1930, Frobenius and members of his expedition undertook comprehensive research into prehistoric paintings and engravings, covering 'vast areas from the Zambezi to the Cape, from the west coast to the slopes of the Drakensberg'. In this time, 'more than 1 100 tracings were taken, showing the peculiarities and differences of style in the provinces of the Union of South Africa, in Southern Rhodesia and South West Africa'.[102] Much to her chagrin, Frobenius had been funded by the state through a grant made by the minister of education D.F. Malan.[103] In Dorothea's view, the state grant of £2 000 was overly generous, and would have been better given to the South African Museum to fund the making of accurate copies.[104] She did not approve of Frobenius's methods (freehand copying of the paintings rather than exact tracing), and argued that his copies were of limited scientific value. At the invitation of the Union government, she had viewed Frobenius's large-scale copies on display in Pretoria.[105] Based on this viewing, she doubted the accuracy of colour, line and size in the reproductions produced by Frobenius and his team of artists.[106] They were 'too highly coloured' and much bigger in scale than the originals, and furthermore in some cases were superfluous duplications of paintings that had already been published – for instance, the copies she and Helen Tongue had produced 22 years ago at Modderpoort and Advance Post.

'Frobenius rushed like a storm through Cape Town en route to Rhodesia,' she remarked in a letter written in November 1928.[107] This attitude of mild interest would harden into irritation and even dislike over the years. She admired the copying work produced by his team, and complimented his researchers for working 'diligently' and for saving 'much beauty, and interesting things' from decay.[108] But her letters to Käthe reflected her growing irritation with Frobenius's theories of an ancient superior civilisation being responsible for Great Zimbabwe and an exotic authorship for bushman art.[109] She disagreed with his assumption that the bushmen merely continued an art and culture that had been developed in antiquity. In her 1932 paper, she contested Frobenius's claim that a 'superior' culture from the East had influenced the art of Southern Rhodesia. While agreeing that sophisticated activities like mining and smelting may have been imported, Dorothea suggested that this contact would have been 'peaceful', arising from 'intermarriage or the employment of one race by the other'.[110] She argued that common-alities of style stretching across widely separated regions implied that the art had been made by people that had at one time occupied most parts of the country, and pointed to continuations in the use of materials and the presence of 'bushman-made' implements in on-site excavations.[111]

Privately Dorothea wrote that a generalised view on the age of the paint-ings was untenable. She noted that light colours tended to be 'non-permanent', while red or orange paintings could be 'very old'.[112] She took issue with Frobe-nius's classification methods. 'His [Frobenius's] "angular wedge style" I do not regard as very old, as white paint can be seen in many of the paintings, and this does not keep for centuries'.[113] She noted that in 'the latest [rock art] pictures, we sometimes see the leather garments and trappings worn by the Bushmen found here a hundred years ago, and still sported by their brethren in the Kal-ahari'.[114] Dorothea brought her ethnographic knowledge to bear, pointing out that, among the depictions of domestic sheep, cattle and horses along with in-digenous animals, in the 'very latest paintings or the last [layer] but one' could be seen representations of 'men who are distinctly Bushmen, Basutos, Zulus or Europeans, recognisable by their bodily characteristics, dress and weapons'.[115] In general, she preferred ethnographic evidence for determining comparative dates of paintings over models aimed at aligning particular pigments and/or painting styles to respective time periods.

In the private space of her personal correspondence, she would strenu-ously set out her aversion to the mixing of fact and fancy, or, in her words, 'proof' with 'conjecture' and 'assumption'.[116] Frobenius, she declared in a 1930 letter to Käthe Woldmann, was a 'brilliant man'. But as a researcher he did 'not clarify which of his assumptions have been proven and which are conjectures. When you ask him directly, has this or that been proven, he gives an honest answer and says "no". He does not lie, he does not wish to deceive; but the uninitiated masses are being deceived, and do not realise where that which has been actually seen and heard ends, and where the wise and sometimes witty assumptions begin'.[117] By 1937, the year before Frobe-nius's death, Dorothea would, again privately, accuse him of being 'ridicu-lous' and of overestimating his own abilities. 'One thing he does understand is how to blow his own trumpet. I would rather not like to read his *Cicerone*,' she wrote to Woldmann in exasperation.[118]

Dorothea's objection to Frobenius's celebrity profile registered in this comment throws into sharp relief her own preference for making a modest contribution. In 1936 she was referring to him as 'privy councillor Frobenius' (*Geheimrat*), and accusing him of 'unchivalrous' behaviour.[119] The source of this enmity appeared to be a proposal by the Berlin State Museum to publish a series of 'bushman texts' that had been translated by Woldmann with Dorothea's written approval. Frobenius had apparently intervened with a request that explanatory material be integrated into the translations. This caused Dorothea to withdraw her approval and permission for the project, which was consequently shelved. Dorothea's insistence that the texts of her father and aunt be offered without comment or interpretation of any kind was an attitude that aligned with her cautious, empirical approach to her own intellectual project.[120]

Seeing for herself

By the time her edited publication of Stow's copies appeared in 1930, Dorothea was adamant that it had been 'irrefutably proven' that 'many of the thousands of paintings in the caves and on the rocks [had been] painted by the Bushmen themselves'.[121] In her 1932 lecture she stated that rock art should be regarded as the 'most important historical documents left us by the early inhabitants of the country'.[122] The proof of 'bushman' authorship was incontrovertible. Her cautious view challenged that of influential prehistorians, archaeologists and artists of the 1920s and 1930s, including the Abbé Breuil, as we have seen, the anatomist and anthropologist Raymond Dart, as well as the artist Walter Battiss, who suggested an ancient foreign authorship for the art and other aspects of bushman culture.[123]

Dorothea's modest, evidence-based view drew on the writings of Stow and earlier travellers in the region, and was supported by her own fieldwork and observation over the preceding 15 years among remnant bushman groups across southern Africa. As she stated in her introduction to the collection of Stow's copies, modernity had ended the painting tradition and this had led to recent doubts about bushman authorship. 'I have not the least doubt that the paintings are the work of Bushmen, nor, as far as I know, has any author up to the beginning of the present century expressed any doubt on the subject.'[124] Fieldwork had provided evidence of the irrevocable impact of modernity in the form of civilisation and the forces of history on bushman lifestyle. It had destroyed not only their painting tradition, but also their 'lore'.[125] As she wrote in *Rock Paintings in South Africa*:

As long as the Bushmen bred in freedom lived, the identity of the painters was undisputed; with their deaths doubts might naturally arise from people asking farm-bred Bushmen about pictures and finding complete ignorance on the subject. Other travellers of today question the wild Bushmen of the Kalahari about the pictures without realising that they and their ancestors have been without the materials for painting as long as they have dwelt on the sand, probably for centuries.[126]

6 | Intimacy and marginality in rock art recording, 1932–1940

In this manner a most primitive race of hunters, the little Bushmen of South Africa, have left their record on the rocks of the land that long was theirs, but that knows them no more...Nor is there any question as to what they are doing, even feeling, so great was the skill of the artists in portraying action in few but telling lines.[1]

Dorothea's interest in rock art scholarship continued after the successful publication of the first batch of Stow's reproductions. She was on a mission to prove that the bushmen were the original inhabitants of southern Africa, and to dispute suggestions that all of Africa's cultural output was derived from an exotic and superior civilisation that had peopled the continent in ancient times. The presence of rock art throughout the country was proof of the earlier widespread existence of bushmen across the land and Dorothea was determined to document the painted record they had left behind. It was time to investigate the rock art in an area she felt had yet to receive the attention of researchers and copyists.

In the wider world, global politics and financial woes had exerted their influence on intellectual life in cities far from the metropolitan centres of Europe and North America. As Dorothea explained to Käthe Woldmann, the depressed economic climate of the 1930s had put an end to the possibility of state money being available for research – even in Cape Town.[2] But Dorothea was not deterred in her aim to document rock art located in the hitherto overlooked swathe of country stretching from Piquetberg (now Piketberg) in the west of the Cape Province, through Paarl, Ceres, Worcester, Swellendam and Riversdale, to the mountains around Oudtshoorn, George and Uniondale. Her interest extended to the Bedford, Albany and Graaff Reinet districts. Stow and Bleek's *Rock Paintings in South Africa* (1930), and Tongue and Bleek's *Bushman Paintings* (1909), had covered rock art in the foothills of the Drakensberg in the eastern Cape, Basutoland (now Lesotho), the Orange Free State (now Free State) and Natal (now KwaZulu-Natal). The project that Dorothea set in motion in her chosen research zone offers an opportunity to examine the social and affective networks that characterise fieldwork, to probe the gap between private and public texts, and to investigate the emotional and interactive processes that underlie the making of knowledge in the field.

This chapter draws on correspondence exchanged in the space of six or seven months in 1932 that gives a textured picture of the informal practices and relationships that govern the making of field-based knowledge. The letters give a sense of the idiosyncratic detail and spontaneity that underlie the lived reality of method in the field, and tell of the making of 'sanitised' official texts in which all experiential information has been written out.[3] The narrative shows how the scholar and her research assistants are inscribed, or present, in their outputs in a variety of subtle ways, and how knowledge flows in both directions between them. It elaborates how methodology develops in organic, pragmatic ways in reaction to the specifics of a particular field site, and how the personalities and energies of research assistants contribute to and influence research results.

Much of this chapter concentrates on the presence of research assistants, and on the implications of informal practices and relationships through which field-based knowledge is made.[4] It aims to provide substance and texture to arguments calling for recognition of the unstable and interactive ways in which knowledge emerges from research in the field. By focusing on the personal details of the research relationship, it calls attention to the processes by which local ways of knowing become intertwined with imported ideas and are recast as empirical fact.[5] Like the British naturalist Alfred Russel Wallace, whom Jane Camerini describes as having 'relatively low social standing and minimal institutional support', Dorothea operated on the margins of established academia.[6] Despite her institutional position as Honorary Reader in Bushman Languages at UCT, she occupied a marginal space not only institutionally in respect of research funding, but also intellectually.[7] Nevertheless, like her institutionally supported (male) colleagues, she established and maintained the networks necessary to achieve her research goals.

In the space of three months early in 1932, Dorothea's assistants produced 138 watercolour rock art reproductions and covered miles of country stretching from Grahamstown to the area now known as the Garden Route. The rock art samples they collected allowed Dorothea to flesh out the survey of rock art that she was scheduled to deliver to the South African Association for the Advancement of Science (SAAAS) later that year.[8] The book that emerged from this project, *More Rock-Paintings in South Africa*, would take eight years to complete, appearing finally in 1940.[9] A decade after the appearance of the Stow book, the thrust of Dorothea's interpretations and theses around rock art reiterated many of those earlier assertions. What was new was her classification of the rock art of southern African into four geographical regions, an idea introduced in her SAAAS lecture of 1932.[10] Her aim was to map paintings into areas based on slight differences she observed in the quality, content and style of paintings. In the earlier book, Dorothea had classified the area under review (Area 2, including the foothills of the Drakensberg in the eastern Cape, Basutoland, the Orange Free State and Natal) as exhibiting by far the greatest number of sites and paintings, featuring 'innumerable, incalculable' superpositions, and surpassing in 'grouping, movement and shading' all of the work found elsewhere.[11] The 1940 publication dealt with paintings in Area 1 (stretching from the mountains of Piquetberg on the west coast of the Cape Province, through Paarl, Ceres, Worcester, Swellendam and Riversdale, to the mountains around Oudtshoorn, George and Uniondale and the Bedford, Albany and Graaff Reinet districts) that she described as 'more primitive'.[12]

In terms of interpretation and meaning, Dorothea reiterated her view that the paintings reflected daily life, cultural activities and historical events (including hunts, dances and masquerades, cattle raids and battles). She conceded that some paintings, especially group scenes, might be illustrations of bushman myths, but only very few conveyed 'magic purpose'.[13] Here she was at odds with her father, who appeared to be in quest of myth illustration in his rather brief and inconclusive rock art sessions with his research subjects at Mowbray.[14] Again she repeated an assertion made in her earlier book. The impression that most of the paintings conveyed a magical purpose was, she argued, a false one based on the fact that the copyist would tend to select for reproduction the more interesting paintings over and above the many run-of-the-mill scenes of daily life. She asserted that the paintings were the work of bushmen who had inhabited most of the country before the arrival of immigrants and settlers. She referred to archaeological evidence to support her argument about authorship and date of paintings in the different areas, and pointed to cultural embellishments depicted in some paintings, such as bows and arrows, karosses and ostrich-eggshell beading, and her own observations of bushmen in the field. Where 'Bantu' spears appeared, along with cattle and horses, she argued that this evidence that the 'Bantu invasion was beginning' meant the most recent paintings could be dated to the second half of the eighteenth century, 'shortly before the Bushmen were detribalised or exterminated'.[15]

Research into prehistory was a gendered activity in which women of the early twentieth century, when they figured at all, typically occupied supportive positions.[16] When included on an expeditionary tour, women undertook copying tasks while their spouses were involved in the work of delineating strata and of excavating, counting and classifying stone tools, human remains and other materials.[17] Both Leo Frobenius and Abbé Breuil relied on female assistants.[18] Institutionally, these prehistorians circulated within the boundaries of formal science and sometimes enjoyed state support. Dorothea, on the other hand, seems to have occupied a peripheral position in relation to the work of prehistory (perhaps because her primary interest lay in the study of languages), as well as to the academy. Her position as honorary reader at UCT did not include financial support. There is evidence to suggest that she felt that the university considered her interest in 'Bushman research' to be marginal and that it therefore had to proceed on a 'voluntary' basis.[19] But her membership of the SAAAS was important to her, and remained a source of intellectual stimulation throughout her career. Notwithstanding these institutional connections, however, her research and field trips were self-funded, and, as we have seen, she tended to travel and work independently of established academic structures.

In terms of resources and output, Dorothea's project was tiny in comparison with the much publicised expeditions carried out by Frobenius, Breuil and others. But her research was of great importance for personal and intellectual reasons. It was as much about her quest to recover and preserve what she could of her vision of premodern _ 'bushman' society as it was an expression of familial loyalty. Scale was not the issue. Dorothea's research proceeded at a private pace amid the larger public and institutional context of prehistory. It was more about quietly working in the background, documenting evidence and salvaging samples of rock art, language and other aspects of culture, than about participating in grand field expeditions and making provocative statements of scientific theory.

Research by correspondence

The archive is silent about why Dorothea took the unprecedented step of engaging research assistants for this project, or indeed why she chose not to venture into the field herself. The reasons may have been circumstantial. It is likely that all her spare moments were consumed with translating notebook texts and preparing material for her series in *Bantu Studies*, but one could also speculate that, at age 62, she no longer felt up to the rigours of work in the field.[20] It is also clear that time was of the essence. Dorothea needed to beef up her knowledge with more comprehensive data. It was just months ahead of her address to the SAAAS.[21]

In February 1932, Dorothea began making arrangements for the Grahamstown-based Van der Riet sisters to try their hand at copying rock art from caves and shelters in the country surrounding their home. Mollie and Joyce were the nieces of Miss Van der Riet, a friend of Dorothea's. They were daughters of the 'late Judge van der Riet'.[22] Their family home, Altadore, was in Grahamstown.[23] It is likely that they were twins, most probably schooled at Diocesan School for Girls, to this day a smart school for girls from elite families.[24] The fact that the sisters were studying art made them ideal candidates for the project.[25] In addition, they were usefully located in the heart of Dorothea's area of interest. She would pay them from the proceeds of sales of her Stow book.[26] The letters written by Joyce to Dorothea between February and July 1932 provide a reflected view of Dorothea's thinking. What stands out in their tone and content is the enthusiasm with which the sisters embraced their task, an enthusiasm that substantially impacted on the research outcome.

From the start, Dorothea insisted that scientific practice be employed. She made sure that the research took place under the watchful eye of Dr John

Hewitt, director of the Albany Museum in Grahamstown, whom she knew well from SAAAS meetings. He had been director for at least 10 years by the time Joyce, following Dorothea's written instruction, called on him to find out more about the rock art of the district.[27] As indicated by the papers he had delivered to SAAAS meetings during the 1920s, Hewitt's interest lay in the human and cultural aspects of the prehistory of the eastern Cape.[28] Through Joyce, Hewitt expressed his support for the project, declaring that none of the 'bushman' paintings in the Albany district had yet been 'properly painted'.[29] He singled out the 'Wilton series' of the district as being especially worthy of copying, and took the opportunity to have a set of copies made for his museum.[30]

Joyce provided precise details regarding the research methods employed: 'We actually traced the drawings off the rock and then painted them on the spot so that they are as exactly alike the originals as it is possible to make them.'[31] In citing this description of methodology in connection with her 1938 funding application to the National Research Council and Board for support to publish the paintings, Dorothea wrote that she 'impressed' on her research assistants that she did not want 'pretty pictures, but accurate copies'.[32] Dorothea directed the sisters to tint the background of their copies to represent the colour of the rock surface, rather than to leave it blank. Where possible, they were also to make pen-and-ink drawings of sites, and take photographs.[33] Thus, armed with a 'very good box camera', as well as a 'plate' camera which they had found 'lying about at home', the sisters agreed to try their hand at photography.[34] In the end, this yielded mixed results. Joyce commented that their 'snaps' were 'disappointing on the whole' and that 'the paintings out in the open did not take as well as the ones we took with a time exposure so that the majority were failures as they were usually in the open'.[35]

Because the archive does not include Dorothea's letters to the Van der Riets, one can only speculate about her response to the wholehearted enthusiasm with which her assistants embraced their task. By the middle of May, both sisters had worn out their shoes and run out of paper and paints, and needed to return home for replacements. Joyce had to resort to writing letters in pencil, as she had no more ink to refill her pen while out in the field.[36] Dorothea must surely have realised how much the Van der Riet sisters' energy contributed to the success of her project. Her appreciation could be measured in the fact that she paid them generously and regularly.

Also, she allowed their names to appear as the main authors of the book. For the young assistants, no doubt it was as much about adventure as about preserving a threatened culture or seeing their names in print. Clearly, the project was worth their while financially, but more so, it spoke to their independent and adventurous spirits and contributed substantially to the detail and quality of the watercolours they produced. Apart from Joyce's 'small art exam in June' and their hockey tour to Johannesburg later that same month, the sisters were 'ready to do exactly what [was] most satisfactory' for Dorothea. They planned to spend the foreseeable months copying the sites that Dorothea specified, and were ready to spend the mid-year vac 'camping out with the car and doing the work you speak of further afield'.[37] Dorothea had a June deadline, however, so by mid-April the sisters had cleared their calendars in order to work exclusively on the project.[38]

Negotiating the field

The correspondence reflects the charm and texture of communications and negotiations that passed back and forth between the assistants and their supervisor as the project got under way. Joyce's letters overflow with excitement. But although she and her sister were ready and able to traverse the country by car (with their mother in tow in some cases), and to stomp miles through rough country armed with all the paraphernalia required for tracing and copying, they were more reticent when it came to putting a price on their efforts.[39] In her introductory letter, Joyce left the matter of payment up to Dorothea, asking only to be paid 'so much a mile for the car and then so much for each set of paintings according to the amount of work in them'. A pencilled note on Joyce's first letter indicates that Dorothea offered to pay the sisters '£1 per sheet (more for difficult ones), £2 for sketch of cave, 5/- for photo'.[40] Her offer was accepted, and Joyce declared that both she and her sister were 'only too willing to finish [the paintings] round Grahamstown', and were keen on travelling further afield later on.[41] At this stage, the sisters were discovering just how many rock art sites existed close to their home. Through Hewitt, they had been told about sites at Alice, as well as about others 'only five or six miles out of town'. Dorothea had a clear idea of which sites she wanted recorded and excluded the 'extraordinarily good' but too 'well known' examples of cave paintings near Cala in the then Transkei that

Joyce's brother had told her about.[42] This site was the same as the one visited by Helen Tongue some 20 years earlier.[43]

Braving a blazing hot eastern Cape day in late February, Joyce and Mollie travelled some 17 miles to Broxley, the farm owned by Mr J. Currie, for their first field encounter. Once there, they walked, climbed and scrambled the necessary distance over rough territory to reach their target, a shelter situated some '5,000 feet above the New Year River', where they made their first set of copies.[44] Hewitt vetted the paintings and pronounced them to be work of 'great fidelity' and better than his own.[45] Thus was produced the first set of four sheets which were duly posted to Dorothea in Cape Town. Joyce and Mollie earned £4.11.10.[46]

'Co-production' of knowledge[47]

From the outset, Dorothea regarded the sisters as her equal partners in the process of knowledge making. No distance in terms of race, culture or gender existed to muddy their interactions.[48] The correspondence shows that the researchers inscribed themselves into Dorothea's project in many ways. While Dorothea controlled the itinerary of sites to a certain extent, such as in the example of Cala, the letters indicate that the sisters were required to make their own decisions throughout. Notwithstanding Dorothea's watchful eye and close involvement, Joyce's letters are shot through with comments and questions that reveal the extent to which the sisters were involved in selecting, influencing and making judgements about the material they were representing. Through the flow of letters, negotiations about methodology were ongoing, with questions related to field practice a common theme.

Early on, Joyce realised that capturing the full number of paintings in shelters was going to be impossible. At Glencraig, for example, there were several caves and many paintings: '[I]t seemed impossible to paint every one so we left out the obviously later ones which were much inferior and even looked as if they had been done in the last few years by the natives living on the farm at present.' Joyce asked outright: 'Is this correct or do you want a record of *every* distinct painting that it is possible to do?' Later in the same letter is revealed a moment in which the researcher's (Joyce's) sense of the aesthetic influenced the research: 'Some of the pages are not as full as they might be but we felt that often to add an odd painting would spoil the group so that if you feel that some of the pages are not "worth" a pound would you pay us according to what you think.' Then there was the problem of preservation: 'Do you want the paintings exactly as they are at the present day because some are so very weather worn that wouldn't it be better to improve them a little in colour I mean not form?'[49]

In the absence of Dorothea's direct answers to Joyce's questions, one must base assumptions on what was produced in the end. But the negotiated, interactive texture of fieldwork is clearly revealed in the letters, as is the fact that the flow of knowledge proceeded in both directions. As much as Dorothea's expertise was sought, at certain times Joyce's letters revealed the extent to which the research assistants weighed in with their own interpretations related to the geographical location and siting of the shelters and caves they visited. Just a month into the trip, Joyce noted that all 'of the paintings we have done so far have been on the side of streams; that seemed essential to the Bushmen.'[50] At Glencraig, the sisters would speculate that since the shelter could be easily seen from a distance, this meant that the artist did not fear unexpected attack.[51] Whether such ideas were the sisters' own or were assimilated in the course of conversation with local people cannot now be known for sure.

During the coming weeks, the extent of the sisters' dependence on informal or local knowledge was to become a feature of their research. Throughout the project, at each farm, town or district they visited, they would approach farmers and townspeople and ask for information about rock art sites. In some cases, contacts were passed on by Dorothea. In others, connections were initiated by the fieldworkers themselves.

This method of involving local networks in the research effort had its pitfalls as well as its positive outcomes. Four weeks into the project, Joyce remarked how their local inquiries elicited either too much information or information that was too vague or contradictory to be of any use. As a result, she complained, they either missed visiting particular sites or were 'sent on wild goose chases all over the veldt [sic]'.[52] From the farm Doorn River near George, Joyce reported being surprised by how little the farmers '[knew] of their own caves'.[53] A month later, at 'New [sic] Bethesda', the sisters again confronted a gap in local knowledge. From this village, which Joyce described as 'a small town thirty odd miles North West of Graaff Reinet', three of the farmers she contacted (from a list of four farms) had no knowledge of paintings on their farms. Joyce's letter explained that the sisters had turned down invitations to search for the paintings because they had heard that 'many of the paintings in the district had been used for target shooting'.[54]

They had better success at the fourth farm, Africander's Kloof, where the paintings were 'numerous' and 'seemed superior'. Time constraints prevented the sisters from extending their search, but they took from the region a list of sites which, Joyce wrote, 'the garage man gave me the day we left'.[55] Details such as this, revealed in Joyce's chatty letter, evoke a sense of the wide scope of interest their project generated in the villages through which they travelled, and the extent to which ordinary people became involved. At some sites, landowners shared their knowledge related to the location and meaning of rock paintings on their lands. At Mountain Top farm 27 miles north-west of Grahamstown, Joyce commented on the presence of 'sheep which Mr Bowker [the farmer] says is an old Cape sheep now hardly seen in South Africa'. She also saw handprints at this site with the 'black figures' underlying these being judged the oldest paintings in the shelter.[56] Joyce's sketch of the shelter appeared in More Rock-Paintings, as did her copy of a group painting.[57] Dorothea thought this group scene was an example of myth illustration involving raindrops, a rainbow, a pool of water (a painted motif more accurately identified in contemporary scholarship as representing the skin bags that bushmen made) and a hare. The hare was a common feature in the folklore of 'every Bushman tribe from whom folklore has been collected to any considerable extent', she would comment later, in a reference to the work of her father and aunt.[58] After Mountain Top, the sisters visited 'Blaaukrantz Drift', 18 miles east of Grahamstown along the Port Alfred road, where they copied two sheets and took photographs.[59] One of these copied images, showing large, elongated figures in red with hook heads, appeared in the book.[60]

The correspondence makes dramatically clear that, for the young women at the rock face, nature loomed large at times, though discussion of its vagaries did not become part of the public texts. Without Joyce's regular letters from the field, one would not know that the sisters fought off ticks, fleas and ants as well as the intense late-summer heat on two visits to Howieson's Poort, the famous site 'seven miles' outside of Grahamstown, where they produced four sheets of copies.[61] Neither would one realise that the extremely hot weather constrained their work at times. Joyce wrote in mid-April that the 'frightfully hot' weather had been a 'decided handicap' to the progress of their work. At Katbosch, they had to contend with 'pouring rain' and 'frightful cold'.[62] Details such as these give a picture of the uncertain, stumbling way by which fieldwork proceeds, demonstrating as well the degree of physical commitment demanded from fieldworkers.

In late April, Joyce and Mollie travelled south-west of Grahamstown to Coldspring (a round trip of 14 miles), where they copied scenes from a shelter alongside a stream and took photographs of the valley.[63] None of this work appeared in the book. Guided by Hewitt, the sisters next made two trips to 'Salem commonage' and braved the discomfort of the sun blazing down on them as they worked. The resulting copies proved worth the effort. In early May, Joyce dispatched the eight sheets produced at Salem, among these a copy featuring a ring of figures with a bigger figure in the centre, which Joyce described as an attempt at composition 'seldom aimed at in their [bushman] work'.[64] Dorothea would describe this as a 'circular dance' featuring women dancing around a male leader in the centre.[65]

The trip to Oudtshoorn proved disappointing at first. Joyce had written to Dorothea's contact, Mrs V.H. North, in search of information about rock art in the area.[66] Dorothea may have suggested they make contact with a Mr Pocock, whom she described as 'a bushman painting enthusiast' in the area. In the end they met him briefly on the day they left.[67] De Hoek, the local name given to the adjoining North farms Groenfontein and Nooitgedacht, was situated about 10 miles west of the Cango Caves and 25 miles from Oudtshoorn on the Prince Albert road.[68] The two-day trip from Grahamstown to Oudtshoorn saw the sisters leaving home early on Friday morning, spending the night at Assegaaibosch, and arriving at De Hoek just after dark the following evening. By 10 May they were ensconced at De Hoek and had visited 'three different lots of caves'.[69] Among these were rock art sites on both the North farms, as well as at Boomplaats and Boesman's Kloof (Figure 6.1). Putting heart and soul into their task, the sisters spent the week working from soon after breakfast until dark. Initially, Joyce wrote that they had 'found nothing really exciting'.[70] The paintings were 'nearly obliterated', and seemed 'very similar' to those near Grahamstown.[71]

Matters improved, however, and by the time the sisters left the North farms, they had visited a 'new' cave on Groenfontein, where they found 'excellent' paintings and many superpositions.[72] The researchers would later describe the paintings as 'very distinct', noting the delicate lines of running or falling buck as an 'outstanding feature of the work' in which the artists had succeeded in portraying an excellent idea of movement.[73] The De Hoek series proved to be one of the main discoveries of the project. Dorothea used three illustrations from De Hoek in the printed version of her lecture, and would include nine copies from this batch in *More Rock-Paintings*.[74]

The pace of research had stepped up considerably by late May. Mollie and Joyce worked hard every day, and exploited every opportunity to visit sites. The paintings at Hell Poort near the Cradock road, for instance, were recorded during a picnic stopover at the site on their way home from a farm dance the previous night.[75] Joyce remarked with satisfaction: 'Everyone here is surprised at the amount we managed to get done but then we worked every day & very hard so really it is not to be wondered at at all.'[76] On 30 May, Joyce acknowledged receipt of a handsome £61 received from Dorothea in return for 34 sheets dispatched previously. Ten days later, they received a further £15 in return for a further 'roll' which Joyce had posted off earlier. Certainly, the work was bringing financial reward, but there was more to it than money. As they themselves acknowledged, Joyce and Mollie were 'becoming very interested in the bushmen & their paintings'.[77] There is evidence too that the project brought metaphysical reward. At Boesman's Kloof, there was a moment in which the fieldworkers were experientially changed by the fieldwork, when Joyce reported how she and her sister had watched transfixed while previously hidden paintings emerged as the afternoon sun lit up the shelter's interior.[78]

Knowing the field

Reading the Van der Riet letters chronologically gives a striking sense of how the sisters gained in confidence as they traversed their 'field' through time and space, revealing their deepening involvement in the work and their growing ability to 'know' the object of their study. For instance, at Misgund, where they stopped in mid-May, Joyce had the self-assurance to proclaim the paintings 'quite different from any we have done before'. The 'large figure, which was about two feet high', was both 'indifferently drawn' and 'out of reach'. They decided to photograph the figure for Dorothea so that she could decide whether or not she wanted a copy.[79] The sisters also copied as well as photographed a bichrome elephant at Misgund, both of which appeared in *More Rock-Paintings*.[80] A couple of weeks later, while on the lookout for engravings near Graaff Reinet, they came across paintings which Joyce described as 'very poor'. The shelters, which were 'filled with spots & crude scribblings', were on the farms Doornplaats (Doorn Plaatz in the book), Katbosch and De Erf, which Joyce described as 'twenty four miles South West of Graaff Reinet'.[81] Two painted copies and one photograph from this series appeared in the book.[82] It was on this segment of the trip that Dorothea asked them to record engravings for Maria Wilman at McGregor Museum.[83] At Steilkrantz, the sisters '[i]n great hopes' walked miles to find rock chippings which Joyce described as disappointing, but which Dorothea evidently felt were worthwhile, as she included three in the book.[84]

After so many weeks and several repeat visits to particular areas, it is not surprising that the sisters were becoming regarded as local experts in the field of bushman research. In one of her last letters, Joyce wrote that it would be easy to continue gathering information for Dorothea since people 'seem to have heard that we are interested & are always ready to tell us of new caves & anything else they happen to know of the bushmen'.[85] She thanked Dorothea sincerely for the opportunity: '... besides the only too needed money, we have enjoyed doing it all most awfully as well'.[86] On 17 June, Joyce dispatched another set of sheets.[87] These were copies from Wilton cave near Alicedale, site of a landmark excavation that Hewitt had been involved in, and that had been described in the Goodwin and Van Riet Lowe book *The Stone Age Cultures of South Africa* just a few years earlier.[88] Joyce included a map on which she had marked painted sites in the Grahamstown district, with a promise that she and Mollie would be happy to record paintings at sites they had heard about near Bedford and in the Fort Beaufort district.[89] In the end, these sites were recorded towards the end of July, too late for inclusion in Dorothea's lecture. She would include bichromes of an eland and an ostrich from this batch in the book.[90]

So the weeks of intensive research came to an end. Dorothea travelled to Durban to deliver her lecture to the SAAAS meeting, which took place from

4 to 6 July. Mollie and Joyce went to their provincial hockey tournament in Jo-hannesburg in 'excellent training' after so much climbing and walking.[91] Three loose, undated sheets of ruled writing paper in the correspondence record Dorothea's painstaking calculations in which she added up her expenses related to the project. Including amounts of £3.10 for her niece Marjorie Bright and a further £1.05 for a 'Miss Hurdus' [*sic*], Dorothea spent £215.9.8.[92] That considerable sum had bought her 150 copied paintings, 138 from the Van der Riet sisters as well as additional copies from the Porterville and Piquetberg mountains contributed by Marjorie and her friend Sheila Fort. After all that effort and expense, it is certain that Dorothea would have stored her precious collection in a safe place while she turned her attention to other pressing tasks. Her attention now was focused on the series of notebook translations that appeared in *Bantu Studies* until 1936. Also, she was assisting Käthe Woldmann with her German translation of texts from *Specimens*.[93]

Packaging field notes

It was not until 1938 that Dorothea returned to the rock art copies. A sep-arately filed collection of correspondence between Dorothea in Newlands and the publishing company Methuen in London attests to two years of negotiations around the production and publication of *More Rock-Paintings in South Africa*.[94] It was either late in 1937 or early in 1938 that Dorothea entrusted her friend and colleague at UCT's Anthropology Department, the archaeologist A.J.H. Goodwin, to approach Methuen in London with her valuable collection.[95] Dorothea's correspondence indicates that she and Goodwin got along socially and professionally.[96] Family memory has it that Dorothea, her two nieces and Goodwin travelled together to an SAAAS meeting on one occasion.[97]

On the rock art book, the preserved correspondence begins in the mid-dle of things. The publishers were looking for a more affordable way to fill the brief, originally estimated at the 'huge' cost of £900.[98] Eventually, after months of discussion, a suitable schedule was agreed on. Two days before Christmas of 1938 Dorothea finally signed a formal contract with Methuen. She returned her signed version to London along with £200 towards the publishing of the book. This was followed up with the National Research Foundation's contribution of £395 by bank draft sent on 31 December, and a request for bromide copies so that Dorothea could, in collaboration with her research assistants, finish her text for the book.[99] The royal-quarto-sized book eventually saw the light of day in 1940. In 80 pages it featured 34 plates containing monochrome, bichrome and polychrome reproductions of paintings, as well as photographs, a sketch and a sketch map of the area covered. The print run was 500 copies.[100]

The archive is silent about Dorothea's reaction to the book. Not even in her private letters did she express how she felt about seeing the rock art copies in print after eight years of effort. She must have been satisfied with – if not extremely proud of – the outcome. It was a handsome publication, following the format of her earlier presentation of Stow's copies. *More Rock-Paintings in South Africa* could certainly hold its own alongside other books on the subject available at the time.[101] Yet, just as the published text elides the contingent aspects and practical difficulties of field research, so too does the finished book gloss over the ruptures and uncontrollable moments underlying the processes of production and publishing. These are apparent only to readers of the Bleek Collection, where Dorothea's papers convey detailed information regarding the laborious process of packaging field notes for publication.

Interestingly, the available correspondence does not make clear who made the final selection of copies for the book. But the astonishing implication is that the publishers did this, perhaps working from an original list provided by Dorothea. This was likely because of the complexities (and cost) of full-colour printing at the time, which directly affected how many colour plates could be included.[102] Given that Mr Godwin was in London at the start of the process, it is possible that he was consulted. Dorothea had appointed him as her envoy and may have entrusted him to deal with more than simply delivering the copies.[103] Either way, the correspondence refers to a list of plates without clarifying who drew this up.[104] Another reference to selection of particular paintings appeared in a letter written almost a year after the start of negotiations, in which Dorothea requested that painting number 66 be substituted by another number, 'perhaps 67'.[105] Much later in the process, Dorothea would repaginate the proofs in an attempt to iron out geographical anomalies that she became aware of after renewing contact with the Van der Riet sisters.[106] In her published introduction, she was careful to make readers aware of two levels of selection – 'first in copying, then in publishing' – that underpinned the final outcome, and consequently influenced the impression created by the paintings collected in the book.[107]

The file of letters makes clear how, behind the scenes, Dorothea liaised with her researchers, wrote texts and captions, checked maps and photographs, numbered bromides, checked proofs and dutifully posted these to London. She was by now resigned to the reality of having to narrow her extensive collection of 150 sheets down to 34 plates, and to the less-than-perfect sequencing of sites due to confusion which had arisen around pagination, layout and the geographical spread of paintings. The letter she addressed to 'Mrs Ginn and Miss Mollie van der Riet' in early January 1939 implied the long period of negotiation which had stretched throughout the previous year. It expressed regret that 'not a third of the collection' would be included in the book.[108]

In keeping with her desire to show representative sampling, Dorothea also regretted not being able to include at least one example from each site visited by the sisters. She would write the complete text only for the two examples from Piquetberg, sites that she herself had visited.[109] She would also supply the explanatory 'Remarks' for all illustrations, but the sisters were asked to provide the remaining text for all of their sites. Dorothea was specific about the form this text should take. Mollie and Joyce should be as definite as possible about farm ownership. Following the format suggested decades earlier by her father and used in the Stow book, Dorothea wanted to give readers a feeling for the landscape in which shelters and paintings were located:

I want a general description of the physical features of each district to precede the 1st plate from that district. Then I want the Locality. – , Site. –, and Description. – given, as I have done. You need not fill up Remarks. –, unless you have something you particularly want to say. I will fill in that part. Description. – should tell of the general work in the cave or shelter.[110]

By now, Joyce was married and living in Walmer, Port Elizabeth, while Mollie was working for the Automobile Association in Grahamstown. Both were happy to help and excited at the prospect of seeing their names in print. Joyce would travel to Grahamstown for a few days so the sisters could work together, and 'Mummie', who had travelled with them on the initial trips to Oudtshoorn and to other local sites all those years back, was also brimming with suggestions.[111] In reality, though, it turned out that in recollecting trips taken and sites recorded seven years previously, the sisters had only a diary and their memories to go on. 'I only wish we had known at the time that this was in store for us, because we would have then taken careful notes,' Joyce wrote.[112] They tried to fill in the gaps by asking farmers on whose farms they had painted to confirm their 'statements'.[113] They asked Dorothea to return the letters Joyce had written. Over two weekends, Joyce and Mollie retraced their steps in the countryside around Grahamstown and beyond. They wrote to municipalities and farmers to confirm landownership.[114] Hewitt helped where he could.[115]

The sisters rounded up as much information as they could, papering over gaps and anomalies as they went along. The seamless text of the published book gives no clue to the places where memory failed and/ or nature had intervened. Despite extensive searching on three different occasions, for instance, Mollie was unable to find a particular group of paintings they had copied at Glencraig.[116] Over the years the area had become overgrown, and Mollie remembered the group in question being 'quite apart from the others in a very small shelter on a slightly lower level'. But, she admitted, 'I cannot be sure as we did so many that I may be mixing it up'. Perhaps too, as Hewitt suggested, motorcars had made a difference, sending clouds of dust across the valley to cover the rocks and hide the paintings.[117] Based on what appeared in the book, the particular group that Dorothea was after may have shown figures using different styles of hunting bow. Dorothea's remarks relating to the only Glencraig group in the book made much of the depiction of 'length of the bow in relation to human figure', and compared the work with 'far superior' copies by Stow of similar paintings from the Thorn and Lower Black Kei rivers.[118] In the end, Mollie was apologetic about the 'little help' they had been able to provide. But she made excellent use of the £10 Dorothea paid her for her share of the work, putting it towards the requirements for her 'A' pilot's licence in time to make use of a special government grant. 'So you see your £10 was indeed a fortune in more ways than one,' she wrote to Dorothea.[119]

While Mollie completed her pilot's training, Dorothea continued to work on the book. She appeared to be oblivious to the gathering clouds of war in Europe. Her research consumed her completely. She assembled rock art samples from around the country, in line with her desire to offer work representing all regions. Sometime in May, she visited the mountains of the western Cape at Bain's Kloof and Gouda, perhaps with Marjorie, who was now married and visiting from Argentina. Dorothea wrote to Käthe Woldmann: '[T]here are still paintings, but much simpler ones, not at all as beautiful as those in the Freestate and in the Eastern Cape. The ones here are mostly in one colour. But the style is the same.'[120]

Cost of war

Dorothea's text and corrected map reached London on 20 May 1939.[121] Queries around the book seemed to drag on forever. The publishers pushed the publication date out to 1940 and, on account of 'war costs', increased the initially agreed cover price of 2 guineas to 45 shillings.[122] If Dorothea found the endless toing and froing frustrating, she did not mention it in her letters. She would need patience and strength, as there was a greater test in store.

Final production began in the last two months of 1939. At last, the end was in sight. In January 1940 Dorothea sent a list of names and addresses of people to whom complimentary copies should be sent. In March she and the National Research Council and Board were still awaiting receipt of the finished book.[123] In terms of Dorothea's funding agreement, twelve copies had to be sent to the Council and Board. Other recipients included Mrs P.E. Ginn, Miss M. van der Riet, Dr Hewitt at the Albany Museum, Mrs R.T. Scott (Dorothea's niece Marjorie, now relocated from Argentina to Groot Drakenstein near Wellington in the western Cape), Sheila Fort and A.J.H. Goodwin in Claremont and Kenilworth respectively, and two copies for herself.[124] Because it was an expensive book, the publishers suggested that not more than 20 review copies be sent out.[125] Publications Dorothea crossed off their list included the *Daily Telegraph*, the *Observer*, the *Sunday Times* and *Connoisseur*. Dorothea's list featured the Royal Anthropological Society's journal, *Antiquity*, *Africa*, *L'Anthropologie*, the *Argus Press* and three US newspapers.[126] With the help of their 'Archaeological Adviser', the publishers drew up a second list of 17 titles, which now included the *American*

Anthropologist, the *American Journal of Archaeology*, the journal of the Royal African Society, *Nature*, *Antiquity* and *Man*.[127] Dorothea would later add, by cable, *Africa Burger* and the *Argus Press* to the list. Locally, Dorothea sent a review copy to the *Cape Times* and the other local dailies and weeklies.

It was in the early months of 1941 that the war, up to now refracted through delays in correspondence and increased costs, had a direct and profound impact on Dorothea's archive. She had in July of the previous year decided to have the reproductions returned to Cape Town.[128] The publishers, centrally situated in the Strand of London, were holding her valuable originals. These were insured against risk of fire but not against 'enemy action'.[129] With the Blitz in full swing, there was a risk of air attack. But sending them home by sea carried as much possibility of disaster. It was a tough call. Dorothea was in a quandary, and even while seeing to practical arrangements such as cover for war risk, she uncharacteristically asked the publishers to second-guess her decision: 'If…circumstances should make you think it wiser to hold the pictures a bit longer, please do so.'[130] The possibility of calamity was at the front of her mind. Full insurance cover, even if expensive, would at least provide cash: '… in the case of their being lost, I should like to be able to have the rock paintings copied again'.[131] Privately, however, she must have known it would not be that simple. She was well aware of the pitfalls associated with retracing sites.

By 15 August 1940 the reproductions, packed in a sturdy wooden 'case', were on the water aboard the *City of Simla*.[132] At that point there was a break in correspondence of about four months. When it resumed towards the end of 1940, the war in the Atlantic was taking its toll on shipping. Mail was slow and haphazard. Late in January 1941 Dorothea was still waiting for news of her case of paintings.[133] Her letter of 21 January to the ship chandlers in Cape Town crossed with that of Methuen, dated 17 January, in which was enclosed an insurance cheque for £222.12.6.[134] The *City of Simla* with all its cargo – including Dorothea's precious collection of rock art reproductions – had been lost at sea.[135] It was one of three cargo and passenger ships sunk in a U-boat attack in the Irish Sea on 20 September 1940.[136]

As shattering as the loss must have been, Dorothea did not waste time regretting her decision to have the collection returned to Cape Town. No doubt she agreed with the publisher's comment that 'no part of the world [seemed] very safe' at the time.[137] Archival documents show that she did not falter in her continuing quest to document the rock art of the country. Immediately she set about arranging to have as many of the paintings recopied as possible.[138] She engaged a new team of copyists for this project, and a new set of reproductions copied in the Swellendam, Oudtshoorn, George and Uniondale districts was produced.[139] The project leader, James Eddie, is not further identified nor does he appear in other contexts in Dorothea's papers. But the collection of copies he and his team produced offers proof that they followed the trail of the Van der Riet sisters to Nooitgedacht, Groenfontein, and Boomplaats near Oudtshoorn, where they copied paintings from the same group of caves and shelters as those featured in *More Rock-Paintings*.[140] They went also to Bushman's Hollow in the Piquetberg mountains, in this case following the trail of Marjorie and Dorothea herself, where they copied paintings from shelters shown in the book.[141] However, they did not make re-productions of painted scenes and groups that featured in the book. Dorothea must have instructed them to concentrate on copying other examples. Eddie's accompanying typed descriptions followed exactly the format devised for the book – 'Locality', 'Site' and 'Description'. But this work differs from the earlier reproductions in its presentation of a blank background in which no attempt has been made to represent the surrounding rock. It seems inexplicable that Dorothea did not request that the background be colour-washed, as she had done earlier in the case of Mollie and Joyce. The resulting reproductions have a lifeless appearance. The same could be said of the project in general, which lacks the experiential detail that added so much charm to the earlier one.

Royalty statements individually numbered and preserved in the Bleek Collection show that *More Rock-Paintings* and the Stow book sold steadily throughout the remaining years of Dorothea's life.[142] Her meticulous record-keeping habits were also sustained right until the end. Three weeks before she died, Dorothea sent £10.2.4 to the Council for Educational, Sociological and Humanistic Research.[143] That letter, dated 8 June 1948, was sent from a new address, The Garth, Southfield Road, Plumstead.[144] It acknowledged the receipt of royalties of £15.13.-, earned in the six months from June to December 1947, an amount which included the fee of 9s6d earned from the reproduction of 'a portion of plate 7' by a 'Mrs Drinker' in her book *Music and Women*.[145]

The last item in C18, itemised as number 86, is an undated 'compliments' slip from Methuen, presumably originally attached to a cheque or statement of account. It refers to enclosed royalties of £20.2.5. Scribbled towards the bottom of this slip of paper, in Dorothea's handwriting and her usual black ink, is a breakdown of the amount into one-third and two-third amounts. After that – silence! Dorothea had died suddenly at her home in Plumstead near Cape Town on 27 June 1948.

7 | Making the Bushman dictionary, 1934–1956

Miss Bleek has been engaged for some time in compiling a dictionary in five languages, all Khoi-San dialects. When she speaks in these tongues it sounds like high-powered knitting needles on low throttle, just clicking over.[1]

Thus was Dorothea introduced in a column in the *Cape Times* of 26 April 1946. The Cape Town daily newspaper was advertising the 'short talk' she was to present at an exhibition of rock art reproductions that would be displayed along with work by Leo Frobenius. The article described Dorothea as 'tall, spare and grey-haired', living 'quietly' near Newlands station, a 'gentle householder' and also a 'world-famous person'. If the audience was lucky, it went on to say, 'Miss Bleek may talk in some of the Khoi-San dialects. She is the only living European with a real mastery of Bushman language.'

At the time, two years before she died, Dorothea was embroiled in the protracted and convoluted process of readying her bushman dictionary manuscript for publication. It was an entanglement that would last past her death. As she had experienced with previous book projects, seeing the dictionary into print was a fraught and time-consuming process. Perhaps she thought of Lucy Lloyd's long-ago struggles to publish *Specimens of Bushman Folklore*, and Stow's *The Native Races of South Africa* some 30 years earlier. Dorothea attended to the delays with customary stoicism and dedication. She was 73 years old by the time she forwarded the all-but-completed manuscript to its publisher, the American Oriental Society of New Haven, Connecticut. She would not live to write the 30-page introduction she had planned, nor to see *A Bushman Dictionary* in print. When it did finally appear, it was welcomed as the crowning achievement of a lifelong pursuit, albeit one that was focused on languages Dorothea herself believed were dying out.

Throughout her career she had been firm in her oft-stated view that the 'tribe' she had spent her life studying was either 'rapidly being absorbed by stronger races or dying out'. The quotation is taken from a letter Dorothea wrote to the linguist Clement Martyn Doke at Wits in May 1932. Its particular context was a response to a query from the Inter-University Committee on African Studies with regard to future funding for 'bushman' research, and it provides testimony to Dorothea's attitude to research. Along with a summary of published research on bushman groups in the southern African region, Dorothea recommended that the languages in the northern part of the Bechuanaland Protectorate, especially around Lake Ngami, be studied and recorded. 'Being a dry difficult country it is still the home of various Bushman tribes of whose speech we only know odd words. A young man who is a good shot would be the best person to do this work, one who would live and hunt with the Bushmen as [the geographer Siegfried] Passarge did; but he should first train himself by the study of the available Bushman material.' The Inter-University Committee was presumably wondering whether to allocate resources to the study of bushman literature, but Dorothea was sceptical: 'It is hopeless to encourage the literary development of the languages, as the people who speak them are either rapidly being absorbed by stronger races or dying out.'[2]

As we have seen, variations of the sentiment expressed in the letter to Doke are repeated throughout Dorothea's scholarship – publicly in her lectures, letters to the press, journal articles and books, and privately in correspondence. It is a constant refrain in the record, and it echoes the attitude expressed decades earlier by Wilhelm Bleek.[3] The motif of vanishing cultures was a persistent theme in Dorothea's scholarship, as it was among many scholars of the late nineteenth and early twentieth centuries. Yet running parallel was her commitment to producing a dictionary of 'bushman' languages, and in so doing to realise the dreams of her father and aunt. Along with the notebooks, the dictionary was part of Dorothea's inheritance. It was both an intellectual and a material legacy that found concrete form in the card indexes and shoeboxes filled with the /Xam lexicon. Physically, the indexes consisted of /Xam words with English translations penned in fine Victorian script on individual sheets of paper specially cut to size that Dorothea had preserved, worked on and later bequeathed, along with the more famous notebooks, to UCT.[4] Together the lexicon and the notebooks were the foundation of Dorothea's dictionary that she expanded to include the language samples she had collected on her field trips.

Dorothea's material inheritance included vocabularies compiled by her father, drawing on the work of others in the field. A set of quarto-sized volumes, handsomely bound for Sir George Grey's collection held at the then Public Library in Cape Town (now the National Library of South Africa's Cape Town campus) and labelled along their spines in embossed gold lettering, preserved what her father had authenticated and compiled alphabetically from /Nusan (or /Nu//en as in Dorothea's Naron mono-graph) samples gathered by the Reverend J.G. Krönlein in the 1860s.[5] A rough title page drawn up by Wilhelm Bleek refers dramatically to 'The Last Mysteries of South Africa, Fragments of an unknown tongue spoken in the waterless desert of the Kāligari which has not been penetrated by Europe-ans'. Handwritten in Wilhelm Bleek's rough script, the vocabulary comprises formal sections with rough notes and pasted-in words in other sections, and occasional additional pencilled notes that suggest the volume was revisited during the 1870s, and later still.

In addition, Dorothea inherited the four-volume /Xam dictionary that Wilhelm and Lucy had begun compiling in 1871 and had continued to up-date for the duration of their 'bushman researches'.[6] The manuscript, in four quarto volumes, bears the title 'Bushman M.S. DICT'.[7] Regular references to notebook page numbers show it compiled as interview work proceeded, with Wilhelm and Lucy pasting vocabulary transcribed onto strips of blue paper in the appropriate alphabetical order on the large pages.[8] In making her dictionary, Dorothea also drew on her father's 1857 vocabulary of the 'Hot-tentot and Bushman dialects' which he had compiled for the Grey Collection.[9]

Thus the dictionary represented the culmination of Dorothea's, her father's and Lucy's intellectual work and was freighted with sentimen-tal meaning. Her father and Lucy had been pasting /Xam words and their translations onto specially sized envelopes and slips of paper, in preparation for alphabetical filing, on the eve of Wilhelm's death in August 1875.[10] In addition to its sentimental meaning , the conceptual importance of the dictionary was fundamental to Dorothea's project of keeping the bush-men 'alive' as a separate ethnic group, achieving a 'true' understanding of their *Geist* or spirit through intensive language study, and tying them to the southern African landscape as its first inhabitants.[11] Whereas the notebooks contained cosmology, folklore and practical information about ways of life, making possible a reconstruction of 'bushman' worlds, the lexicon contained the conceptual building blocks of those worlds. In the German linguistic tradition in which Dorothea remained entrenched, language could provide the key to unlocking the 'essence' of other 'cultures'.

Compiling and Publishing

As early as the mid-1930s Dorothea had solicited advice from colleagues, including Louis Maingard, professor of French at Wits, and Clement Doke, the recently appointed professor of Bantu languages, also at Wits.[12] An earlier mention of the dictionary crops up in December 1933 in a letter to the musicologist Percival Kirby.[13] Dorothea was busy transcribing /Xam words from the notebooks into alphabetic form. Her comment arose at the end of a more general discussion in response to Kirby's query about the /Xam word *!kummi* that he had found in a marginal note in one of Lloyd's notebooks referring to 'a certain musical instrument played by women'. Dorothea's response was based on linguistic and ethnographic knowledge. She wrote that she had 'never come across a stringed instrument played only by women', but there was the possibility of a link between Kirby's word and the /Xam word for 'beads'. It 'may have been that women used a string with a few beads at the end to whirl round; that would give much the same sound as the *!goin !goin*, to which reference is made in the next sentence. But this is just a conjecture.'[14] Her concluding remark confirmed that work on the dictionary was well under way: 'I still have a number of MS notebooks of my aunt's to enter in the dictionary. Should I come on any more information about the *!kummi*, I will let you know.'

Dorothea's letters confirm that she worked consistently on the dictionary in parallel with her fieldwork and publishing projects through the 1930s. 'I am continually working on the comparative dictionary of the Bushman languages, a very long piece of work,' she wrote to Käthe Woldmann in 1936.[15] Her correspondence records a request made probably in 1934 by Professor Diedrich Westermann, director of the International Institute of African Languages and Cultures in London.[16] Later correspondence records Westermann's request that Dorothea compile a 'dictionary of all recorded words in all Bushman languages and dialects'.[17] In an undated typescript that could be a first draft of her introduction to the dictionary, Dorothea acknowledged that the work was 'begun in 1934 at the request of Professor Westermann'. It was 'an endeavour to collect all words in any Bushman language that have been written down by any author'. She took this injunction seriously. 'This has entailed much searching for the small lists of words included by missionaries, officials, travellers and hunters in their volumes on other subjects, besides putting together the larger vocabularies published in several Bushman languages,' she wrote.[18] The page of introductory notes is followed by Dorothea's list of references in both manuscript and published form, as well as her classification of dialects and their relation to geographical regions. These appear almost unchanged in the published dictionary.[19]

Making the dictionary was a massive task. The aim to include 'all Bushman languages and dialects' may have been too ambitious. Or perhaps Dorothea interpreted Westermann's brief too widely.[20] Decades later, in his introduction to the published work, Professor J.A. Engelbrecht commented that Dorothea's aim to 'include every list of Bushman words that had ever been recorded' meant that 'unsupported data' had been included, and that some of the material lacked 'precision' and hence was of 'historical value' only.[21] Its encyclopaedic scope created a series of obstacles in regard to orthography and layout that translated into serious editing and technical delays when the time came to print the manuscript. Dorothea had complex orthographic requirements about how the languages in her dictionary should be accurately presented.[22] The linguistic complexity of transcribing her language samples with their intricate and varying signs and diacritics meant that a typewriter with specially made keys had to be created to type the manuscript. In the end it had to be 'photostatically' reproduced rather than typeset.[23]

While working on the dictionary, Dorothea was regularly submitting articles to the journal *Bantu Studies*. Its editor, John David Rheinallt Jones, had indicated that he would be willing to accept 'Khoisan material' despite the journal's name. Dorothea's submissions were based on translations of notebook texts organised under the general title 'Customs and Beliefs of the /Xam Bushmen'. It had always been part of her plan to publish as much as she could of the material that her father and aunt had collected. This would be published with as little editing as possible in keeping with Dorothea's wish that translations from the collection of her father and aunt be published without interpretation.[24] In line with her concern that the scholars of Europe could misinterpret the texts of 'natural' people like the bushmen, Dorothea was insistent that the notebook texts be allowed to speak for themselves.

In January 1930, Dorothea wrote to Käthe Woldmann that she was about to publish a piece 'about the customs and superstitions of the Bushman as these relate to the baboon'.[25] This would be the first of nine contributions.[26] In it, as in her 1929 folklore article, she made the point that animals loomed large in bushman folklore, and that humans were less prominent. She emphasised that for the bushmen, the 'dividing line between mankind and the animal world' was never deep. 'In any case there is no great divide between man and animals in their thinking,' she remarked to Woldmann.[27]

Perceptively, Dorothea noted that in attributing human characteristics to baboons (and to other animals), the bushmen revealed their own 'frame of mind' and the deep-seated beliefs that influenced their way of life and world view – for example, their belief that sensations in the body could foretell danger in a way that mimicked the behaviour of some animals.[28] Baboons were clearly a matter of great fascination for Dorothea, as they were for the bushmen. 'I highly respect the baboons, our local large ape variety,' she told Woldmann in the course of a letter addressing the possibility of humans having descended from primates. 'To me the descent of humans from ape-like beings brings no problems if you allow for long periods of gradual development. Not because I do not value the wild uncultivated races, but because I highly respect the baboons, our local large ape variety.' In this instance, her views were based on careful field-based observation rather than on theoretical postulation. Thus they did not 'bear any relation to Darwin's school of thought'.[29]

Other topics addressed in her submissions were 'lions' and 'game animals'.[30] The importance of rain for bushmen was reflected in Dorothea's decision to submit three articles on the subject, ranging from general tales about the rain to more specific customs dealing with rain making and omens.[31] Next she submitted two articles on the subject of 'sorcerors'. The first of these (Part 7) was the longest of all of her submissions.

It has been described as the 'richest single source of insight into /Xam cosmology'.[32] The submissions on 'sorcerors' included some of the comments Dia!kwain had made about Joseph Orpen's and other rock art reproductions shown to him by Wilhelm Bleek in 1874 and 1875. She thus endorsed her father's earlier suggestion of a link between rock art and bushman spiritual beliefs. Dorothea's final submission to *Bantu Studies* dealt with the special speech of the bushmen, indicating her own interest in the association between language and a people's *Geist*.[33]

Understandably, compiling the dictionary was challenging in a context in which a spoken language was to be rendered in written form. Dorothea's years in the field had suggested to her that, for non-native speakers at least, classifying meaning on the basis of sound alone was an ambiguous process. She did not spend time worrying about the potential for confusion between sound and meaning, nor about the power of the researcher to define and fix particular sounds to particular meanings. But she was extremely sensitive to the possibility for error in a situation where the language and folklore was 'translated' by those with different (European) thought processes. However, it turned out that the ambiguities presented by different sounds and duplicated meanings became a problem when the task was word classification and lexicography instead of the explication of folk tales. Dorothea consulted other expert linguists, but even they could not offer clarification. It seemed that all that laboratory science could do was confirm the sometimes contradictory findings of those in the field. Doke's 'mechanical analysis of sounds' in his phonetics laboratory at UCT confirmed Dorothea's and Maingard's statements that there were many variations in bushman sounds.[34] This occurred 'not only with the same speaker pronouncing the same word differently at different times', but when different speakers were tested, there were also 'many variations, naturally occurring in the clicks and vowels'.[35]

By 1935, Dorothea had worked through the notebooks and begun on the lexicon. In October, she wrote Kirby to let him know she had come across another reference to *!kummi*.[36] At the same time, she was attending to larger issues concerning layout and presentation. Towards the end of 1935, she wrote to Maingard asking for advice about orthography and the arrangement of vocabularies.[37] Maingard took more than a year to reply, causing uncharacteristic anxiety on Dorothea's part.[38] Perhaps the delay was because Maingard's Korana dictionary was in the throes of publication at the time. She needed Maingard's advice about structuring her material, layout, spelling, phonetics and orthography. When finally he responded, Maingard provided the practical advice she required and advised her to use the International Phonetic Association symbols as far as possible.[39] He complimented Dorothea on her 'judgment and thoroughness' and offered to send her any of the books that he had suggested she consult.

In 1936–1937 the Empire Exhibition in Johannesburg gave Dorothea a worthwhile opportunity for research. Like its predecessors in London in 1924 and 1925, South Africa's Empire Exhibition was intended as a showcase for the country's achievements and assets in the tradition of 'world's fairs' such as London's Crystal Palace show in 1851. The South African version included 'tribal' exhibits, including one featuring bushmen who had been brought to Johannesburg by the hunter and 'bushman activist' Donald Bain from his camp near Tweerivieren.[40] The group of about 70 bushmen were accommodated at Wits University's research farm Frankenwald between September 1936 and January 1937. While about 30 bushmen performed at the exhibition each day, the rest were available for study by anatomists and anthropologists from Wits who were continuing a programme of physical measurement and medical examination they had begun some months back at Bain's camp in the Kalahari.[41] Dorothea joined the anatomist Professor Raymond Dart, among others, for her sojourn at Frankenwald. She produced a paper afterwards on the /'Auni, a dialect of the Lower Nossop language, and she added language samples provided by Bain to her dictionary even though this meant integrating many new words into already completed sections.[42] She did this gladly, she wrote to Woldmann: 'I am delighted by the knowledge I am gaining.'[43] She returned as soon as possible to the dictionary, now to add Kirby's and Doke's word lists to her manuscript.[44]

Dorothea persevered with her dictionary work through the war years. It was an anxious time for her. She lost contact with her sister Mabel, who had remained in Germany with her family.[45] Even though she had put aside work on the unpublished notebook texts, it would take her 'a couple of years more' to complete the dictionary manuscript.[46]

In April 1943, Dorothea reported to Doke: 'After the lateral & retroflex clicks, I have words beginning in ≠ to do – & then must revise the whole.'[47] In July 1944, Maingard wrote to assure Dorothea that his enthusiasm for her work had not slackened.[48] He dealt with her queries concerning the use of capital letters, symbols and orthography.[49] Two months later he again reassured her, confirming that he considered it an honour 'to be allowed to see the Dictionary in the process of being made and a great privilege to be asked to help'.[50] At this point, Maingard had made corrections to Dorothea's first draft, and the dictionary in manuscript form was on its way to completion. Its 'Bushman–English' part amounted to '1 157 foolscap pages of typescript'; the English–Bushman part, to be used 'as an index to the other, to 120 pages'.[51] Compiled over the past 10 years, it was 'an endeavour to gather all the linguistic material collected by all writers on any Bushman language, including the many fragments found in the works of early travellers and missionaries'. It included 'three groups of Languages, the Southern Bushman group with fifteen different dialects, the Northern Bushman group with seven different dialects, the Central Bushman group also with seven dialects'.[52] In total, 'twenty-eight languages and dialects', some of a few words only, others with a 'fair sized vocabulary' and a few with a 'large one', were represented.[53]

In mid-1945, Dorothea began looking for funding to cover the printing and – even more challenging – for a press with sufficient technical capacity to take on the job of printing her dictionary. She enlisted the help of Isaac Schapera, at that point the director of UCT's School of African Life and Languages and chairman of the university's Publications Committee. It seems she had forgiven his 'dishonorable conduct' 10 years previously, when she had accused him (in a letter to Maria Wilman) of skimming the best off her not-yet-published book on the Naron.[54] On his suggestion, she approached the famous Lovedale Press at Alice in the eastern Cape. Six months later, Lovedale returned an estimate of £1 000.[55] At the same time, she began the laborious process of recopying the entire manuscript – a task 'necessitated by changing the spelling of her "examples" into phonetic spelling', which Maingard had recommended to reduce printing costs.[56] It was to be the first of several compromises of her original orthographic requirements.[57] She pressed on in her search for funding and, on the advice of Maingard, approached the newly renamed Department of African Studies[58] at Wits and the National Research Board.[59] Maingard and Doke would support her application.[60]

152

Finding a publisher

In September 1945, Dorothea put her dictionary work aside for a time, and went to help settle Marjorie and Dick on their newly purchased small farm, Columé, in Wellington.[61] This village, situated in the mountains beyond Paarl and known for its wine production, lies about an hour from Cape Town by road. Dorothea spent a month helping Marjorie with the house and two small children while Dick worked at establishing the farm. An entry in Dick's daily journal described Dorothea, then 72 years old, as 'not very fit; with her Bushman dictionary not quite finished ... a great-hearted lady who has helped us not only materially, but also by her cheery companionship, hard work and quiet confidence'.[62] Dorothea cut her visit short, however, as she was afraid of falling ill in the 'primitive' conditions on the farm.[63] Her departure left the Scotts the poorer, Dick wrote. 'Marj and I and the children are very deeply attached to her.'[64] Dick Scott's journal entry provides a sense of a close-knit family group of which Dorothea was an important part.

She returned to La Rochelle and her dictionary on 1 October. By January 1946 she knew that the National Research Board had granted £500 towards the dictionary. She stepped up her efforts to find a printer, and sent a detailed outline of the dictionary and its publishing and typesetting requirements to Oxford University Press (OUP) in Cape Town, and another to Lovedale following up on the estimate she had received two years before.[65] Doke and Maingard, meanwhile, tried without success to find a suitable printer in Johannesburg.[66] Now, it seemed, the aftermath of the war became more tangible. Lovedale was unable to print the dictionary for 'at least two to three years' because of difficulties in finding suitable paper and a lack of adequate machinery. OUP's printer (Austin's in England) was flatly unable to take on the job, due to a 'backlog of work' and an 'uncertain' labour situation.[67] Schapera contacted his colleague Melville Herskovits at Northwestern University in Chicago, and through him the linguist Zellig Harris, at the time editor of the American Oriental Society's journal.[68] That organisation indicated it would be 'proud to publish this important work', and would cover any costs above the estimated £1 000.[69] But Dorothea was cautious. She would consult her colleagues in Johannesburg.[70] Both Maingard and Doke urged her to accept the offer even though the typesetting machine would not be able to accommodate some of the 'odd letters' in her text. Finally she accepted, despite having hoped the work would be 'wholly South African'.[71]

After that, Dorothea's life would experience substantial changes. Her sister Helma died on 30 May 1947, after months of deteriorating health during which Dorothea had carried much of the load of care.[72] By December 1947 La Rochelle was sold, and Dorothea, Marjorie, Dick and the two little girls, as well as two Scottish terriers, had moved to The Garth in Plumstead, just a few suburbs south of Newlands.[73] Dorothea's other niece, Dorothy, by then married to a British officer who had been stationed in India during the war, had meanwhile returned to Cape Town with her five-month-old son to help pack up La Rochelle. But the move, and the auction of furniture and other items remaining at La Rochelle, took place while Dorothy was in hospital. She had been admitted late in 1947 for surgery to remove a brain tumour. She died early the following year.[74]

These tragedies and upheavals appeared to have little impact on Dorothea's dictionary work.[75] On 19 June 1947, about a month after Helma's death, Dorothea sent her manuscript dictionary, 'all but the introduction, which I shall not finish until I know what explanations of type I may have to give', to Schapera. She enclosed a cheque for her personal contribution of £250, and the same amount from UCT.[76] Schapera, in turn, dispatched the manuscript to the US by 'registered book post', and the money by airmail. Both were received in good order.[77] Dorothea agreed to a print order of 500 copies (cloth-bound) that included 25 review copies and 10 copies for each of the funders; agreed to the display of acknowledgements; and took responsibility for proofreading the manuscript herself.[78] A day before Christmas Eve 1947, she received the contract, which she signed and returned the day after Boxing Day.[79]

Dorothea must have felt a great sense of relief to know that at last the deal was signed and sealed and the manuscript posted. She may well have expected that her book would be published within a year or two at the most. She had one or two queries about the agreement, in particular regarding who would pay for corrections, and who would pay the $3 600 cost earmarked for 'publishing and marketing'.[80] But by the time Harris wrote to address her questions nearly seven months later, Dorothea had died. She never got to read his (mistaken) promise of a speedy end to the project: 'The trials are behind us now, and I expect that we will be able to proceed promptly to the completion of the book.' How wrong he was. It would be eight years more before the book appeared. Dorothea was spared the news that her orthographic requirements were not going to be met.[81]

From Bleek to Scott

From this point the dictionary functions as an archival 'bridge' in the Bleek Collection – its final production and publication eight years after Dorothea's death on 27 June 1948 was the culmination of a process in which the custodianship of the Bleek and Lloyd collection changed hands. Marjorie stepped in and took charge of seeing the complex manuscript through the final production process. This is not surprising. We have seen evidence of the strong bond between them.

Marjorie's correspondence attests to the extent of her efforts to have the dictionary published.[82] It was a labour of commitment, loyalty and respect, following in a tradition by now well established in the Bleek lineage. Taking up the baton so late in the production process, Marjorie may not have expected to become as embroiled in the project as she was in the months and years that followed. The correspondence shows the lengths to which she had to go to tie up loose ends, not to mention the delays that occurred during the proofreading process in the US. By the time Marjorie took charge, she had a demanding career in the sciences. Dorothea's and Marjorie's careers had followed similar trajectories for years, as illustrated by their simultaneous appearance in the group photograph taken at the South African Association for the Advancement of Science (SAAAS) meeting in Durban in 1932, where Dorothea had delivered her presidential address on rock art (Figure 7.1).

In 1948 Marjorie was an entomologist based at the Department of Zoology at UCT. She had little time for the onerous task of reading pages of words in /Xam, !Kung and the other orthographies with their detailed English translations.[83] When Maingard withdrew from the project due to pressure of work and the 'remissness' of the US publisher in taking almost a year to return pages for proofing, Marjorie called on her husband, Dick Scott, for help.[84]

In February 1950, the manuscript typist Helen Hause wrote from Chicago to apologise for the long delay in returning pages. She had been away in Africa doing fieldwork, and was shocked on her return to find that her replacement had done nothing. Hause would continue without delay. But there were problems around typography, and changes were required.[85] Dick was an experienced proofreader, having worked for the *Buenos Aires Herald*. Proofreading the dictionary turned out to be a project to which Dick devoted much time and energy, without seeing the final result. He worked on what Harris mailed to them intermittently, and then took leave for two months in June and July 1950 to work full-time on the proofs. On 1 August 1950, he mailed his corrected proofs to Harris. Seven months later, when Dick died suddenly in February 1951, there had still been no word from Chicago.[86]

After Dick's death there were further delays. In August 1951, Hause wrote to say she had taken a teaching position at Northwestern University and was only able to work on the dictionary 'in between times'.[87] More delays ensued. One cannot imagine how Marjorie reacted to this. Recently bereaved of both her husband and her beloved aunt, and with two young daughters and a career to look after, she had her hands full. But likely she felt the same loyalty and obligation to completing Dorothea's project that Dorothea had in turn felt about her own scholarly legacy. Marjorie immediately took on the task of proofreading after Dick's death.

At the time Marjorie stepped in to work on the dictionary, the project already involved networks spanning two continents. Manuscripts, master copies and page proofs had crossed and recrossed the Atlantic, back and forth from Cape Town and Johannesburg to Philadelphia, New Haven and Chicago. And apart from the geographic connection, the production of the dictionary linked Bleek family scholarship, albeit peripherally, with American scholarship through the involvement of Zellig Harris. Harris, founding figure in American linguistics during the 1950s, and the teacher and mentor of Noam Chomsky, was the editor of Dorothea's *A Bushman Dictionary*. In their brief correspondence there had been no mention of linguistics. Harris had yet to be fully recognised for his paradigm-changing methods of transformational and discourse analysis that sought to analyse the deep structure of written, vocal and sign languages, and was concerned with the analysis of naturally occurring speech rather than invented examples.[88] It is intriguing to wonder what Dorothea would have thought of this theoretical and abstract approach to linguistics. Ever the pragmatist, she may have dismissed anything she considered tainted by philosophy. But she might have been interested in learning more about Harris's lifelong interest in the further evolution or refinement of language as a force for international cooperation and social amelioration.

Publishing the dictionary in the United States brought additional complications for Marjorie. The manuscript was bulky and was being mailed between the two continents in sections. Delays were frequent, and there was also potential for parts of the manuscript to go missing, as occurred in October 1951, when a delay in letter writing caused confusion over the whereabouts of part of the manuscript.[89] Marjorie must have breathed a sigh of relief when the finished dictionary finally appeared in 1956. She could certainly claim credit for being critical to its arrival after so much time had elapsed. Even arranging for the introduction to be written had been a saga of its own. Maingard had withdrawn from the project and Schapera had emigrated to Britain, so Marjorie approached Professor J.A. Englebrecht of the Department of Bantu Studies at the University of Pretoria to write the introduction to the dictionary.[90]

Engelbrecht was working on Bleek material at the time. His edited and revised version of Wilhelm Bleek's *Zulu Legends*, based on materials he had found in the Grey Collection at the Public Library, was published in 1952.[91] References in two of Engelbrecht's letters indicate that he took over the final proofreading of Hause's retyped copy of the dictionary.[92] But to some extent Engelbrecht was working in the dark. He had not been involved in the earlier stages of the process, and while he may have been knowledgeable about Wilhelm Bleek, it is not clear that he knew much about Dorothea.

Be that as it may, Engelbrecht took to his task with painstaking dedication. Over the many months during which he compiled his rather short introduction to the dictionary, Marjorie had to send him virtually everything that was available in print on Dorothea, including correspondence and copies of her published works. Engelbrecht also requested copies of Wilhem Bleek's *A Brief Account of Bushman Folklore and Other Texts*, as well as Lucy Lloyd's *A Short Account of Further Bushman Material Collected*. He declared his intention to 'wade through' the entire dictionary manuscript so as to be accurate beyond reproach in his review of Dorothea's transcriptions.[93] 'My only reason for acting as I do (incidentally putting you to a great deal of trouble too) is that I want to be sure of my facts as my own experience (and that of others as well) tells me that some people can become really unpleasant when others do a piece of work which they claim as their sole privilege,' he wrote to Marjorie in August 1952. Engelbrecht made it clear that he would not be writing a 30-page introduction as Dorothea had envisaged. Much of what he wanted to say had already been said elsewhere.[94]

In his introduction, Engelbrecht admired Dorothea's stated intention and the extra effort it had required to produce a comprehensive work. As we have seen, however, he critiqued some of the material for its lack of precision, leaving it of historical value only.[95] Dorothea's comprehensive and comparative approach was going out of style. Her colleague Clement Doke likewise critiqued the author's inability to bring 'critical discrimination to bear upon the vast material she has used'.[96] But Doke celebrated the dictionary as a 'monumental piece of work' that represented the successful completion of what had seemed 'an insuperable task' for the printer. He wrote at the end of his review: 'Miss Bleek has done linguistics a great service. Her labours have preserved much in Bushman languages which would certainly have been lost without her devoted research and recording. This valuable Bushman Dictionary is a fitting monument to her scholarship and disinterested industry.'[97]

Thus closed the chapter on a particular kind of research in southern Africa. The study of bushmen would continue, and the dictionary remains a standard reference work in southern African linguistics. The work is widely consulted by scholars of history, anthropology, rock art and archaeology, not to mention folklorists. Dorothea would have been pleased to know that her book was available in libraries around the world. An online search of international library catalogues reveals that there are at least 130 copies of *A Bushman Dictionary* available internationally.[98] In South Africa, the Africana Library in Kimberley, three libraries attached to Vista University (Mamelodi, Bloemfontein, Port Elizabeth), and universities including Rhodes, North West and Cape Town each hold one copy; in all, South African institutions hold a total of 15 copies. Namibia appears to be the only other African state owning the publication, with one copy held by the Ministry of Education and Culture, and another by the National Library of Namibia. In the United States, institutions holding a copy include the University of Minnesota (Twin Cities), most of the Ivy League universities (including Yale, Harvard and Princeton) as well as Northwestern, Berkeley, Johns Hopkins, Pennsylvania, Duke and Rutgers. Off campus, the American Museum of Natural

History and the Metropolitan Museum of Art hold copies, as do the Library of Congress and the Queens Borough, New York and Cleveland public libraries. In Europe, the library of the Musée de l'Homme has a copy, as do several other French institutions including Saint Denis/Reunion–Droit Lettres; the universities of Leiden and Nijmegen in the Netherlands; Gottingen and Hamburg universities in Germany; and two libraries in Denmark. Several copies are held in Australia (universities of Melbourne and Sydney and the National Library of Australia); New Zealand (National Library of New Zealand and the Porirua Public Library); and Canada (universities of Montreal, Regina, Toronto and Calgary). In Britain, the dictionary can be found at Westminster and the Royal Borough of Kensington and Chelsea libraries, as well as at Oxford, Cambridge, Edinburgh and Glasgow university libraries. There are copies in two libraries in Japan, and one in Israel's national library collection.

Conversation in writing

Along with paying homage to the memory of her father and aunt and continuing their intellectual legacy, Dorothea fervently believed that language provided the key to understanding the 'culture' and the particular 'natural' 'souls' of bushmen people whom she had spent her life studying. Her cautious brand of scholarship was firmly anchored in fieldwork, and in the methods of gathering rock art samples and for the making of comparative models of language distribution, which would support her claim that the bushmen had been the earliest inhabitants of southern Africa. In their halcyon days, the bushmen's foraging lifestyle had allowed them the time to perfect their rock art, and to indulge in their rich traditions of storytelling, dressing up and play-acting. But, Dorothea argued in her lectures and publications, their lifestyle was irrevocably threatened by the forces of modernity and the arrival of different groups of people in the landscape. Yet a more nuanced, intimate view of her thoughts and ideas emerges through her private correspondence with Käthe Woldmann that continued for nearly two decades. An examination of these letters reveals that, among other things, Dorothea had no time for Leo Frobenius, philosophy or the teachings of Rudolf Steiner.

We return to the year 1927, just a year after Dorothea had moved to La Rochelle with Helma and her family. She had competed two fieldwork sojourns to Sandfontein and her six-month-long journey through Angola. A letter dated 27 April finds Dorothea responding to Käthe's query about her prospects of finding a research job in South Africa. At the same time, she enquired after a copy of *Specimens*.[99] So began a conversation that was centrally animated by the mythology and folk tales told by people who at that time were unproblematically designated bushmen.

The correspondence traces how the two women shared with each other their interests in mythology, legend, human origins and, most particularly, the bushmen. But they approached these topics from different perspectives. Woldmann was enmeshed in ideas about lost cities, 'root races' and spiritual science, all aspects of the esoteric movement known as anthroposophy that was founded by the Austrian mystic, architect and scholar Rudolf Steiner (1861–1925). Käthe lived in Dornach, the town near Basel, Switzerland, in which Steiner had established his cultural centre, the Goetheanum, in 1913.[100] She was well placed to be influenced by Steiner's ideas that drew on theosophy, German idealism and the teachings of Johann Wolfgang von Goethe. But Dorothea demanded proof and evidence. She was unequivocal in her disdain for this kind of theoretical thinking. 'Philosophy is not my cup of tea,' she wrote.[101]

The context of this declaration was Dorothea's response to 'two essays of Dr Steiner' that Käthe had sent to her.[102] Dorothea wrote: 'I read them [the essays] with interest as it provided me with some insight into the way of thinking of his followers and his entire movement. It is however totally foreign to me.' She did not approve of the way books dealing with the 'prehistory of mankind seem not to differentiate between proven facts and conjectures'. She was scandalised by Steiner's suggestion that 'our forebears in ancient times "viewed not only their own sensory perceptions as their own experiences but also those of their forbears"...Everyone is inclined to draw a picture of the past in order to place that little knowledge that we have in some sort of context; but why refer to a picture (conjecture) as proven fact? That appears far too unscientific to me!'[103]

She was equally unimpressed by Ernst Uehli's essays that appeared in the journal *Das Goetheanum* that Woldmann sent next. A Waldorf educationist and student of Steiner from 1905, Uehli (1875–1959) was a prominent figure in the first generation of anthroposophists and the founding editor of two leading journals of anthroposophy in the 1920s and 1930s.[104] Dorothea criticised the lack of sources he provided to prove his 'Atlantis theory'. Atlantis and Lemuria were two 'lost continents' from which 'root races' (or stages in human evolution) had emerged.[105] But Dorothea was pleased to be kept up to date with 'some of the thinking in Europe'.[106] Käthe Woldmann was her link to this strain of European ideas. The correspondence shows that Woldmann never gave up on her project of keeping Dorothea informed of the latest in anthroposophical currents of thought swirling in Europe at the time.

Dorothea's opinions on race, descent and evolution surface in an earlier letter to Woldmann, this one written in January 1930. She was responding to Woldmann's taking issue with the idea of evolution,[107] preferring perhaps the notion of preordained stages in human evolution or the 'root races' doctrine of Steiner and his cohorts. In Dorothea's view, while 'races' could be positioned within a specific hierarchy of development, this did not tally with the root-races theory of selective intellectual advancement based on esoteric spiritual enlightenment. 'What you are saying about the proof or lack of proof in connection with the theory of Descendenz (evolution) does not make sense to me,' Dorothea wrote. 'Pygmies and Bushmen are in relation to us the "original man" [*Urmenschen*]; that means they represent the earliest type of man that still exists.' Dorothea's response drew on the science of archaeology. This was the context in which she expressed her admiration for baboons, and which gave credence to the many notebook texts about baboons that she was at that time preparing for submission to *Bantu Studies*.

Dorothea held that 'Bushmen and pygmies' were much more developed in comparison with the 'original specimen of mankind', whether they were 'a special part of the creation, or whether they descended from the animal world'. The proof of this was the stone tools which were found all over the world and in greater concentrations in South Africa. It was not certain or confirmed whether the implements originated from 'an earlier race or a few races', but what was certain was that they did not belong to the 'Bushmen of the last centuries'. 'The geological strata in which these implements were found point to a very old age for most of them,' she told Woldmann.[108] Nevertheless, 'our bushmen' were capable of change through interaction with the environment. The 'discovery of the poison for the bow and arrow must have brought about a similar change to their lives as the discovery of

161

gunpowder for our forebears'.[109] As far as evolution was concerned, Dorothea was open-minded:

> To me the descent of humans from ape-like beings brings no problems
> if you allow for long periods of gradual development. Not because I do
> not value the wild uncultivated races, but because I highly respect the
> baboons, our local large ape variety. Primitive man is certainly not bad,
> also generally not stupid. He is very stupid concerning some aspects – and
> much more advanced than us – concerning other aspects. But also the
> baboon is not bad and not at all as stupid as many think he is. For the
> Bushman himself the idea would not be unfamiliar or repulsive. Soon
> I am hoping to publish about the customs and superstitions of the Bush-
> man as these relate to the baboon and I will send you a copy.[110]

In 1932, Woldmann wrote to Dorothea hoping to obtain permission for
Professor Richard Karutz, director of the museum at Lübeck and noted
anthroposophist, to quote from Bleek and Lloyd's published versions of
/Xam folklore in an unspecified project.[111] When she received the letter,
Dorothea was hard at work on her rock art survey, finalising the paper
she would present to the SAAAS in Durban just two months hence. She
did not like the idea of 'armchair scholars' who had not seen the country
or its people, having free access to the notebook stories. But Woldmann
had visited South Africa in the past, so Dorothea gave permission for
citation with strict conditions: 'Of course he [Karutz] should not quote
complete stories without source references; also he should not distort
them. These things are dealt with much better by people who have seen
the country and its people themselves; the armchair scholars often lose
their bearings.'[112] Whether she was aware of the extent to which Karutz
was involved in Steiner's brand of mysticism and esoteric philosophies
is not clear. Either way, Dorothea again dismissed Woldmann's efforts to
interest her in Steiner:

> I am not able to share the Atlantis-craze. 'Secret-sciences' are not my cup
> of tea. What has been gained from the insights of a clairvoyant has to be
> proven with concrete evidence, and not the other way round. And that the

evidence can be interpreted in many ways can be seen from the 'Atlantis case'. However, everyone has his dreams, and I would not like to destroy these.[113]

In 1936, Woldmann made another attempt to interest Dorothea in the legends of Atlantis and the writings of Ernst Uehli, and sent her his book on 'Atlantis'.[114] Dorothea was slightly more impressed this time: 'The beginning interests me greatly; I have as yet not read such a coherent history of the different discoveries and the theories connected with those.' But then she reached the 'difficult' chapters dealing with Steiner's 'history of the Atlantic mysteries'. Now the argument was too fanciful: 'Children's fairy tales, folktales I enjoy, but so-called "scientific" tales I do not like. Science should separate precisely that which is hypothetical from proven facts.'[115] Elsewhere, Dorothea took issue with 'Mr [Wolfgang] Moldenhauer's' attempts to link 'African paintings' or the rock art of Africa to the now submerged 'Atlantic and Lemuric cultures' using arguments he had drawn from Steiner: 'In his circle the works of Steiner are probably so well known that he does not think of those readers who do not know them. He should write more simply, not so academically, then his views would be clearer.'[116]

On another occasion, Dorothea dismissed Moldenhauer's use of concepts outlined by Steiner: 'The reports of Moldenhauer in [*Das*] *Goetheanum* are very interesting, as far as I am able to understand them, but the young writer is so academic, particularly concerning the findings of Frobenius, that I can barely follow him. Where is "Lemuria"? What are "Formlinge"? What is meant by "atavistic clairvoyance"?' These ideas, she declared, were indicative of a new wave of thinking in Germany which did not impress her. She did not like the theoretical direction anthropology was taking in Europe. It appeared that Dorothea was uncomfortable about the increasingly brutal and anti-humanist ideologies of the Third Reich, the race-based methodologies of physical anthropology, and the esoteric anthroposophist theories of evolutionary development and racially determined human intelligence that increasingly in the pre-World War II period seemed to show affinities with raw and exclusionary forms of racism: 'Over the last ten to 15 years a set of new terminologies pertaining to cultures appears to have been developed in Germany. "Atlantic and Lemuric cultures", Erythräea, etc.[117] They are often used by Moldenhauer in a way that the uninitiated cannot follow.' As before,

Moldenhauer was bringing rock art and 'atavistic clairvoyance' into conversation with the mythic lands of Lemuria and Atlantis. 'I cannot believe that natural people have such thoughts that he describes,' she wrote.[118]

Her correspondence with Dorothea suggests that Käthe Woldmann was swept up in the teachings of Rudolf Steiner and the esoteric theories in relation to spiritualism, human origins, limitless intelligence, and racial and cultural differences that he had gathered together under the rubric of anthroposophy. Dorothea was less convinced. We have seen how she regularly expressed her disdain for theoretical and philosophical thinking. Ever the rationalist, she responded cautiously to Woldmann's enthusiastic sharing of the theories of Steiner and his followers. In many ways, Dorothea's responses indicated a liberal belief in freedom of thought and a kind of sensitivity to the environment that was unusual for its time, although the precise political context she was referring to remains obscure. 'Hopefully the tendency to persecute those that do not think as the comrades will pass by and the sense of freedom will prevail. A world where everyone thinks the same would be a rather boring place,' she wrote to Woldmann in March 1936.[119]

Conclusion

That Dorothea welcomed debate and was open to a degree of new thinking seems apparent from the lively tone of the correspondence explored above. It is clear that she took the trouble to read and engage with the ideas presented to her. She was grateful for the effort taken to send essays (often published in *Das Goetheanum*) and books. But she was more comfortable with scholarship based on observation, evidence, documentation and measurement. Time and again in her correspondence and publications, she reiterated her belief in proof based on experience. She had organised her scholarship and research around fieldwork, and she remained suspicious of philosophy, theory and conjecture, and of the 'armchair scholars' of Europe.

Amid the unknowns and gaps in this archive and the clash of new thinking in Europe and South Africa in the years leading up to and during World War II, Dorothea seems to have stuck staunchly to her German intellectual traditions. She regarded bushmen as 'natural' rather than 'cultural'.[120] Within the bounds of the 'natural', however, her knowledge of bushman folklore and rock art was evidence for her that their originality and creativity

164

was greater than that of, for example, the 'black races', whom, following the racial biases expressed by her father, she relegated to a lower order within the *Naturvölker*, the 'natural' or 'primitive' peoples of the world. There is no doubt that her thinking kept within the bounded typologies of 'race' and 'tribe' that were current at the time. However, she was adamant that understanding bushman languages and use of vocabulary was the key to unlocking their essence. We have seen that she did not think 'European thinking' could legitimately be applied to interpreting the ideas of 'the little people' whose 'childlike position' had confined them to a simple, practical existence, attitude and way of life in a previously free, pure and independent world in which nothing was 'absolutely good or bad'.[121]

So it seems that Dorothea never abandoned the idea that the 'bushmen' were childlike, innocent, little people, containing an essential core in their being that could be discerned through careful observation and a comprehensive understanding of their language. Having evolved (in response to the environmental conditions in which they lived and through contact with new arrivals in their territories) to a certain level, they were now doomed to extinction. However, Dorothea's continued work on their language, history (via the study of rock art) and culture ensured that knowledge of bushmen and their prior claim to the country would continue into the future. Dorothea's scholarship fulfilled her debt of honour to the beloved father whom she barely knew and of gratitude to the intellectual work of her aunt who had been her mentor. At the same time it continued to keep the idea of 'bushman' alive as a field of academic inquiry across a range of disciplines including history, archaeology, linguistics, anthropology, traditional and contemporary literatures, and folklore. In so doing, she contributed to keeping a place open into the future for the continued presence of the notion 'bushman' in the racial landscape of South Africa.

For Dorothea, observation and field-based evidence were the cornerstones of her intellectual project. Her scholarship was about salvaging, collecting and comparing evidence rather than interpretation. One could say that Dorothea's subject matter was the 'old way of life', as the fieldwork record presented here shows. Her cautious, collect-at-all-costs imperative and her style of fieldwork were out of favour by the 1930s, when she was in her 60s and her career in the field was largely over. The revolution in fieldwork

165

and the move to sociological and psychological approaches to the study of societies passed Dorothea by. Her private letters confirm her anti-theoretical stance. Her roots in German empiricism may have been the source of her dislike of philosophy, and of her picky insistence on how the notebook texts were presented – not only orthographically, but also that they appear as in the original, without annotation or embellishment. She argued that most rock art should be understood at face value, as a 'historical document' left by the earliest inhabitants of southern Africa and as proof of their earlier claim to the country. Language was likewise a means of tying the various 'bushman tribes' to the landscape as original inhabitants.

This book has portrayed a detailed account, drawn from archival documents and published works, of the rock art and language fieldwork projects of Dorothea Bleek. The account focuses on interactions and encounters at different times in her career, and provides a sense of her larger project of paying homage to a familial quest and publicly mapping bushmen as the original inhabitants of southern Africa. Through the record of these achievements, Dorothea's intellectual contribution to scholarship in southern Africa has been reassessed, and recognition paid to her rock art research and fieldwork for the pioneering knowledge that she produced. Her scholarly project lay in her insistence on bushman authorship of rock art and in linking it to daily life, social interaction, history and myth illustration, and in drawing on the folklore collected by her father and aunt to explain its meaning. These methods and ideas were products of their time and a particular mode of thinking linked to nineteenth-century German traditions. They may have been overtaken in subsequent innovative and seminal new interpretations, especially in the area of rock art. Nevertheless, Dorothea's sustained contribution to fieldwork in southern Africa, and the creative, de-centred and diverse nature of her institutional and social networks, remain worthy of acknowledgement and warrant greater recognition in relation to larger disciplinary legacies and histories of thought in southern Africa.

Notes

Introduction

1. Bleek to Woldmann, 21 February 1936. Käthe Woldmann Papers, University of Cape Town Libraries, Manuscripts and Archives Department, hereafter BC 210, Box 4.

2. W. Bleek. 1875. Second Report Concerning Bushman Researches. Presented to the Cape Parliament. See also L. Lloyd. 1889. *A Short Account of Further Bushman Material Collected. Third Report Concerning Bushman Researches.* London: David Nutt.

3. Wilhelm Bleek's intellectual background and family history are best explored in A. Bank. 2006. *Bushmen in a Victorian World: The Remarkable Story of the Bleek-Lloyd Collection of Bushman Folklore.* Cape Town: Double Storey, especially Chapter 1. For a detailed study on German philology and its relation to the emergence of African studies during the nineteenth century, see S. Pugach. 2012. *Africa in Translation: A History of Colonial Linguistics in Germany and Beyond, 1814–1945.* Ann Arbor: University of Michigan Press. For more on Wilhelm Bleek's intellectual milieu in particular, see R. Thornton. 1983. ' "This Dying Out Race": W.H.I. Bleek's Approach to the Languages of Southern Africa'. *Social Dynamics* 9 (2), 1–10; see also M. Di Gregorio. 2002. 'Reflections of a Nonpolitical Naturalist: Ernst Haeckel, Wilhelm Bleek, Friedrich Müller and the Meaning of Language'. *Journal of the History of Biology* 35, 79–109.

4. For a history of the Hamitic hypothesis and the theory that all development in sub-Saharan Africa was the work of a (fairer-skinned) branch of Caucasian immigrants, see E. Sanders. 1996. 'The Hamitic Hypothesis: Its Origin and Functions in Time Perspective'. *Journal of African History* 10 (4), 521–532.

5. See, for example, book-length accounts in Bank, *Bushmen in a Victorian World*; also N. Bennun. 2004. *The Broken String: The Last Words of an Extinct People.* London: Viking; as well as contributions to edited collections, including J. Deacon and T. Dowson. Eds. 1996. *Voices from the Past: /Xam Bushmen and the Bleek and Lloyd Collection.* Johannesburg: Wits University Press; and P. Skotnes. Ed. 1996. *Miscast: Negotiating the Presence of the Bushmen.* Cape Town: UCT Press.

6. For folklore, foundational works are R. Hewitt. 1986. *Structure, Meaning and Ritual in the Narratives of the Southern San*. Hamburg: Helmut Buske; M. Guenther. 1999. *Tricksters and Trancers: Bushman Religion and Society*. Bloomington: Indiana University Press. More recently, see M. Wessels. 2010. *Bushman Letters: Interpreting /Xam Narratives*. Johannesburg: Wits University Press. For rock art interpretation, foundational works in the discipline are J.D. Lewis-Williams. 1981. *Believing and Seeing: Symbolic Meanings in Southern San Rock Art*. London: Academic Press; and P. Vinnicombe. 1976. *People of the Eland: Rock Paintings of the Drakensberg Bushmen as a Reflection of Their Life and Thought*. Pietermaritzburg: University of Natal Press.

7. Bank, *Bushmen in a Victorian World*, 32.

8. For a fine-grained analysis of the faltering beginnings of the project, see A. Bank. 2002. 'From Pictures to Performance: Early Learning at the Hill'. *Kronos* 28, 66–101.

9. The entire collection comprises 110 Lucy Lloyd /Xam notebooks, 17 Lloyd (mostly) !Kung notebooks and 28 Wilhelm Bleek /Xam notebooks. It also includes two Korana and !Kung notebooks compiled by Jemima Bleek. There are four Lloyd Korana notebooks in the Maingard Collection at the University of South Africa. See http://lloydbleekcollection.cs.uct.ac.za/researchers.html (accessed 20 August 2013).

10. See Bank, *Bushmen in a Victorian World*, especially Chapter 13 and 351–371.

11. For a history of the dispossession of the Cape San, see M. Adhikari. 2010. *The Anatomy of a South African Genocide: The Extermination of the Cape San Peoples*. Cape Town: UCT Press; N. Penn. 1996. ' "Fated to Perish": The Destruction of the Cape San', in Skotnes, *Miscast*, 81–91.

12. A. Bank. 2000. 'Evolution and Racial Theory: The Hidden Side of Wilhelm Bleek'. *South African Historical Journal* 43, (1), 7. For more on this debate, see the discussion in M. Wessels. 2008. 'New Directions in /Xam Studies: Some of the Implications of Andrew Bank's *Bushmen in a Victorian World: The Remarkable Story of the Bleek-Lloyd Collection of Bushman Folklore*'. *Critical Arts* 22 (1), 69–82; see also S. Moran. 2009. *Representing Bushmen: South Africa and the Origin of Language*. Rochester: University of Rochester Press.

13. See http://www.unesco.org/webworld/mdm/en/index_mdm.html (accessed 28 October 2011) for the *Memory of the World* register, where the collection is titled 'The Bleek Collections of San (Bushman) Studies'. In 1997, when the

Bleek Collection was added, the register was limited in scope. The list given here indicates how the project has burgeoned since its inception in the 1990s, in keeping with contemporary and postcolonial attitudes to archives, memory and heritage. Recent additions suggest a purposeful effort towards redress and the inclusion of material previously regarded as marginal. These include court papers from the Rivonia Treason Trial (added in 2007); materials relating to the slave trade across 11 countries gathered under the title 'Ports of Call' (2007); the John Marshall Ju/'hoan Bushman Film and Video Collection 1950–2000 (2009); and Documentary Heritage on the Resistance and Struggle for Human Rights in the Dominican Republic 1930–1961 (2009).

14. Draft motivation, undated typescript, 3–4; draft typescript attached to letter from Nigel Penn dated 27 September 1996, 3; facsimile from Peter Coates (of the South African Library's Preservation Department) of draft joint nomination form attached to letter from University Librarian A.S.C. Hooper, 14 October 1996, 5; all in Bleek Collection, University of Cape Town Libraries, Manuscripts and Archives Department, hereafter BC 151, *Memory of the World* Programme. See also J. Deacon. 2005. 'Foreword', in J. Hollmann. Ed. *Customs and Beliefs of the /Xam Bushmen*. Johannesburg: Wits University Press, xiii–xv, where the /Xam language is described as 'South Africa's Latin'. For more on the making of the Bleek Collection, see J. Weintroub. 2006. 'From Tin Trunk to World Wide Web: The Making of the Bleek Collection'. Unpublished MPhil dissertation, University of Cape Town; and J. Weintroub. 2013. 'On Biography and Archive: Dorothea Bleek and the Making of the Bleek Collection'. *South African Historical Journal* 65 (1), 70–89.

15. The /Xam words featured on the South African coat of arms are *!ke e: /xarra //ke* (people who are different come together). See A. Barnard. 2004. 'Coat of Arms and the Body Politic: Khoisan Imagery and South African National Identity'. *Ethnos* 69 (1), 5–22; see also B. Smith, J.D. Lewis-Williams, G. Blundell and C. Chippindale. 2000. 'Archaeology and Symbolism in the New South African Coat of Arms'. *Antiquity* 74, 467–468. The Linton panel of rock art was removed from the farm Linton in the Maclear district, eastern Cape, in 1917. It is now in the collection of the Iziko South African Museum in Cape Town, where it forms part of the museum's permanent rock art display.

16. Exhibitions and performances inspired by the /Xam notebooks and the Mowbray research project include the 1996 Miscast exhibition at the South African

National Gallery in Cape Town, the Lantern Festival celebrations at Clanwilliam in the Western Cape, as well as the Jazzart/Magnet Theatre production *Rain in a Dead Man's Footprints*. See P. Skotnes. 2002. 'The Politics of Bushman Representation', in P. Landau and D. Kaspin. Eds. *Images and Empires: Visuality in Colonial and Postcolonial Africa*. Los Angeles and London: University of California Press, 253–274; M. Martin. 1996. 'Bringing the Past into the Present: Facing and Negotiating History, Memory, Redress and Reconciliation at the South African National Gallery'. South African Museums Association conference, Durban; P. Skotnes and M. Fleishman. 2002. *A Story is the Wind: Representing Time and Space in San Narratives*. Cape Town: LLAREC; Magnet Theatre Company. 2004. *Rain in a Dead Man's Footprints*, http://www.magnettheatre.co.za/productions/view?magnet_production_id=19 (accessed 20 July 2012).

17. W. de Kock. Ed. 1968. *Dictionary of South African Bibliography*, Vol. I. Johannesburg: National Council for Social Research, 80–85; J.D. Lewis-Williams. Ed. 2000. *Stories that Float from Afar: Ancestral Folklore of the San of Southern Africa*. Cape Town: David Philip.

18. Skotnes, *Miscast*.

19. D. Bleek. Ed. 1923. *The Mantis and His Friends: Bushman Folklore Collected by the Late Dr. W.H.I. Bleek and the Late Dr. Lucy C. Lloyd*. Cape Town: Maskew Miller. For an annotated collection of Dorothea's submissions to *Bantu Studies*, see J. Hollmann. Ed. 2005. *Customs and Beliefs of the /Xam Bushmen*. Johannesburg: Wits University Press. For an assessment of the current state of /Xam (or !Ui) linguistics, see M. du Plessis. 2014. 'A Century of the "Specimens of Bushman Folklore": 100 Years of Linguistic Neglect', in J. Deacon and P. Skotnes. Eds. *The Courage of //Kabbo: Celebrating the 100th Anniversary of the Publication of 'Specimens of Bushman Folklore'*. Cape Town: UCT Press.

20. H. Phillips. 1993. *The University of Cape Town 1918–1948: The Formative Years*. Cape Town: UCT Press, 27.

21. Dia!kwain and /Han≠kass'o were two of several /Xam-speaking men from the northern Cape who shared their language, folklore and cosmologies with Wilhelm and Lucy during the 1870s. Dia!kwain was living in the Bleek household when Wilhelm died in August 1875, while /Han≠kass'o spent some weeks at Mowbray in 1871 before returning to work with Lucy for two years from 1878. The !Kung youngsters, aged between about six and 19 years, had been raided from their home territories in northern Namibia. They worked

with Lucy between 1879 and 1882, producing a collection of drawings and watercolours which Lucy annotated. See P. Skotnes. 2007. *Claim to the Country: The Archive of Wilhelm Bleek and Lucy Lloyd*. Cape Town and Athens, OH: Jacana and Ohio University Press, 236–271; also J. de Villiers. 2012. 'Tamme's Country: An Intertextual Reading of the !Kun-Lloyd Archive'. Unpublished MA dissertation, University of the Western Cape.

22. For Dorothea's use of the terms 'idle' and 'improvident', see G. Stow and D. Bleek. Eds. 1930. *Rock Paintings in South Africa from Parts of the Eastern Province and Orange Free State*. London: Methuen, xxiii–xxv. See also D. Bleek. 1932. 'A Survey of Our Present Knowledge of Rockpaintings in South Africa'. *South African Journal of Science* 29, 72–83.

23. J.D. Lewis-Williams. 1996. ' "The Ideas Generally Entertained with Regard to the Bushmen and Their Mental Condition" ', in Skotnes, *Miscast*, 307–310.

24. For Dorothea's views on rock art authorship, see BC 151, D3.6, D.3.19 and E5.1.26. For early twentieth-century views on foreign civilisations in southern Africa, see R. Derricourt. 2011 *Inventing Africa: History, Archaeology and Ideas*. New York: Pluto Press, 48–68, 106–110; S. Dubow. 1996. 'Human Origins, Race Typology and the Other Raymond Dart'. *African Studies* 55 (1), 1–30.

25. On the issue of selectivity in rock art recording, see J. van der Riet, M. van der Riet and D. Bleek. 1940. *More Rock-Paintings in South Africa*. London: Methuen, xiii–xv. (The full title reads: *More Rock-Paintings in South Africa: From the Coastal Belt between Albany and Piquetberg, Mainly Copied by Joyce and Mollie van der Riet; with Notes by the Same and an Introduction and Explanatory Remarks by Dorothea F. Bleek*).

26. Encroachment theory would become a dominant feature of South African history during Nationalist Party rule in the middle decades of the twentieth century, and feed into the 'empty land' myth of the 1940s–1980s. For a comprehensive view of South African historiography and the contributions of Stow and Theal, see C. Saunders. 1988. *The Making of the South African Past: Major Historians on Race and Class*. Cape Town: David Philip. For a critical interrogation of the peopling of southern African landscapes, see N. Etherington. 2011. 'Barbarians Ancient and Modern'. *American Historical Review* 116 (1), 31–57; and P. Landau. 2010. *Popular Politics in the History of South Africa, 1400–1948*. Cambridge: Cambridge University Press.

27. See, for example, Stow and Bleek, *Rock Paintings in South Africa*, vii–xxviii; BC 151, D3.6, 3–4.

28. See G. Stow. 1905. *The Native Races of South Africa: A History of the Intrusion of the Hottentots and Bantu into the Hunting Grounds of the Bushmen, the Aborigines of the Country*. London: Swan Sonnenschein. For more on Stow's rock art research, see A. Solomon. 2006. 'Roots and Revolutions: A Critical Overview of Early and Late San Rock Art Research'. *Afrique & Histoire* 2 (6), 77–110; and P. Skotnes. 2008. *Unconquerable Spirit: George Stow's History Paintings of the San*. Johannesburg: Jacana.

29. See Bleek, *The Mantis*. Dorothea's introduction promised a bushman version of the text so that 'students of the language could compare the original with the translation', but this never materialised.

30. D. Bleek. 1928. *The Naron: A Bushman Tribe of the Central Kalahari*. London: Cambridge University Press; and D. Bleek. 1929. *Comparative Vocabularies of Bushman Languages*. London: Cambridge University Press.

31. D. Bleek. 1928–1930. 'Bushman Grammar: A Grammatical Sketch of the Language of the /Xam-ka-!k'e'. *Zeitschrift für Eingeborenen-Sprachen* 19, 81–98; 20, 161–174; see also D. Bleek. 1927. 'The Distribution of Bushman Languages in South Africa'. *Festschrift Meinhof*, Hamburg, 55–64.

32. See Hollmann, *Customs and Beliefs*, for an annotated collection of these translations.

33. For a historicised reading of Van der Post's writings on bushmen, see E. Wilmsen. 2002. 'Primal Anxiety, Sanctified Landscapes: The Imagery of Primitiveness in the Ethnographic Fictions of Laurens van der Post'. *Visual Anthropology* 15, 143–201. For the Marshall family, see, for example, E. Marshall Thomas, 1959. *The Harmless People*. New York: Knopf. For a reflection on the writing of romantic ethnographies, see M. Shostak. 1989. ' "What the Wind Won't Take Away": The Genesis of *Nisa: The Life and Words of a !Kung Woman*', in Personal Narratives Group. *Interpreting Women's Lives, Feminist Theory and Personal Narratives*. Bloomington: Indiana University Press.

34. Lewis-Williams, *Believing and Seeing*.

35. Vinnicombe, *People of the Eland*. A tribute to and contemporary reassessment of Vinnicombe's scholarship can be found in contributions to P. Mitchell and B. Smith. Eds. 2009. *The Eland's People: New Perspectives in the Rock Art of the Maloti-Drakensberg Bushmen: Essays in Memory of Patricia Vinnicombe*. Johannesburg: Wits University Press.

36. For a collection of essays addressing this debate, see G. Blundell, C. Chippindale and B. Smith. Eds. 2010. *Seeing and Knowing: Understanding Rock Art With and Without Ethnography*. Johannesburg: Wits University Press.

37. H. Kuklick. 2011. 'Personal Equations: Reflections on the History of Fieldwork, with Special Reference to Sociocultural Anthropology'. *Isis* 102 (1), 2.

38. Kuklick, 'Personal Equations', 2–4.

39. Kuklick, 'Personal Equations', 20.

40. See E. Krige. 1960. 'Agnes Winifred Hoernlé: An Appreciation'. *African Studies* 19 (3), 138–144; R. Gordon. 1987. 'Remembering Agnes Winifred Hoernlé'. *Social Dynamics* 13 (1), 68–72. Hoernlé's student Monica Hunter (Wilson), who began fieldwork in Pondoland in the early 1930s as Dorothea's time was winding down, is likewise remembered for her decades of teaching and for her academic and social roles, rather than for her extensive fieldwork. This lacuna is being addressed. See A. Bank. 2008. 'The "Intimate Politics" of Fieldwork: Monica Hunter and Her African Assistants, Pondoland and the Eastern Cape, 1931–1932'. *Journal of Southern African Studies* 34 (3), 557–574; and A. Bank and L. Bank. Eds. 2013. *Inside African Anthropology: Monica Wilson and Her Interpreters*. Cambridge: Cambridge University Press.

41. Kuklick, 'Personal Equations'; N. Jacobs. 2006. 'The Intimate Politics of Ornithology in Colonial Africa'. *Comparative Studies in Society and History* 48, 564–603; J. Camerini. 1996. 'Wallace in the Field'. *Osiris* 11, 44–65; L. Shumaker. 2001. *Africanising Anthropology: Fieldwork, Networks, and the Making of Cultural Knowledge in Central Africa*. Durham, NC: Duke University Press.

42. N. Zemon Davis. 1995. *Women on the Margins: Three Seventeenth-Century Lives*. Cambridge, MA: Harvard University Press, 210.

43. Zemon Davis, *Women on the Margins*, 64–65.

44. Zemon Davis, *Women on the Margins*, 38–45.

45. D. Driver. 1995. 'Lady Anne Barnard's Cape Journals and the Concept of Self-Othering'. *Pretexts: Studies in Literature and Culture* 5, 46–65.

46. S. Marchand. 1997. 'Leo Frobenius and the Revolt against the West'. *Journal of Contemporary History* 32 (2), 153.

47. C. Rassool. 2002. 'Beyond the Cult of "Salvation" and "Remarkable Equality": A New Paradigm for the Bleek-Lloyd Collection'. *Kronos* 32, 251.

48. For more on the establishment of institutions of science and arts in South Africa, see S. Dubow. 2006. *A Commonweath of Knowledge, Science, Sensibility and White South Africa 1820–2000*. Oxford: Oxford University Press.

49. J. Kaplan. 1978. 'The "Real Life" ', in D. Aaron. Ed. *Studies in Biography*, Harvard English Studies 8, 1–8. See also V. Woolf. 1942. 'The Art of Biography', in *The Death of the Moth and Other Essays*. New York: Harcourt Brace Jovanovich, 187–197.

50. Kaplan, 'The "Real Life" ', 1.

51. Aaron, *Studies in Biography*, vii.

52. M. Beard. 2000. *The Invention of Jane Harrison*. Cambridge, MA, and London: Harvard University Press, 94–97. For the use of letters to construct a social history of three South African women, see S. Marks. Ed. 1987. *Not Either an Experimental Doll: The Separate Worlds of Three South African Women*. Bloomington: Indiana University Press.

53. Beard, *Invention*, 123–124 (parentheses in original).

54. Beard, *Invention*, 123–124.

55. Beard, *Invention*, 10.

56. Beard, *Invention*, 10–12.

57. Beard, *Invention*.

58. The expression 'life-writing' is used in the sense coined by Virginia Woolf as a means of questioning the project of seamless biography writing, and of signalling the unknowability and the hidden kernel which lies at the heart of the written representation of any life. See Woolf, 'The Art of Biography', 187–189.

59. H. Lee. *Virginia Woolf*. London: Vintage, 1997.

60. Lee, *Virginia Woolf*, 4.

61. Lee, *Virginia Woolf*, 4.

62. See J. Weintroub. 2006. ' "Some Sort of Mania": Otto Hartung Spohr and the Making of the Bleek Collection'. *Kronos* 32, 114–138.

63. E. Eberhard. 1996. 'Wilhelm Bleek and the Founding of Bushman Research', in Deacon and Dowson, *Voices from the Past*, 49–65.

64. BC 210, Box 4.

65. See Beard, *Invention*. For complications arising from conflicts between rights to privacy, the expectations of descendants and the judicious use of private letters in biography writing, see E. Mendelson. 1987. 'Authorised Biography and Its Discontents', in Aaron, *Studies in Biography*, 9–26.

66. Bleek and L. Lloyd. Eds. 1938. *Das wahre Gesicht des Buschmannes in seinen Mythen und Märchen*. (The True Face of the Bushmen in their Myths and Stories) Trans. K. Woldmann. Basel: Kommissionverlag Zbinden & Hügin.

67. Bleek to Woldmann, 6 June 1928. BC 210, Box 4.

68. Bleek to Woldmann, 11 April 1927. BC 210, Box 4. The letter states: 'I can re-member you and your brother very well and know that you have made some very good copies of Bushman paintings.' Photographs of Woldmann's rock art reproductions are preserved as glass negatives in BC 210.
69. Bleek to Woldmann, 5 November 1931; 29 December 1933. BC 210, Box 4.
70. Bleek to Woldmann, 13 July 1936; 13 December 1936; 18 February 1938. BC 210, Box 4.
71. Bleek to Woldmann, 1 December 1938. BC 210, Box 4.
72. Woldmann lost contact with her brother at some point during the 1930s, but they were later reunited. See Bleek to Woldmann, 13 March 1934; 31 December 1936; 29 November 1937. BC 210, Box 4.
73. Jaeger lived in Halle, which became part of East Germany after World War II. Bleek to Woldmann, 5 March 1929; 18 February 1928. BC 210, Box 4.
74. On Woldmann's health, see Bleek to Woldmann, 1 March 1928; 6 June 1928; 29 November 1937. BC 210, Box 4.
75. M. Maynes, J. Pierce and B. Laslett. 2008. *Telling Stories: The Use of Personal Narratives in the Social Sciences and History.* Ithaca, NY, and London: Cornell University Press. For a recent example of biography in anthropological writing, see Bank and Bank, *Inside African Anthropology.*
76. C. Rassool, 2004. 'The Individual, Auto/biography and History in South Africa'. Unpublished PhD thesis, University of the Western Cape, 248.
77. Rassool, 'Auto/biography', 272.
78. Rassool, 'Auto/biography', 283.
79. Rassool, 'Auto/biography', 248. The many biographies of Nelson Mandela are obvious examples here.
80. The release in October 2010 of the 'intimate and personal' and previously hidden early adulthood of Nelson Mandela (officially sanctioned by the Nelson Mandela Centre of Memory) seeks consciously to reverse this trend. See N. Mandela. 2010. *Conversations with Myself.* London: Pan Macmillan. But see also D. Smith. 2010. *Young Mandela.* London: Weidenfeld & Nicolson.
81. For biographies of female literary figures, see those dealing with Bessie Head and Nadine Gordimer. Antjie Krog's 2003 (auto)biography *A Change of Tongue* (Cape Town: Struik) represents an unusual blending of the political and the personal in a postmodernist narrative in which silences and contradictions play an important part.

82. D. Birkett and J. Wheelwright. 1990. ' "How Could She?" Unpalatable Facts and Feminists' Heroines'. *Gender and History* 2 (1), 49–56.

83. Birkett and Wheelwright, 'Unpalatable', 50.

84. Birkett and Wheelwright, 'Unpalatable', 56.

85. Birkett and Wheelwright, 'Unpalatable', 56.

Chapter 1

1. *Grau, theurer Freund, ist alle Theorie / Und grün des Lebens goldner Baum.* Bleek to Woldmann, 8 February 1932. Käthe Woldmann Papers, University of Cape Town Libraries, Manuscripts and Archives Department, hereafter BC 210, Box 4.

2. The University of Cape Town was established at its present location on Cecil Rhodes's estate on the slopes of Devil's Peak in 1928 when part of the campus moved from its earlier location at the top of Government Avenue in upper Cape Town, now Hiddingh Campus.

3. See contributions to P. Skotnes. Ed. 1996. *Miscast: Negotiating the Presence of the Bushmen.* Cape Town: UCT Press, 15–23; see also A. Bank. 2006. *Bushman in a Victorian World: The Remarkable Story of the Bleek-Lloyd Collection of Bushman Folklore.* Cape Town: Double Storey, especially Chapter 13.

4. W. Bleek and L. Lloyd. Eds. 1911. *Specimens of Bushman Folklore.* London: George Allen & Co.

5. P. Scott Deetz. 2007. *Catalog of the Bleek-Lloyd Collection in the Scott Family Archive.* Williamsburg, VA: Deetz Ventures, Inc., 37.

6. See Jemima's letter to Sir George Grey in which she records her desperate feelings of grief. Bleek Collection, University of Cape Town Libraries, Manuscripts and Archives Department, hereafter BC 151, C10.17. Transcribed in P. Skotnes. Ed. 2007. *Claim to the Country: The Archive of Lucy Lloyd and Wilhelm Bleek.* Cape Town and Athens, OH: Jacana and Ohio University Press, 281–287.

7. Bank, *Bushmen in a Victorian World*, Chapter 10.

8. Dia!kwain's owl story is noted in Bleek and Lloyd, *Specimens*, xvi.

9. The Korana (also Kora) were a mix of nomadic peoples from different parts of southern Africa who by the nineteenth century had organised themselves into formidable mounted raiding groups under various leaders. Many lived along

the Orange or Gariep River. Their marauding activities intensified conflict on the colonial frontier, culminating in the Korana wars of 1869 and 1878. For critical engagement with the hybrid identities of groups occupying the interior of the Cape Colony and its frontier regions during the nineteenth century, see M Leśniewski. 2010. 'Guns and Horses, c 1750 to c 1850: Korana – People or Raiding Hordes?' *Werkwinkel Journal of Low Countries and South African Studies* 5 (2), 11–16; see also P. Landau. 2010. *Popular Politics in the History of South Africa, 1400–1948.* Cambridge: Cambridge University Press.

10. For Lloyd's comments on the boys' skills at drawing, and the story of Dia!kwain's sketch of the ostrich for Wilhelm Bleek, see Bleek and Lloyd, *Specimens,* xiii–xv.

11. Lloyd's interviews with the !Kung boys yielded 15 notebooks. For Wilhelm Bleek's desire to collect language samples from 'bushmen met with beyond Damaraland' and more on the !Kung children, see Bleek and Lloyd, *Specimens,* xii–xiv. For more on Coates Palgrave's commission and travels in what is now Namibia, see W. Hartmann, J. Silvester, and P. Hayes. Eds. 1998. *The Colonising Camera: Photographs in the Making of Namibian History.* Cape Town: UCT Press, 10–12.

12. The watercolours and drawings received a great deal of academic and popular attention from the late 1990s onwards. They were exhibited at the South African National Gallery in Cape Town, from April to June 2003, and internationally. See M. Szalay. Ed. 2002. *The Moon as Shoe: Drawings of the San.* Zurich: Scheidegger and Spiess.

13. BC 151, 2008 additions, Bright-Bleek letters #210.

14. Scott Deetz, *Catalog,* 24.

15. Scott Deetz, *Catalog,* 24.

16. Scott Deetz, *Catalog,* 24–25.

17. Scott Deetz, *Catalog,* 24, 38–39.

18. Scott Deetz, *Catalog,* 37–38.

19. See Bleek to Kirby, 23 July 1936. Percival Kirby Papers, University of Cape Town Libraries, Manuscripts and Archives Department, hereafter BC 750, Correspondence A.

20. Scott Deetz, *Catalog,* 25 n24. She was buried at Diano Marina on the Gulf of Genoa.

21. Scott Deetz, *Catalog,* 25 n24.

22. Scott Deetz, *Catalog*, 25 n24, 73.

23. See Bleek and Lloyd, *Specimens*, xvi, for Lloyd's acknowledgement of Edith Bleek's assistance.

24. E. Bleek and D. Bleek. 1909. 'Notes on the Bushmen', in M. Tongue. 1909. *Bushman Paintings*. London: Clarendon Press.

25. See Scott Deetz, *Catalog*, 25 n24; also Bank, *Bushmen in a Victorian World*, 2. Sara Pugach argues that the opening of Berlin's *Seminar für Orientalische Sprachen* in 1887 signalled a shift in the location of colonial knowledge about Africans from the missionary field to the metropolitan centre. See S. Pugach. 2012. *Africa in Translation: A History of Colonial Linguistics in Germany and Beyond, 1814–1945*. Ann Arbor: University of Michigan Press, 60. Pugach's study of the seminar's development has been unable to confirm Dorothea's presence at any of the courses offered in its early years (email correspondence, S. Pugach, 2 April 2013).

26. For more on the use of the body as instrument of science in fieldwork, see H. Kuklick. 2011. 'Personal Equations: Reflections on the History of Fieldwork, with Special Reference to Sociocultural Anthropology'. *Isis* 102 (1), 1–33.

27. H. Glenn Penny. 2008. 'Traditions in the German Language', in H. Kuklick. Ed. *A New History of Anthropology*. Oxford: Blackwell, 79–95; M. Bunzl and H. Glenn Penny. 2003. 'Introduction: Rethinking German Anthropology, Colonialism, and Race', in M. Bunzl and H. Glenn Penny. Eds. *Worldly Provincialism: German Anthropology in the Age of Empire*. Ann Arbor: University of Michigan Press, 1–30; A. Zimmerman. 2001. 'Looking Beyond History: The Optics of German Anthropology and the Critique of Humanism'. *Studies in History and Philosophy of Biological and Biomedical Sciences* 32 (3), 385–411.

28. Arising towards the end of the eighteenth century, German cosmopolitanism refers to a complex set of theories springing from the view that all human beings belong to a single moral community. See P. Kleingeld. 1999. 'Six Varieties of Cosmopolitanism in Late Eighteenth-Century Germany'. *Journal of the History of Ideas* 60 (3), 505–524.

29. Glenn Penny, 'Traditions', 82–85.

30. Glenn Penny, 'Traditions', 86.

31. Glenn Penny, 'Traditions', 86.

32. Glenn Penny, 'Traditions', 85–87.

33. Glenn Penny, 'Traditions', 85–87.

34. Glenn Penny, 'Traditions', 89–93.

35. See Zimmerman, 'Beyond History'; see also A. Zimmerman. 2001. *Anthropology and Antihumanism in Imperial Germany*. Chicago and London: University of Chicago Press, 1–11.

36. Bleek to Péringuey, 25 November 1920. Iziko South African Museum correspondence, B 60; Maria Wilman Collection, McGregor Museum (hereafter MMKD) 2591/6.

37. A. Kuper. 2005. *The Reinvention of Primitive Society: Transformations of a Myth*. London and New York: Routledge.

38. Kuper, *Reinvention*, 121.

39. Kuper, *Reinvention*, 120–123.

40. See, for example, BC 151, A3.8, 201; A3.16, 274, 280–81; A3.29, 431.

41. Bleek to Woldmann, 6 June 1928. BC 210, Box 4.

42. Bleek to Woldmann, 28 November 1928. BC 210, Box 4.

43. Bleek to Woldmann, 5 April 1929. BC 210, Box 4.

44. Zimmerman, *Anthropology and Antihumanism*; Zimmerman, 'Beyond History', 385–411.

45. See Zimmerman, 'Beyond History', 390–393.

46. Zimmerman, 'Beyond History', 390–393. See also J. Whitman. 1984. 'From Philology to Anthropology in Mid-Nineteenth-Century Germany', in G. Stocking. Ed. *Functionalism Historicised: Essays on British Social Anthropology*. Madison: University of Wisconsin Press.

47. Zimmerman, 'Beyond History', 390–393.

48. Zimmerman, 'Beyond History', 391.

49. See Bleek and Lloyd, *Specimens*, xvi, for Lloyd's acknowledgement of Dorothea's help with 'copying many of the manuscripts and making the Index to this volume'.

50. See T. Güldemann. 2005. 'Introduction', in J. Hollmann. *Customs and Beliefs of the /Xam Bushmen*. Johannesburg: Wits University Press, 385–387.

51. S. Dubow. 2006. *A Commonwealth of Knowledge: Science, Sensibility and White South Africa 1820–2000*. Oxford: Oxford University Press.

52. Tongue, *Paintings*.

53. E. Bleek and D. Bleek, 1909. 'Notes on the Bushmen', in Tongue, *Paintings*.

54. For historical archaeology on the ancestral lands of //Kabbo and the other interlocutors, see J. Deacon. 1986. ' "My Place is the Bitterpits": The Home Territory of Bleek and Lloyd's /Xam San Informants'. *African Studies* 45, 135–155.

55. BC 151, A3.1.

56. BC 151, A3.1.

57. BC 151, A3.1, 4ff.

58. BC 151, A3.2.

59. BC 151, E5.1.8. For genealogy on Hokan, see BC 151, A3.3, 134–137. For more on this trip, see A. Bank. 2006. 'Anthropology and Fieldwork Photography: Dorothea Bleek's Expedition to the Northern Cape and the Kalahari, July to December 1911'. *Kronos* 32, 77–113.

60. MMKD 2644; BC 151, A3.4, 222.

61. D. Bleek. 1929. *Comparative Vocabularies of Bushman Languages*. Cambridge: Cambridge University Press, 1.

62. Phrase taken from P. Weinberg. 1997. *In Search of the San*. Johannesburg: Porcupine Press. See also H. Brody. 2013. *Tracks across Sand: The Dispossession of the ‡Khomani San of the Southern Kalahari*. London: Face to Face Media.

63. Dorothea's notebook refers to 'Witdraai' and 'Koopan'. See BC 151, A3.4, 223ff. For recent ethnographic writing emanating from Wit Draai (presently a farm as well as a police post), see K. Tomaselli. 2005. *Where Global Contradictions Are Sharpest: Research Stories from the Kalahari*. Amsterdam: Rosenberg Publishers, and other titles by the same author. Wit Draai was also the erstwhile home of the late 'San elder' Dawid Kruiper, and remains an impoverished settlement frequented by ethnographers and others on their way into the Kalahari.

64. D. Bleek. 'Scotty Smith'. Undated typescript. BC 151, E5.2.1.

65. M. Legassick and C. Rassool. 2000. *Skeletons in the Cupboard: South African Museums and the Trade in Human Remains, 1907–1917*. Cape Town and Kimberley: Iziko and McGregor Museum; S. Dubow. 1995. *Illicit Union: Scientific Racism in Modern South Africa*. Johannesburg: Wits University Press; S. Dubow. 1996. 'Human Origins, Race Typology and the Other Raymond Dart'. *African Studies* 55 (1), 1–30. For more on the activities of Wilman and Lennox, see C. Quigley. 2001. *Skulls and Skeletons: Human Bone Collections and Accumulations*. Jefferson, NC: McFarland, 231–234.

66. BC 151, A3.4, 222.

67. BC 151, A3.4, 230.

68. BC 151, A3.4, 230.

69. BC 151, A3.4, 230.

70. BC 151, J2.1.

71. Bleek, *Comparative Vocabularies*, 1–2. The /'Auni people whom Dorothea met along

the lower Nossop River close to the Namibian and Botswana borders with South Africa spoke /'Au or /'Auo, a language she thought was similar to Nama but distantly related to /Xam. See A. Trail. 2002. 'The Khoesan Languages', in R. Mesthrie. Ed. *Language in South Africa*. Cambridge: Cambridge University Press, 42–43.

72. BC 151, A1.1. The Reverend J.G. Krönlein, a missionary who established the Beersheba Mission Station in the Kalahari, provided Wilhelm Bleek with a collection of Nama stories that formed the basis of his *Reynard the Fox in South Africa; or, Hottentot Fables and Tales*. See Bank, *Bushmen in a Victorian World*, 32–35; T. Güldemann. 2006. 'The San Languages of Southern Namibia: Linguistic Appraisal with Special Reference to J.G. Krönlein's Nuusaa Data'. *Anthropological Linguistics* 4, 369–395.

73. BC 151, A3.4, 224.

74. Bleek, *Comparative Vocabularies*, 2.

75. BC 151, A3.6; A3.7; A3.8.

76. T. Güldemann. Ed. 2000. *The //!ke or Bushmen of Griqualand West: Notes on the Language of the //!ke or Bushmen of Griqualand West by Dorothea F. Bleek*. Working Paper 15, Khoisan Forum. Köln: Institut für Afrikanistik.

77. BC 151, J2.2.

78. BC 151, J2.2. Lestrade, who became an employee of the Union government's Native Affairs Department, studied linguistics in Hamburg under the acclaimed linguist and champion of the Hamitic hypothesis Carl Meinhof. See Pugach, *Africa in Translation*, 175–185; see also D. Hammond-Tooke. 1997. *Imperfect Interpreters: South Africa's Anthropologists, 1920–1990*. Johannesburg: Wits University Press.

79. Bleek, *Comparative Vocabularies*, 1–2.

80. BC 151, A3.6, 16–23.

81. Bleek, *Comparative Vocabularies*, 2–3. For more on Louis Fourie's ethnological work among the bushmen of Namibia, see A. Wanless. 2007. 'The Silence of Colonial Melancholy: The Fourie Collection of Khoisan Ethnologica'. Unpublished DPhil thesis, University of the Witwatersrand.

82. Broadly, the language classification set out in Dorothea's comparative grammar was as follows: 1. Southern (the /Xam spoken by the 'colonial bushmen' interviewed by her father and aunt). 2. Northern (the Naron and !Kung spoken by people she met in Angola, and by the boys from the northern parts of South West Africa that Aunt Lucy had hosted in Mowbray). 3. Central (/'Au or /'Auo, similar to Nama, and spoken by some of the people she had met at Sandfontein).

83. I. Schapera. 1930 [1980]. *The Khoisan Peoples of South Africa*. London: Routledge, vii.

84. Maingard to Bleek, 5 April 1938. BC 151, C16.7.

85. D. Bleek. 1932. 'A Survey of Our Present Knowledge of Rockpaintings in South Africa'. *South African Journal of Science* 29, 72–83.

86. Bleek to Woldmann, 21 February 1936. BC 210, Box 4.

87. D. Bleek. 1929. 'Bushman Folklore'. *Africa* 2 (3), 302–313.

88. Bleek to Woldmann, 22 January 1930. BC 210, Box 4.

89. Bleek to Woldmann, 9 April 1931. BC 210, Box 4.

90. Bleek, 'Survey'.

91. P. Scott Deetz and M. Scott Roos. 2010. 'Memories of Growing Up with "Aunt D"', email communication.

92. Scott Deetz, *Catalog*, 48. Henry Hepburn Bright died in 1930.

93. Scott Deetz, *Catalog*, 48, 59.

94. Scott Deetz, *Catalog*, 59.

95. Scott Deetz, *Catalog*, 59. Sketch plan produced by Marjorie Scott; embellished by Patricia Scott Deetz in 2007.

96. See E. Rosenthal and A. Goodwin. 1953. *Cave Artists of South Africa*. Cape Town: A.A. Balkema; also Patricia Scott Deetz, personal communication, July 2010.

97. Bleek to Scott, 10 December 1937. In the collection of Patricia Scott Deetz.

98. Bleek to Woldmann, 18 February 1938. BC 210, Box 4.

99. Bleek to Scott, 10 December 1937. In the collection of Patricia Scott Deetz.

100. Bleek to Scott, 7 September 1939. In the collection of Patricia Scott Deetz.

101. Dorothea enjoyed driving, and taking friends and family out on trips. She loved owning the latest model of motor vehicle. See Scott Deetz and Scott Roos, 'Memories'.

102. The list of Dorothea's assets indicated that she owned an Austin motor car at the time of her death in 1948, attesting to the independence and mobility that Dorothea counted as important and that she continued to enjoy until the end of her life. See BC 151, 2008 additions #185.

103. Part of this closeness is reflected in the fact that Dorothea left the major part of her estate to Marjorie Scott. This included her Austin motor car worth £80 000, properties in L'Agulhas and at Onrus River, and a portfolio of shares and investments, including shares in an Argentinian company. See BC 151, 2008 additions #185.

Chapter 2

1. M. Tongue. 1909. *Bushman Paintings*. London: Clarendon Press, 32. Emphasis in original.

2. Tongue, *Paintings*, 32.

3. Tongue, *Paintings*, 32.

4. Tongue, *Paintings*, 32.

5. F. Christol. 1897. *Au Sud de l'Afrique*. Paris: Berger-Levrault. Christol visited the area before 1882 and is remembered for arranging the removal of parts of a painting from a cave on the farm Ventershoek near Wepener in the Orange River Colony. Fragments from the famous 'cattle raid' scene were donated by Christol to the Musée de l'Homme in Paris and to the Musée de Neuchâtel in Switzerland. See P. Mitchell. 2010. Review: *Vols de Vaches à Christol Cave: Histoire Critique d'une Image Rupestre d'Afrique du Sud. Africa* 80 (4), 664–666. The physical removal of rock art was an acceptable practice in the early twentieth century. See L. Henry. 2007. 'A History of Removing Rock Art in South Africa.' *South African Archaeological Bulletin* 62 (185), 44–48.

6. Tongue, *Paintings*, 33.

7. Tongue, *Paintings*, 30.

8. Tongue, *Paintings*, 17.

9. Tongue, *Paintings*, 31, Plate XL.

10. Tongue, *Paintings*, 31.

11. Tongue, *Paintings*, 33.

12. J. Orpen. 1874. 'A Glimpse into the Mythology of the Maluti Bushmen'. *Cape Monthly Magazine* 9, 1–11.

13. W. Bleek. 1874. 'Remarks by Dr Bleek'. *Cape Monthly Magazine* 9, 11–13.

14. Wilhelm Bleek's interest in the work of rock art copyists of the day is discussed in A. Bank. 2006. *Bushmen in a Victorian World: The Remarkable Story of the Bleek and Lloyd Collection of Bushman Folklore*. Cape Town: Double Storey, Chapter 12. See also J.D. Lewis-Williams and S. Challis. 2011. *Deciphering Ancient Minds: The Mystery of San Bushman Rock Art*. London: Thames & Hudson.

15. Bleek to Woldmann, 9 April 1931. Käthe Woldmann Papers, University of Cape Town Libraries, Manuscripts and Archives Department, hereafter BC 210, Box 4.

16. For Lucy's purchase of Stow's manuscript and reproductions and her efforts

to have the manuscript published, see Bank, *Bushmen in a Victorian World*, 376–380; and K. Schoeman. Ed. 1997. *A Debt of Gratitude: Lucy Lloyd and the 'Bushman Work' of G.W. Stow*. Cape Town: South African Library.

17. Tongue, *Paintings*, 11/b2, 14.

18. Tongue, *Paintings*, 19–21.

19. D. Bleek. 1932. 'A Survey of Our Present Knowledge of Rockpaintings in South Africa'. *South African Journal of Science* 29, 72–83.

20. For a comprehensive review of rock art copying activity in the Maloti-Drakensberg region between 1870 and 1910, see P. Vinnicombe. 1976. *People of the Eland: Rock Paintings of the Drakensberg Bushmen as a Reflection of Their Life and Thought*. Pietermaritzburg: University of Natal Press, 116–123.

21. Orpen, 'Mythology'. For a transcription of the Qing/Orpen text, see M. McGranaghan, S. Challis and J.D. Lewis-Williams. 2013. 'Joseph Millerd Orpen's "A Glimpse into the Mythology of the Maluti Bushmen": A Contextual Introduction and Republished Text'. *Southern African Humanities* 25, 137–166. For a close reading of the Orpen/Qing encounter and its significance for rock art scholarship, see Lewis-Williams and Challis, *Deciphering Ancient Minds*. See also P. Mitchell and S. Challis. 2008. 'A First Glimpse into the Maloti Mountains: The Diary of James Murray Grant's Expedition of 1873–1874'. *Southern African Humanities* 20 (1), 401–463.

22. For more on Schunke's reproductions, see Bank, *Bushmen in a Victorian World*, 322–339.

23. For a fuller account of the work of Brother Otto first in Natal and later at the Kei River, see A. Flett and P. Letley. 2007. 'Brother Otto Mäeder: An Examination and Evaluation of His Work as a Rock Art Recorder in South Africa'. *Southern African Humanities* 19, 103–121. For the provenance of his photographs, copies and samples, see Vinnicombe, *People of the Eland*, 118–119. See also B. Huss and O. Mäeder. 1925. 'The Origin of the Bushman Paintings at the Kei River'. *South African Journal of Science* 22, 496–503.

24. Tongue, *Paintings*, Preface, b2.

25. There is a large literature on precolonial histories of the eastern Cape region. See, for example, N. Mostert. 1992. *Frontiers: The Epic of South Africa's Creation and the Tragedy of the Xhosa People*. London: Pimlico; C. Crais. 1992. *The Making of the Colonial Order: White Supremacy and Black Resistance in the Eastern Cape, 1770–1865*. Johannesburg: Wits University Press; R. Ross. 'Hermanus Matroos, aka Ngxukumeshe: A Life on the Border'. *Kronos* 30, 47–69.

26. Stow's reproductions and research methods are documented in P. Skotnes. 2008. *Unconquerable Spirit: George Stow's History Paintings of the San.* Johannesburg: Jacana. For commentary on Wilhelm Bleek's use of rock art, see Bank, *Bushman in a Victorian World*, 303–339. For a general account of the growth of interest in prehistory at the Cape in the late nineteenth century, see S. Dubow. 2004. 'Earth History, Natural History and Prehistory at the Cape, 1860–75'. *Comparative Studies in Society and History* 46, 207–233. For an examination of rock art copying practices that describes the work of past and present copyists, including Orpen, the artist Walter Battiss, the Abbé Breuil, Harald Pager and Patricia Vinnicombe, see N. Leibhammer. 2009. 'Originals and Copies: A Phenomenological Difference', in P. Mitchell and B. Smith. Eds. *The Eland's People: Essays in Memory of Patrica Vinnicombe.* Johannesburg: Wits University Press, 43–59.

27. A. Willcox, 1956. *Rock Paintings of the Drakensberg, Natal and Griqualand East.* London: Max Parrish; H. Pager. 1971. *Ndedema: A Documentation of the Rock Paintings of the Ndedema Gorge.* Graz: Akademische Druck.

28. S. Mguni. 2012. 'Five Years of Southern African Rock Art Research', in P. Bahn, N. Franklin and M. Strecker. Eds. *Rock Art Studies News of the World IV.* Oxford: Oxbow Books, 99–112. See also N. Shepherd. 2002. 'Disciplining Archaeology: The Invention of South African Prehistory, 1923–1953'. *Kronos* 28, 127–145.

29. Both Pager and Willcox relied on the research assistance of their spouses. Pager's wife, Shirley Ann, accompanied him on his two-year field stint in the Drakensberg, while Willcox acknowledged his wife (not named) for 'carrying her rucksack countless miles of heavy going' and for not objecting 'even to spending part of her honeymoon in Bushman rockshelters'. See Willcox, *Rock Paintings*, Acknowledgements. See also Acknowledgments in Pager, *Ndedema*.

30. Mguni, 'Five Years'.

31. For a personal recollection recounting Vinnicombe's 'explicit desire to make rock art acceptable to professional archaeology' through the use of statistical methods and an analytical approach, see J.D. Lewis-Williams. 2009. 'Patricia Vinnicombe: A Memoir', in Mitchell and Smith, *The Eland's People*, 16.

32. L. Meskell. 2009. 'Contextualising *People of the Eland*', in Mitchell and Smith, *The Eland's People*, 29.

33. Meskell, 'Contextualising', 29.

34. Meskell, 'Contextualising', 29–41.

35. J.D. Lewis-Williams. 1981. *Believing and Seeing: Symbolic Meanings in Southern San Rock Art*. London: Academic Press, 15–16.

36. Lewis-Williams, *Believing and Seeing*, 15–16.

37. Lewis-Williams, *Believing and Seeing*, 18.

38. Lewis-Williams, *Believing and Seeing*, Chapter 3. For a view on 'pan-San' cosmology, see J.D. Lewis-Williams. 1984. 'Ideological Continuities in Prehistoric Southern Africa: The Evidence of Rock Art', in C. Schrire. Ed. *Past and Present in Hunter Gatherer Societies*. London: Academic Press. For recent discussion of interpretive method based on a rock art scene studied by Dorothea, see J.D. Lewis-Williams and D. Pearce. 2012. 'Framed Idiosyncrasy: Method and Evidence in the Interpretation of San Rock Art'. *South African Archaeological Bulletin* 67, 75–87. For an interpretation drawing on /Xam folklore, see J.D. Lewis-Williams. 2013. 'From Illustration to Social Intervention: Three Nineteenth-Century /Xam Myths and Their Implications for Understanding San Rock Art'. *Cambridge Anthropological Journal* 23 (2), 241–262.

39. For explication of cognitive archaeology and the shamanistic interpretation of rock art, see J.D. Lewis-Williams. 2002. *A Cosmos in Stone: Interpreting Religion and Society through Rock Art*. Oxford: AltaMira Press, especially Chapter 5, 'Through the Veil', 97–117, and Chapter 7, 'Seeing and Construing', 133–161. See also J.D. Lewis-Williams and T. Dowson. Eds. 1994. 'Aspects of Rock Art Research: A Critical Retrospective', in T. Dowson and J.D. Lewis-Williams. Eds. *Contested Images: Diversity in Southern African Rock Art Research*. Johannesburg: Wits University Press, 201–221. For a discussion on ethnographic analogue, see D. Pearce. 2012. 'Ethnography and History: The Significance of Social Change in Interpreting Rock Art', in B. Smith, K. Helskog and D. Morris. Eds. *Working with Rock Art: Recording, Presenting and Understanding Rock Art Using Indigenous Knowledge*. Johannesburg: Wits University Press.

40. See, for example, Bleek to Woldmann, 26 December 1930. BC 210, Box 4; D. Bleek. n.d. 'The Record of the Rocks in South Africa'. BC 151, E5.1.26, 2, and D3.6, 3–4. The evolutionary view in which those cultures deemed to be 'primitive' represented humanity in the childhood phase of its development found popular expression in the work of E. Tylor. 1871 [1920]. *Primitive Culture*. London: John Murray. See also L. Frobenius. 1909. *The Childhood of Man*. Trans. A. Keane. London: Seely & Co.

41. J.D. Lewis-Williams. 1996. ' "The Ideas Generally Entertained with Regard to the Bushmen and Their Mental Condition" ', in P. Skotnes. Ed. *Miscast: Negotiating*

the Presence of the Bushmen. Cape Town: UCT Press, 307–310; Vinnicombe, *People of the Eland*, 348.

42. Lewis-Williams, ' "Ideas" ', 308–309.

43. W. Battiss. 1939. *The Amazing Bushman.* Pretoria: Red Fern Press; W. Battiss. 1952. *Bushman Art.* Pretoria: Red Fern Press.

44. Rock Art Research Institute, http://web.wits.ac.za/academic/science/geography/ rockart/ (accessed 20 July 2010).

45. Bleek, 'Survey'.

46. For a sample of the literature on rock art, identity and social change, see S. Challis. 2012. 'Creolisation on the Nineteenth-Century Frontiers of Southern Africa: A Case Study of the AmaTola "Bushmen" in the Maloti-Drakensberg'. *Journal of Southern African Studies* 38, 265–280; S. Ouzman. 2005. 'The Magical Arts of a Raider Nation: Central South Africa's Korana Rock Art'. *South African Archaeological Society Goodwin Series* 9: 101–113; G. Blundell. 2004. *Nqabayo's Nomansland: San Rock Art and the Somatic Past*, Studies in Global Archaeology 2, Sweden: Uppsala University. For additional historically situated readings, see R. Yates, A. Manhire and J. Parkington. 1994. 'Rock Painting and History in the South-Western Cape', and J. Loubser and G. Laurens. 1994. 'Depictions of Domestic Ungulates and Shields: Hunter/Gatherers and Agro-Pastoralists in the Caledon River Valley Area', both in Dowson and Lewis-Williams, *Contested Images*, 29–60 and 83–118; chapters in C. Chippindale and P. Taçon. Eds. 1998. *The Archaeology of Rock-Art.* Cambridge: Cambridge University Press, including S. Ouzman. 'Towards a Mindscape of Landscape: Rock-Art as Expression of World-Understanding', 30–41; P. Jolly. 'Modelling Change in the Contact Art of the South-Eastern San, Southern Africa', 247–267. For a feminist interpretation of rock art, see A. Solomon. 1996. 'Some Questions about Style and Authorship in Later San Paintings', in Skotnes, *Miscast*, 291–295; A. Solomon. 1994. ' "Mythic Women" ': A Study in Variability in San Rock Art and Narrative', in Dowson and Lewis-Williams, *Contested Images*, 331–371.

47. For a visual representation of this process, see Vinnicombe, *People of the Eland*, 126–127.

48. Vinnicombe, *People of the Eland*, 125–127.

49. Vinnicombe, *People of the Eland*, 126.

50. H. Balfour. 1909. 'Preface', in Tongue, *Paintings*, 6.

51. For instance, Helen took the 'post-cart from Indwe' to reach Cala commonage in the district of Tembuland (Tongue, *Paintings*, 23). The notes end with thanks to Mrs Clark of Clark Siding near Dordrecht for her 'ever open house' which 'provided headquarters from which to visit the neighbouring districts', and to 'Miss Chandler of Bloemfontein', who lent her cottage at Modderpoort for the same purpose (Tongue, *Paintings*, 35).

52. Tongue, *Paintings*, 32. Emphasis added.

53. Tongue, *Paintings*, 13. Emphasis added.

54. Tongue, *Paintings*, 14, 17. Emphasis added.

55. The full title reads *Bushman Paintings Copied by M. Helen Tongue; with a Preface by Henry Balfour.*

56. G. Stow and D. Bleek. Ed. 1930. *Rock Paintings in South Africa from Parts of the Eastern Province and Orange Free State.* London: Methuen, xii. Compare with P. Skotnes. 1996. 'The Thin Black Line: Diversity and Transformation in the Bleek and Lloyd Collection and the Paintings of the Southern San', in J. Deacon and T. Dowson. Eds. *Voices from the Past Voices from the Past: /Xam Bushmen and the Bleek and Lloyd Collection.* Johannesburg: Wits University Press, 234–244. For further discussion of contemporary practices of rock art recording, redrawing and republishing, of the distance between the copies and the original painting and site, and the impact of these on issues of interpretation and meaning, see J. Wintjes. 2011. 'A Pictorial Genealogy: The Rainmaking Group from Sehonghong Shelter'. *Southern African Humanities* 23, 17–54; and Leibhammer, 'Originals and Copies', in Mitchell and Smith, *The Eland's People*, 43–59.

57. Stow and Bleek, *Rock Paintings in South Africa*, xi.

58. Bleek to Woldmann, 6 June 1928. BC 210, Box 4.

59. Stow and Bleek, *Rock Paintings in South Africa*, xi.

60. Bleek to Woldman, 6 June 1928.

61. Tongue, *Paintings*, 14.

62. Tongue, *Paintings*, 19–20.

63. Tongue, *Paintings*, 20, 21.

64. Tongue, *Paintings*, 14, 16, 18.

65. Anglican missionaries of the St Augustine brotherhood have occupied the site at Modderpoort since the late 1860s. For a fine-grained reading of the site's hybrid uses and spiritual meanings, see D. Coplan. 2003. 'Land from

the Ancestors: Popular Religious Pilgrimage along the South Africa–Lesotho Border'. *Journal of Southern African Studies* 29 (4), 984–990.

66. Tongue, *Paintings*, 26.

67. Tongue, *Paintings*, 26.

68. Tongue, *Paintings*, 25–27.

69. Tongue, *Paintings*, 27.

70. Tongue, *Paintings*, 28.

71. G. Stow. 1905. *The Native Races of South Africa*. London: Swan Sonnenschein, 119–120.

72. Tongue, *Paintings*, 28, Plate 37.

73. Tongue, *Paintings*, 27.

74. Tongue, *Paintings*, 21–22.

75. Collotype refers to an early colour-reproduction process which allowed shaded rather than blocked colours to be reproduced.

76. Tongue, *Paintings*, collotypes 1 and 2.

77. Tongue, *Paintings*, 16.

78. Tongue, *Paintings*, 16.

79. Tongue, *Paintings*, 17.

80. Tongue, *Paintings*, 30.

81. Tongue, *Paintings*, 19–23.

82. See Blundell, *Nqabayo's Nomansland*, 40–45, for evidence of an artist making paintings in the Tsolo region during the early decades of the twentieth century.

83. Tongue, *Paintings*, 22.

84. Tongue, *Paintings*, 20.

85. Tongue, *Paintings*, 32.

86. Tongue, *Paintings*, 21–22.

87. For more on the effacement of the place of assistants in archaeology, see N. Schlanger. 2010. 'Manual and Intellectual Labour in Archaeology: Past and Present in Human Resource Management', in S. Koerner and I. Russell. Eds. *Unquiet Pasts: Risk Society, Lived Cultural Heritage, Re-designing Reflexivity*. London: Ashgate, 161–171; N. Shepherd. 2003. ' "When the Hand that Holds the Trowel is Black": Disciplinary Practices of Self-Representation and the Issue of "Native" Labour in Archaeology'. *Journal of Social Archaeology* 3 (3), 334–352. For field assistants in anthropology and the natural sciences, see A. Bank. 2008. 'The "Intimate Politics" of Fieldwork: Monica Hunter and Her

African Assistants, Pondoland and the Eastern Cape, 1931–1932'. *Journal of Southern African Studies* 34 (3), 557–574; A. Bank and L. Bank. Eds. 2013. *Inside African Anthropology: Monica Wilson and Her Interpreters.* Cambridge: Cambridge University Press.

88. Tongue, *Paintings*, 35.

89. Tongue, *Paintings*, 25–26. The Black Watch is a reference to the so-nicknamed Scottish infantry regiment of the British Army that served in the Cape Colony during the Second South African War.

90. Tongue, *Paintings*, 26–27.

91. Tongue, *Paintings*, 14. This cave had been visited by Stow.

92. Tongue, *Paintings*, 14.

93. Tongue, *Paintings*, 19–20.

94. Tongue, *Paintings*, 19.

95. Tongue, *Paintings*, 19. See also E. Bleek and D. Bleek. 1909. 'Notes on the Bushmen', in Tongue, *Paintings*.

96. Tongue, *Paintings*, 33–35.

97. Tongue, *Paintings*, 29, 33. Stow had copied engravings at a site on the banks of the Great Riet River that he identified as Blaauw Bank, now known as Driekopseiland. See D. Morris. 2008. 'Driekopseiland Rock Engraving Site, South Africa: A Precolonial Landscape Lost and Re-membered', in A. Gazin-Schwartz and A. Smith. Eds. *Landscapes of Clearance: Archaeological and Anthropological Perspectives.* Walnut Creek, CA: Left Coast, 87–111.

98. Tongue, *Paintings*, 33–34.

99. Tongue, *Paintings*, 33.

100. Bleek, 'Survey', 78–79.

101. See Bleek, 'Notes', 36–44. For a scientific examination of rock art samples to establish types of pigment used, see B. Segal. 1935. 'A Possible Base for "Bushman" Paint'. *Bantu Studies* 9, 49–51. Dorothea's comments on the quality of certain colours anticipated those made years later by the artist Walter Battiss, who argued that the paints were derived with great knowledge of natural pigments, and made to render a quality of colour that could not be matched by modern manufacture. See Battiss, *Bushman Art*, 9.

102. Bleek, 'Notes', 37.

103. J. van der Riet, M. van der Riet and D. Bleek. 1940. *More Rock-Paintings in South Africa.* London: Methuen, xvi.

104. D. Bleek. n.d. 'The Record of the Rocks in South Africa'. BC 151, E5.1.26, 2. The reference to the last bushman artist perishing in battle is from Stow, *Native Races*, 230.

105. Bleek, 'Notes', 37.

106. Bleek, 'Notes', 36–37.

107. Lucy Lloyd and her sister Fanny were living in Berlin at about the time of the exhibition. See Bank, *Bushmen in a Victorian World*, 378.

108. For a history of rock painting in Europe, see H. Breuil. 1952. *Four Hundred Centuries of Cave Art*. Trans. M. E. Boyle. Montignac and Dordogne: Centre d'Études et de Documentation Préhistoriques.

109. R. Teukolsky. 2009. 'Primitives and Post-Impressionists: Roger Fry's Anthropological Modernism', in *The Literate Eye: Victorian Art Writing and Modernist Aesthetics*. Oxford: Oxford University Press, 192–233.

110. Balfour was the first and longest-serving curator of the Pitt Rivers Museum at Oxford, holding the position from 1885 to 1939, and also president of the Royal Anthropological Institute for a term. See F. Larson. 2007. 'Anthropology as Comparative Anatomy: Reflecting on the Study of Material Culture during the Late 1800s and the Late 1900s'. *Journal of Material Culture* 12 (1), 89–112.

111. Balfour, 'Preface', 4.

112. Balfour, 'Preface', 5. For more on circumstances leading to the proclamation of the Act, see M. Legassick and C. Rassool. 2000. *Skeletons in the Cupboard: South African Museums and the Trade in Human Remains, 1907–1917*. Cape Town and Kimberley: Iziko South African Museum and McGregor Museum. The authors argue that the Act was designed to stop the international trade in human remains, as well as to protect rock art and other 'bushman relics' within the country.

113. Balfour, 'Preface', 6. Balfour congratulated Tongue and Bleek on their production of '100 admirable copies made with great care and accuracy'. Compare Balfour's opinion of Tongue's fine copies with the Abbé Breuil's dismissive description of them as 'charming', expressed in H. Breuil. 1955. *The White Lady of the Brandberg*. London: Trianon Press, 2.

114. W. Bleek, 'Remarks'.

Chapter 3

1. Bleek Collection, University of Cape Town Libraries, Manuscripts and Archives Department, hereafter BC 151, A3.6.

2. Jemima died at Sir Lowry's Pass Village at the home of her youngest daughter, Helma, and her husband, Henry Hepburn Bright. She was buried in Somerset West on 27 October 1909.

3. A. Bank. 2006. 'Anthropology and Fieldwork Photography: Dorothea Bleek's Expedition to the Northern Cape and the Kalahari, July to December 1911'. *Kronos* 32, 77–113.

4. A. Bank. 2006. *Bushmen in a Victorian World: The Remarkable Story of the Bleek-Lloyd Collection of Bushman Folklore*. Cape Town: Double Storey, 386.

5. See Bank, *Bushmen in a Victorian World*, 389–390.

6. Her sister Mabel, now Jaeger, was living in Halle, Germany, in 1929. See Bleek to Woldmann, 3 May 1929. Käthe Woldmann Papers, University of Cape Town Libraries, Manuscripts and Archives Department, hereafter BC 210, Box 4.

7. P. Scott Deetz. 2007. *Catalog of the Bleek-Lloyd Collection in the Scott Family Archive*. Williamsburg, VA: Deetz Ventures, Inc., 46, 48.

8. Bleek to Woldmann, 6 June 1928; 28 July 1930. BC 210, Box 4.

9. H. Glenn Penny. 2008. 'Traditions in the German Language', in H. Kuklick. Ed. *A New History of Anthropology*. Oxford: Blackwell, 85–87.

10. The search by German humanists of the mid- to late-nineteenth century for essences of 'nature' compared with 'culture' began to take on ideas of educability, as Whitman describes in his discussion of philological *Psychologie*. See J. Whitman. 1984. 'From Philology to Anthropology in Mid-Nineteenth-Century Germany', in G. Stocking. Ed. *Functionalism Historicised: Essays on British Social Anthropology*. Madison: University of Wisconsin Press, 219–224. Compare with the positivist view of Glenn Penny in 'Traditions', 79–95; also M. Bunzl and H. Glenn Penny. 2003. 'Introduction: Rethinking German Anthropology, Colonialism, and Race', in Glenn Penny and Bunzl. Eds. 2003. *Worldly Provincialism: German Anthropology in the Age of Empire*. Ann Arbor: University of Michigan Press, 1–30.

11. S. Dubow. 1995. *Illicit Union: Scientific Racism in Modern South Africa*. Johannesburg: Wits University Press.

12. J.D. Lewis-Williams. 2008. 'A Nexus of Lives: How a Heretical Bishop Contributed to Our Knowledge of South Africa's Past'. *Southern African Humanities* 20,

463–475; Bank, *Bushmen in a Victorian World*, Chapter 1; R. Thornton. 1983. '"This Dying Out Race": W.H.I Bleek's Approach to the Languages of Southern Africa'. *Social Dynamics* 9 (2), 1–10; S. Pugach. 2012. *Africa in Translation: A History of Colonial Linguistics in Germany and Beyond, 1814–1945*. Ann Arbor: University of Michigan Press.

13. P. Harries. 2007. *Butterflies and Barbarians: Swiss Missionaries and Systems of Knowledge in South-East Africa*. Johannesburg: Wits University Press; P. Harries. 2000. 'Field Sciences in Scientific Fields: Ethnology, Botany and the Early Ethnographic Monograph in the Work of H-A Junod', in S. Dubow. Ed. *Science and Society in Southern Africa*. Manchester: University of Manchester Press; P. Harries. 1991. 'Exclusion, Classification and Internal Colonialism: The Emergence of Ethnicity among the Tsonga-Speakers of South Africa', in L. Vail. Ed. *The Creation of Tribalism in Southern Africa*. Los Angeles: University of California Press, 85–87. For a classic study of the evangelical project in southern Africa, see J. Comaroff and J. Comaroff. 1991. *Of Revelation and Revolution: Christianity, Colonialism and Consciousness in South Africa*. Chicago: University of Chicago Press.

14. Harries, *Butterflies and Barbarians*, 113.

15. Harries, *Butterflies and Barbarians*, 164.

16. For a detailed treatment of the language work of Henri-Alexandre Junod and Swiss missionaries among the Tsonga, see Harries, *Butterflies and Barbarians* and 'Field Sciences'.

17. Pugach, *Africa in Translation*, 22–26.

18. Pugach, *Africa in Translation*, 37.

19. Pugach, *Africa in Translation*, 29–33.

20. Pugach, *Africa in Translation*, Chapter 1.

21. On increasing objectification in the practice of *Ethnologie*, see A. Zimmerman. 2001. *Anthropology and Anti-humanism in Imperial Germany*. Chicago and London: University of Chicago Press. Zimmerman argues that classical German humanist philosophies of the late nineteenth century were overtaken by the rise of a narrowly scientific, object-focused, anti-humanist approach that came to dominate German cultural studies in the ensuing decades. See also A. Zimmerman. 2001. 'Looking Beyond History: The Optics of German Anthropology and the Critique of Humanism'. *Studies in History and Philosophy of Biological and Biomedical Sciences* 32 (3), 385–411.

22. Pugach, *Africa in Translation*, 3–5.

23. Pugach, *Africa in Translation*, 191.

24. Pugach, *Africa in Translation*, 172–185. For more on the involvement of South African anthropologists and academic institutions in addressing the 'native question', see S. Dubow. 2006. *A Commonwealth of Knowledge: Science, Sensibility and White South Africa 1820–2000*. Oxford: Oxford University Press; D. Hammond-Tooke. 2001. *Imperfect Interpreters: South Africa's Anthropologists 1920–1990*. Johannesburg: Wits University Press.

25. Pugach, *Africa in Translation*, 191.

26. D. Jeater. 1995. 'The Fruits of the Tree of Knowledge: Power versus Pollution in Official Attitudes towards African Vernaculars in Southern Rhodesia, 1890–1993'. Seminar paper, Wits Institute for Advanced Social Research; D. Jeater. 1994. 'The Way You Tell Them: Language, Ideology and Development Policy in Southern Rhodesia'. Paper presented at the Journal of Southern African Studies Conference on 'Paradigms Lost, Paradigms Regained? Southern African Studies in the 1990s'.

27. Jeater, 'The Way You Tell Them'.

28. Jeater, 'The Way You Tell Them'. Emphasis in original.

29. Jeater, 'The Way You Tell Them'.

30. My use of the term 'anti-humanist' follows Zimmerman, *Anthropology and Anti-humanism*, 1–11.

31. M. Beard. 2000. *The Invention of Jane Harrison*. Cambridge, MA: Harvard University Press, 123–124.

32. For location on Google Maps, see http://www.maplandia.com/botswana/southern-region/ngwaketse-west/kakia/ (accessed 22 July 2010).

33. BC 151, A3.6.

34. BC 151, A3.7, A3.8.

35. D. Bleek. 1929. *Comparative Vocabularies of Bushman Languages*. London: Cambridge University Press, 2.

36. BC 151, A3.6.

37. Bleek, *Comparative Vocabularies*, 2.

38. BC 151, A3.6, entry for 23 June.

39. BC 151, A3.6, entries for 5, 7, 8, 21 July for presents; 30 June and 1 July for purchases.

40. P. Carstens, G. Klinghardt and M. West. 1987. *Trails in the Thirstland: The Anthropological Field Diaries of Winifred Hoernlé*. Cape Town: Centre for African Studies.

41. A. Tucker. 1913. 'Richtersveld: The Land and Its People'. Public lecture delivered in Johannesburg.

42. See W. Mitchell. 1994. 'Imperial Landscape', in W. Mitchell. Ed. *Landscape and Power*. Chicago: University of Chicago Press, 4–34. See also Dorothea's diary entries for 23, 27 June and 6 July; BC 151, A3.6. For a feminist perspective on representations of landscape in travel writing and in the writings of women travellers, see A. Blunt. 1994. *Travel, Gender and Imperialism: Mary Kingsley and West Africa*. New York and London: Guilford Press.

43. M. Pratt. 1992. *Imperial Eyes: Travel Writing and Transculturation*. London: Routledge, 76; Blunt, *Travel, Gender and Imperialism*.

44. See album at BC 151, J2.1: No. 250–300. All the images in this album are available online at http://www.lib.uct.ac.za/mss/existing/DBleekXML/website/ (accessed 28 January 2009).

45. BC 151, A3.6, 31 July.

46. For the potential of photography for broadening simplified interpretations of colonial histories, see E. Edwards. 2001. *Raw Histories: Photographs, Anthropology and Museums*. Oxford: Berg. On visual history more generally, see P. Hayes and A. Bank. Eds. 2001. 'Judging Books by Their Covers'. *Kronos* 27, Visual History Special Issue, 1–14.

47. BC 151, A3.6, 26 June.

48. BC 151, A3.6, 29 June, 30 June, 1 July.

49. BC 151, A3.6, 5 July, has Ompilletsi translating from a Masarwa woman 'who could speak her language'. On 10 July, Dorothea 'got Ompilletsi to translate and took down words & sentences especially pro-nouns' from a 'group of Masarwa' who came to the wagon. Two days before their return to Khanye, on 30 July, Dorothea spent a '[q]uick morning getting Masarwa with Ompilletsi translating'. For his father's cattle post, see 28 July.

50. BC 151, A3.6.

51. BC 151, A3.6, diary entry 23 June. For Vollmer's activities, see entries for 26, 30 June and 18, 20 July. For her cold, see 12, 14 July.

52. BC 151, A3.6, diary entry 29 June. For lists of photographs taken and curios purchased, see 70–79. For list of body measurements, see 86.

53. BC 151, A3.6, diary entries 24, 29 June; 10, 14, 24, 30 July.

54. See Carstens, Klinghardt and West, *Trails*, for instances in Winifred Hoernlé's diary, which also includes references to taking walks beyond or behind the wagon, or, in Hoernlé's case, climbing surrounding hills.

55. Both Wilhelm Bleek's 'pepper pot' pistol and Jemima Lloyd's 'little hand gun' are in the collection of Andrew Roos (Patricia Scott Deetz, personal communication, 9 July 2010). According to Deetz, the family guns were kept in a locked deed box in a safe at their lawyer's office. It is likely the gun that Dorothea took to Angola was in this collection, but was later mistakenly destroyed by British customs officials when the guns were taken to England to be inherited by one of Deetz's nephews.

56. Patricia Scott Deetz, personal communication, 26 July 2010.

57. BC 151, A3.6, 4 July.

58. BC 151, A3.6, 2 July.

59. BC 151, A3.6, diary entries for 25 and 27 June mentioned 'McIntyre's wagons'. Other passing wagons mentioned on 27 June and 5 July. At Kakia they outspanned alongside McIntyre, presumably a man travelling alone, and later shifted their camp to 'his tree' when he moved on: see entries for 12, 15, 19 July: 'McIntyre turned up in evening had supper'; and 20 July, when McIntyre 'breakfasted & dined with us & helped translate. Good man.' And the Openshaw family camped nearby: 13 and 15 July: 'Elder Openshaw will try to photograph men naked'; 16, 17 July: 'Openshaws came to supper'; 18 July: 'Mr Openshaw photographed two men'.

60. Péringuey cited in A. Coombes. 2004. *History After Apartheid: Visual Culture and Public Memory in a Democratic South Africa*. Johannesburg: Wits University Press, 216–220. See also C. Rassool. 2015. 'Re-storing the Skeletons of Empire: Return, Reburial and Rehumanisation in Southern Africa'. *Journal of Southern African Studies* 41 (3), 659–660. The French-born Péringuey (1855–1924) trained as an entomologist specialising in Coleoptera. He became director of the South African Museum in 1906.

61. Coombes, *History After Apartheid*, 219.

62. For a history of the South African Museum's attempts to highlight the invasive practice of life casting and to deconstruct the diorama's portrayal of bushmen as pristine hunter-gatherers inhabiting a timeless rural past, see Coombes, *History After Apartheid*, 219–230. See also P. Davison. 2001. 'Typecast – Representations of the Bushmen at the South African Museum'. *Public Archaeology* 1, 3–20.

63. BC 151, A3.8, 172.

64. For a detailed account of Wilhelm Bleek's faltering interactions with his earliest interlocutors, see Bank, *Bushmen in a Victorian World*, Chapter 3; A. Bank. 2002. 'From Pictures to Performance: Early Learning at the Hill'. *Kronos* 28, 66–101.
65. BC 151, A3.8, 161.
66. BC 151, A3.8, 177, 179, 181, 183.
67. BC 151, A3.6, 86.
68. BC 151, A3.6.
69. BC 151, A3.6, 86.
70. BC 151, A3.6, 3 July.
71. BC 151, A3.8, 240.
72. BC 151, A3.8, 219–220.
73. In this instance, Dorothea's notes have the open-ended quality of inscription, rather than the objective and controlled mode of transcription. See the discussion around modes of writing in the field in J. Clifford. 1990. 'Notes on Field(notes)', in R. Sanjek. Ed. *Fieldnotes: The Makings of Anthropology*. Ithaca, NY: Cornell University Press, 47–70.
74. N. Chaudhuri and M. Strobel. Eds. 1992. *Western Women and Imperialism: Complicity and Resistance*. Bloomington and Indianapolis: Indiana University Press. For an analysis of the effect of gender in travellers' perceptions and writings about foreign landscapes, see S. Blake. 1992. 'A Woman's Trek: What Difference Does Gender Make?', in Chaudhuri and Strobel, *Western Women and Imperialism*, 19–34.
75. See contributions in P. Romero. Ed. 1992. *Women's Voices on Africa: A Century of Travel Writings*. Princeton, NJ, and New York: Markus Wiener. Compare with contemporaneous travel writing on Africa written from an intellectual perspective, as in M. Perham. 1974. *African Apprenticeship*. New York: Homes & Meier. For an examination of Canadian women's travel writing and its progression in style through decades of colonialism, see C. Cavanaugh and R. Warne. 2000. Eds. *Telling Tales: Essays in Western Women's History*. Vancouver and Toronto: UBC Press. For a systematic examination of the gendered nature of women's travel writing, see Blunt, *Travel, Gender and Imperialism*. For a contrasting mode of travel writing highlighting passion and exuberance, see M. Fountaine. 1980. *Love among the Butterflies: The Travels and Adventures of a Victorian Lady*. Boston: Little, Brown.

76. Glenn Penny, 'Traditions', 86–89, argues that Adolf Bastian was a leading proponent of fieldwork that remained an essential feature of German ethnology until the early twentieth century. For more on fieldwork traditions in Britain and America, and the early twentieth-century expeditions of Malinowski and Boas in particular, see G. Stocking. 1992. *The Ethnographer's Magic and Other Essays in the History of Anthropology*. Madison: University of Wisconsin Press.

77. But contemporary language study now described as sociolinguistics recognises the 'fluid, multilingual nature of communication', and the 'essentially dynamic nature of language use in any society'. See R. Mesthrie. 2002. 'South Africa: A Sociolinguistic Overview', in R. Mesthrie. Ed. *Language in South Africa*. Cambridge: Cambridge University Press, 11–26.

78. These methods were typical of the research practice employed by early anthropologists as well as linguists working at the time. See, for example, I. Schapera. 1926. 'A Preliminary Consideration of the Relationship between the Hottentots and the Bushmen'. *South African Journal of Science* 23, 833–866; C. Doke. 1933. 'Preliminary Investigation into Native Languages'. *Bantu Studies* 7; G. Lestrade. 1934. 'European Influences upon the Development of Bantu Language and Literature', in I. Schapera. Ed. *Western Civilisation and the Natives of South Africa*. London: Routledge, 105–127.

Chapter 4

1. Bleek Collection, University of Cape Town Libraries, Manuscripts and Archives Department, hereafter BC 151, A3.13, 57–58.

2. D. Bleek. 1928. *The Naron: A Bushman Tribe of the Central Kalahari*. London: Cambridge University Press, 1.

3. Bleek, *Naron*, 1.

4. For a larger discussion on this point, see S. Pugach. 2012. *Africa in Translation: A History of Colonial Linguistics in Germany and Beyond, 1814–1945*. Ann Arbor: University of Michigan Press.

5. A. Coombes. 2004. *History After Apartheid: Visual Culture and Public Memory in a Democratic South Africa*. Johannesburg: Wits University Press, 216.

6. Coombes, *History After Apartheid*, 215–217.

7. E. Edwards. 1997. 'Making Histories: The Torres Strait Expedition of 1898'. *Pacific Studies* 20 (4), 14.

8. G. Stocking. 1992. *The Ethnographer's Magic and Other Essays in the History of Anthropology*. Madison: University of Wisconsin Press, 12–59.

9. For a detailed reading of Monica Hunter's fieldwork in Pondoland, see A. Bank. 2008. 'The "Intimate Politics" of Fieldwork: Monica Hunter and Her African Assistants, Pondoland and the Eastern Cape, 1931–1932'. *Journal of Southern African Studies* 34 (3), 557–574.

10. For a thorough investigation of Monica Wilson's career and scholarship, her place in the 'unofficial' history of southern and central African anthropology, and her collaborations with research assistants and students, see A. Bank and L. Bank. Eds. 2013. *Inside African Anthropology: Monica Wilson and Her Interpreters*. Cambridge: Cambridge University Press.

11. Bleek to Woldmann, 5 April 1929. Käthe Woldmann Papers, University of Cape Town Libraries, Manuscripts and Archives Department, hereafter BC 210, Box 4.

12. BC 151, A3.12.

13. Bleek to Péringuey, 25 November 1920. Iziko South African Museum correspondence, hereafter SAM, B 60.

14. Bleek to Péringuey, 25 November 1920.

15. Bleek, *The Naron*, 1.

16. Bleek to Péringuey, 6 December 1920. SAM, B 60.

17. Bleek to Péringuey, 6 December 1920.

18. BC 151, A3.6, entry for 15 July.

19. Bleek to Péringuey, 22 November 1920. SAM, B 60. Emphasis added.

20. Recent scholarship in the history of anthropology exhibits a reliance on biography as context for studies examining histories of thought and scholarship both past and present. See, in particular, Stocking, *Ethnographer's Magic*. For a personalised account of the intertwining of biography and scholarship, see H. Kuper. 1984. 'Function, History, Biography: Reflections on Fifty Years in the British Anthropological Tradition', in G. Stocking. Ed. *Functionalism Historicised: Essays on British Social Anthropology*. Madison: University of Wisconsin Press, 192–213.

21. For an extended history of South West Africa and the German presence there, see G. Steinmetz. 2007. *The Devil's Handwriting: Precoloniality and the German Colonial State in Qingdao, Samoa, and Southwest Africa*. Chicago: University of Chicago Press.

22. For a description of networks of trade and cooperation among !Kung and others in the Kalahari region that draws on Dorothea's *Naron* monograph, see R. Gordon. 1984. 'The !Kung in the Kalahari Exchange: An Ethnohistorical Perspective', in C. Schrire. Ed. *Past and Present in Hunter Gatherer Studies.* London: Academic Press, 195–224; J. Denbow. 1984. 'Prehistoric Herders and Foragers of the Kalahari: The Evidence for 1500 Years of Interaction', 175–193, in the same volume.

23. BC 151, A3.12, 4–5, for vocabulary related to men curing skins and making and wearing '*veldschoen*' while 'women look for the *veldkos* & bring the water', and for vocabulary related to forms of *veldkos* – 'something like a pumpkin', ant eggs, locusts, oinkies, tortoises, fruit from a 'big tree' – and for phrases relating to living shelters, the making of fires, food and cooking, and clothing.

24. BC 151, A3.12, 53.

25. For Dia!kwain's stories related to childhood interactions with newcomers to his territory, see A. Bank. 2006. *Bushmen in a Victorian World: The Remarkable Story of the Bleek-Lloyd Collection of Bushman Folklore.* Cape Town: Double Storey, 269–275.

26. For reference to Vedder, see D. Bleek. 1929. *Comparative Vocabularies of Bushman Languages.* London: Cambridge University Press; Bleek to Woldmann, 26 November 1928 and 28 July 1930. BC 210, Box 4. In both cases the reference is to Vedder's grammatical sketch and small vocabulary of !Kū published in 1911 in the journal *Zeitschrift fur Kolonialsprachen* 1 (1).

27. For Stow (*Native Races*, 49, 70, 108, 208 and 230), see BC 151, A3.10, 07; A3.12, 13, 16, 17. For references to *Specimens* (352), see BC 151, A3.10, 010; A3.13, 65.

28. For Passarge, see BC 151, A3.12, 20; A3.13, 74; A3.16, 142, 143 (Sandfontein); A3.22, 113 (Angola).

29. BC 151, E5.1.47 to E5.1.49 and D3.24.

30. BC 151, D3.24.

31. Bleek to Woldmann, 26 December 1930. BC 210, Box 4.

32. Bleek to Woldmann, 26 December 1930.

33. It is suggested that Sandfontein could be /Noixas, located south of today's Kalkfontein in western Ghanzi, Botswana. See M. Guenther. 1996. 'From "Lords of the Desert" to "Rubbish People": The Colonial and Contemporary State of the Nharo of Botswana', in P. Skotnes. Ed. *Miscast: Negotiating the Presence of the Bushmen.* Cape Town: UCT Press, 323.

34. Bleek, *The Naron*, 1.

35. Bleek, *The Naron*, 3.

36. E. Edwards. 2001. *Raw Histories: Photographs, Anthropology and Museums*. Oxford: Berg; Bank, *Bushmen in a Victorian World*, Chapter 4; M. Godby. 1996. 'Images of //Kabbo', in Skotnes, *Miscast*, 115–128; and C. Webster. 2000. 'The Portrait Cabinet of Dr Bleek: Anthropometric Photographs by Early Cape Photographers'. *Critical Arts* 14 (1), 1–14.

37. L. Hart. 2002. The San (Bushman) Photographs of Dorothea Bleek: The Complete 312 Images. BC 151. Available online at http://www.lib.uct.ac.za/manuscriptsarchives/resources/digital-resources/the-san-photographs-of-dorothea-bleek/ (accessed 12 June 2014).

38. The two photographs illustrating Dorothea's *Naron* monograph were taken by James Drury.

39. A. Bank. 2006. 'Anthropology and Fieldwork Photography: Dorothea Bleek's Expedition to the Northern Cape and the Kalahari, July to December 1911'. *Kronos* 32, 77–113.

40. Bank, 'Anthropology and Fieldwork Photography'. For detail on Wilhelm Bleek's involvement in Huxley's project, see Edwards, *Raw Histories*, Chapter 6.

41. Bleek to Kirby, 7 May 1936; Bleek to Kirby, 17 May 1936. Percival Kirby Papers, University of Cape Town Libraries, Manuscripts and Archives Department, hereafter BC 750, Correspondence A; BC 151, E5.1.17 to E5.1.21.

42. BC 151, E5.1.18, 70.

43. Bleek to Woldmann, 28 July 1930.

44. Bleek to Kirby, 22 April 1935. BC 750, Correspondence A.

45. SA Museum Director (Gill) to Bleek, 18 April 1936. SAM, B 23.

46. These displays are in what is problematically referred to as the museum's 'Ethno-Wing'. See L. Witz. 2006. 'Transforming Museums on Postapartheid Tourist Routes', in I. Karp, C. Kratz, L. Szwaja and T. Ybarra-Frausto. Eds. *Museum Frictions: Public Cultures/Global Transformations*. Durham, NC: Duke University Press, 115–123.

47. Bleek to Wilman, 14 March 1921. Maria Wilman Collection, McGregor Museum (hereafter MMKD) 2591/6.

48. Bleek to Wilman, 6 May 1921. MMKD 2591/3.

49. Bleek to Wilman, 6 May 1921.

50. Bleek to Wilman, 6 May 1921.

51. Bleek, *Comparative Vocabularies*, 2.

52. Bleek to Wilman, 17 April [no year but likely 1921]. MMKD 2591/2.
53. Bleek, *The Naron*, 2.
54. Bleek, *The Naron*, 2.
55. BC 151, E5.1.3.
56. BC 151, D3.5, D3.5.1, E5.1.3. Dorothea's formulation of bushman languages into Southern, Central and Northern groups remains at the base of contemporary linguistic analyses and delineations of southern African Khoesan languages. See R. Vossen. Ed. 2013. *The Khoesan Languages*. Oxford: Routledge, 3. But, for a critique of linguistics scholarship that proceeds on the basis of 'pre-theoretical assumptions of ancientness' and of language divergence premised on perceptions of physiological and cultural difference, see M. du Plessis. 2014. 'The Damaging Effects of Romantic Mythopoeia on Khoesan Linguistics'. *Critical Arts* 28 (3), 569–592.
57. UCT's Vacation School was an extramural programme aimed at public education. It continues as the university's annual Summer School.
58. D. Bleek. 1928. 'Bushmen of Central Angola'. *Bantu Studies* 3 (2), 105–125.
59. Bleek, 'Central Angola'. She published a version of this paper in German in *Archives for Anthropology* 21 (1/2).
60. Pocock applied to join Dorothea on the journey (Patricia Scott Deetz, personal communication). She was a botanist lecturing at Rhodes University at the time and later became a worldwide authority on algae.
61. *Oudtshoorn Courant*, 8 June 1925; 10 June 1925; 17 July 1925. *Cape Times*, 5 December 1925; 19 December 1925. 'Museum gets diary of walk across Africa'. *Eastern Province Herald*, January 1926 (n.d.). Clippings in the collection of Patricia Scott Deetz.
62. For a photograph of a *machila*, see M. Cushman. 1944. *Missionary Doctor: The Story of Twenty Years in Africa*. New York: Harper, 152–153; K. Schestokat. 2003. *German Women in Cameroon: Travelogues from Colonial Times*. New York: Peter Lang, 108.
63. J. Fabian. 2000. *Out of Our Minds: Reason and Madness in the Exploration of Central Africa*. Berkley: University of California Press, Chapters 5 and 7.
64. See M. Pocock, *Cape Times*, 19 December 1925: 'Sometimes when the natives refuse to sell for either money or salt, a piece of calico will purchase all that is needed. At the present time…even the commonest of print is so expensive in this part of Angola – a yard costing as much as 20 days' wages – that it is practically never seen except at the mission stations or trading posts.'

65. See 'Museum gets diary'. Pocock presented her diary to the Albany Museum in Grahamstown, but it is now missing. Patricia Scott Deetz, personal communication, June 2010.

66. Bleek, 'Central Angola', 125.

67. For a first-hand account of missionary work in central Angola in the 1920s, see Cushman, *Missionary Doctor*. For more on the presence of missionaries and women in Africa during the early decades of the twentieth century, see Schestokat, *German Women in Cameroon*.

68. Bleek, 'Central Angola', 105.

69. Bleek, 'Central Angola', 109.

70. Bleek to Woldmann, 26 December 1930.

71. Bleek, 'Central Angola', table of measurements, 106. Many of her notebooks contain tables of measurements – for example, A3.22, 1–5. For use of physical attributes in relation to southern African people in other scholarship being produced at the time, see I. Schapera. 1930. *The Khoisan Peoples of South Africa*. London: Routledge & Keegan Paul, 51–59, that draws on Dorothea's Angola research.

72. For the history of anthropometry and physical 'science' in South Africa, see S. Dubow. 1995. *Illicit Union: Scientific Racism in Modern South Africa*. Johannesburg: Wits University Press. For an argument suggesting that the physical attributes associated with the term 'bushman' result from their marginal economic status and structural underdevelopment, see E. Wilmsen. 1989. *Land Filled with Flies: A Political Economy of the Kalahari*. Chicago: University of Chicago Press; also R. Gordon and S. Sholto Douglas. 2000. *The Bushman Myth: The Making of a Namibian Underclass*. Boulder, CO: Westview Press. The authors consider the role of anthropology in producing particular physical stereotypes. Physical anthropology at South African universities, and directed at 'bushmen' in particular, continued into the 1950s. For a provocative discussion of the Wits Kalahari 'Research Laboratory' and its role in making 'bushman' a separate field of study in the South African academy, see C. Rassool and P. Hayes. 2002. 'Science and the Spectacle: //Khanako's South Africa, 1936–1937', in W. Woodward, P. Hayes and G. Minkley. Eds. *Deep hiStories: Gender and Colonialism in Southern Africa*. New York: Rodopi.

73. See, for example, Bleek, 'Central Angola', 106–107; D. Bleek. 1931. 'The Hadzapi or Watindega of Tanganyika Territory'. *Africa* 4 (3), 274; Bleek, *Comparative*

Vocabularies, 6–7, where Dorothea makes the association between language and race in relation to skin colour, dialect and physical features: 'infantile limbs are peculiar to all', profile, jaw and mouth, cheekbones, noses.

74. But see R. Herbert. 2002. 'The Socio-history of Clicks in Southern Bantu', in R. Mesthrie. Ed. *Language in South Africa*. Cambridge: Cambridge University Press, 297–315, for a discussion about the polyvalent and varied social forces that are at work in language evolution.

75. Bleek, 'Central Angola', 125.

76. In 1933 Dorothea wrote that she had not organised a 'scientific expedition' that year as she was 'too old'. See Bleek to Woldmann, 29 December 1933. BC 210, Box 4.

77. Her final fieldwork excursion was to the Wits Field School at Frankenwald in 1936. See notebooks BC 151, A3.29, A3.30 and A3.32.

78. BC 151, A3.27 and A3.28 (these notebooks include many blank pages); E5.1.16; J2.1 (photographs).

79. Bleek to Kirby, 20 July 1931. BC 750, Correspondence A.

80. Bleek to Woldmann, 22 January 1930; also 28 July 1930 and 9 April 1931. BC 210, Box 4.

81. Bleek to Woldmann, 22 January 1930. The name 'Sandawe' remains in use to reference people of central Tanzania who continue to speak a 'click' language.

82. P. Romero. 1992. *Women's Voices on Africa: A Century of Travel Writings*. Princeton, NJ: Princeton University Press, 105–122.

83. Bleek, 'Hadzapi'.

84. Bleek, 'Hadzapi', 274.

85. For more on Wilhelm Bleek's opinions on skin colour, see A. Bank. 2000. 'Evolution and Racial Theory: The Hidden Side of Wilhelm Bleek'. *South African Historical Journal* 43, 163–178.

86. M. Finkel. 2009. 'The Hadza'. *National Geographic* 216 (6), 94, 104.

87. For this information, she cites J.F. Bagshawe. 1925. 'The Peoples of the Happy Valley, Part II'. *Journal of the Royal African Society* 24, 117–130.

88. Bleek, 'Hadzapi', 276.

89. Bleek, 'Hadzapi', 278–280.

90. Bleek, 'Hadzapi', 280.

91. For an elaboration of South African academic and state-aligned research institutions emerging during the opening decades of the twentieth century,

see S. Dubow. 2006. *A Commonwealth of Knowledge: Science, Sensibility and White South Africa 1820–2000*. Oxford: Oxford University Press.

92. D. Hammond-Tooke, 1997. *Imperfect Interpreters: South Africa's Anthropologists 1920–1990*. Johannesburg: Wits University Press; A. Kuper, 1999. 'South African Anthropology: An Inside Job', in *Among the Anthropologists: History and Context in Anthropology*. London: Athlone Press, 45–70.

93. Schapera, *Khoisan Peoples*.

94. Schapera, *Khoisan Peoples*, Introductory Note.

95. Bleek to Woldmann, 5 March 1929. BC 210, Box 4.

96. The identity of early groups at the Cape remains a matter of debate among historians, archaeologists and linguists played out in arguments over use of the terms 'Khoi' and 'San', a revised focus on the pastoralist Khoekhoe and Iron Age farmers, and in scholarship around the peopling of southern Africa more widely. For an opening salvo in the debate, see R. Elphick. 1985. *Khoikhoi and the Founding of White South Africa*. Johannesburg: Ravan Press; R. Thornton 1983. 'Narrative Ethnography in Africa, 1850–1920: The Creation and Capture of an Appropriate Domain for Anthropology'. *Man* 18 (3), 502–520. For contemporary rehearsals, see P. Jolly. 1996. 'Between the Lines: Some Remarks on "Bushman" Ethnicity', 197–209; and C. Schrire. 1996. 'Native Views of Western Eyes', 343–353, both in Skotnes, *Miscast*; J. Parkington. 2007. '//Kabbo's Sentence', in P. Skotnes. *Claim to the Country: The Archive of Wilhelm Bleek and Lucy Lloyd*. Cape Town and Athens, OH: Jacana and Ohio University Press, 75–89. See also K. Sadr. 2008. 'Invisible Herders? The Archaeology of Khoekhoe Pastoralists'. *Southern African Humanities* 20, 179–203; B. Heine and C. König. 2008. 'What Can Linguistics Tell Us about Early Khoekhoe History?' *Southern African Humanities* 20, 235–248; K. Sadr and F. Fauvelle-Aymar. Eds. 2008. 'Khoekhoe and the Origins of Herding in Southern Africa'. *Southern African Humanities* 20 (1), 93–132; and other contributions to the special issue. See also contributions to N. Swanepoel, A. Esterhuysen and P. Bonner. Eds. 2008. *Five Hundred Years Rediscovered: Southern African Precedents and Prospects*. Johannesburg: Wits University Press.

Chapter 5

1. D. Bleek. 1932. 'A Survey of Our Present Knowledge of Rockpaintings in South Africa'. *South African Journal of Science* 29, 77.

2. Bleek to Woldmann, 26 November 1928. Käthe Woldmann Papers, University of Cape Town Libraries, Manuscripts and Archives Department, hereafter BC 210, Box 4.

3. G. Stow and D. Bleek. Ed. 1930. *Rock Paintings in South Africa from Parts of the Eastern Province and Orange Free State.* London: Methuen, vii.

4. D. Bleek. 1921/1927/1938? 'The Probable Age of Bushman Paintings in the Union of South Africa'. Corrected typescript. BC 151, D3.19.

5. BC 151, D3.4.1.

6. BC 151, D3.4.1, D3.4.2 and D3.4.3.

7. Bleek to Woldmann, 6 June 1928 (Winburg, O.F.S). BC 210, Box 4. For the charcoal rubbings found and copied near Sandfontein, see D. Bleek. 1928. *The Naron: A Bushman Tribe of the Central Kalahari.* London: Cambridge University Press, 41, where she describes the site at BabiBabi 'about half an hour's walk from Mr van der Spuy's house'. The reproductions are in the collection of the Iziko South African Museum.

8. Lucy Lloyd to Fanny Stow, 2 June 1882. For correspondence related to Lucy's undertaking and correspondence with Fanny Stow, see K. Schoeman. Ed. 1997. *A Debt of Gratitude: Lucy Lloyd and the 'Bushman Work' of G.W. Stow.* Cape Town: South African Library, 108–120.

9. Stow and Bleek, *Rock Paintings in South Africa.* The Carnegie Trust funded the publication.

10. For a detailed review of the accuracy of the copying methods employed by Stow and Bleek, see T. Dowson, S. Ouzman, G. Blundell and A. Holliday. 1994. 'A Stow Site Revisited: Zastron District, Orange Free State', in T. Dowson and J.D. Lewis-Williams. Eds. *Contested Images: Diversity in Southern African Rock Art Research.* Johannesburg: Wits University Press, 177–188.

11. For more on intellectual trends in prehistory, see S. Dubow. 1996. 'Human Origins, Race Typology and the Other Raymond Dart'. *African Studies* 55 (1), 1–30; and R. Derricourt. 2011. *Inventing Africa: History, Archaeology and Ideas.* London: Pluto Press. On foreign authorship, see S. Impey. 1926. *Origin of the Bushmen and the Rock Paintings of South Africa.* Johannesburg: Juta. See discussion on Impey in M. Burkitt. 1928. *South Africa's Past in Stone and Paint.* Cambridge: Cambridge University Press, 126–130. For a positioning of southern African rock art in relation to the art of southern Europe, see I. Schapera. 1925. 'Some Stylistic Affinities of Bushman Art'. *South African Journal of Science* 22, 504–515.

12. Stow and Bleek, *Rock Paintings in South Africa*, xi.

13. D. Bleek. 1929. 'Bushman Folklore'. *Africa* 2 (3), 302–313.

14. Stow and Bleek, *Rock Paintings in South Africa*, xi.

15. Bleek, 'Bushman Folklore', 302.

16. Bleek, 'Bushman Folklore', 305.

17. Stow and Bleek, *Rock Paintings in South Africa*, xxv.

18. Stow and Bleek, *Rock Paintings in South Africa*, xxv; BC 151, D3.19; Bleek, 'Survey', 77.

19. Dorothea's view on the connection between leisure time and art production has been supported by the folklorist Mathias Guenther, who argues that the 'simplicity of the techno-economic domain' of 'bushman' society fostered the rich, dynamic and complex nature of its expressive cultures. See M. Guenther. 1994. 'The Relationship of Bushman Art to Ritual and Folklore', in Dowson and Lewis-Williams, *Contested Images*, 257–273.

20. Stow and Bleek, *Rock Paintings in South Africa*, xxiv–xxv.

21. Bleek, 'Probable Age'. For further discussion of dating, see Burkitt, *South Africa's Past*, and Schapera, 'Some Stylistic Affinities'.

22. Bleek, 'Probable Age'.

23. Stow and Bleek, *Rock Paintings in South Africa*, xi.

24. Stow and Bleek, *Rock Paintings in South Africa*, xii–xiii.

25. Stow and Bleek, *Rock Paintings in South Africa*, xx.

26. Burkitt, *South Africa's Past*, Chapter 7; Bleek, 'Survey', 79–80.

27. Burkitt, *South Africa's Past*, 110–115.

28. Burkitt, *South Africa's Past*, 111.

29. Burkitt, *South Africa's Past*, 111.

30. Burkitt, *South Africa's Past*, 43; A. York Mason. 1933. 'Rock Paintings in the Cathkin Peak Area, Natal'. *Bantu Studies* 7, 131–159.

31. Balfour, 1909. 'Preface', in H. Tongue. *Bushman Paintings*. Oxford: Clarendon Press; W. Battiss. 1939. *The Amazing Bushman*. Pretoria: Red Fern Press; W. Battiss. 1952. *Bushman Art*. Pretoria: Red Fern Press.

32. Stow and Bleek, *Rock Paintings in South Africa*, xix.

33. Stow and Bleek, *Rock Paintings in South Africa*, xvii–xviii. But see A. Bank. 2006. *Bushmen in a Victorian World: The Remarkable Story of the Bleek-Lloyd Collection of Bushman Folklore*. Cape Town: Double Storey, Chapter 12.

34. BC 151, D3.6, 3. The *Cape Times* article contained a response to Professor E.L.

Schwarz's earlier article calling for a clearer definition of the term 'bushman'. For a scholarly engagement with Schwarz, see I. Schapera. 1927. 'The Tribal Divisions of the Bushmen'. *Man* 27, 68–73, where Schapera drew on Dorothea's North, South and Central language classification to make his arguments.

35. From a substantial literature on chronology and dating, see J. Loubser. 2010. 'Layer by Layer: Precision and Accuracy in Rock Art Recording and Dating', in G. Blundell, C. Chippindale and B. Smith. Eds. *Seeing and Knowing: Understanding Rock Art With and Without Ethnography*. Johannesburg: Wits University Press, 149–165; A. Mazel. 2009. 'Unsettled Times: Shaded Polychrome Paintings and Hunter-Gatherer History in the Southeastern Mountains of Southern Africa'. *Southern African Humanities* 21, 85–115; P. Mitchell. 2009. 'Hunter-Gatherers and Farmers: Some Implications of 1,800 Years of Interaction in the Maloti-Drakensberg Region of Southern Africa'. *Senri Ethnological Studies* 73, 15–46.

36. Stow and Bleek, *Rock Paintings in South Africa*, xiv.

37. Stow and Bleek, *Rock Paintings in South Africa*, xiv–xv.

38. Stow and Bleek, *Rock Paintings in South Africa*, xiv–xv.

39. Stow and Bleek, *Rock Paintings in South Africa*, xx.

40. Stow and Bleek, *Rock Paintings in South Africa*, xxi.

41. Stow and Bleek, *Rock Paintings in South Africa*, xxi.

42. For more on //Kabbo's ancestral lands, see J. Deacon. 1986. ' "My Place is the Bitterpits"; The Home Territory of Bleek and Lloyd's /Xam San Informants'. *African Studies* 45, 135–155, which describes the defined sense of territory that the Bleek-Lloyd interlocutors expressed about their homes, particularly in the case of //Kabbo.

43. Stow and Bleek, *Rock Paintings in South Africa*, xviii.

44. Stow and Bleek, *Rock Paintings in South Africa*, xvii.

45. Stow and Bleek, *Rock Paintings in South Africa*, xxvi–xxvii.

46. Explanations recorded by Stow to accompany his paintings are available in P. Skotnes. 2008. *Unconquerable Spirit: George Stow's History Paintings of the San*. Johannesburg: Jacana.

47. Bleek to Woldmann, 6 June 1928.

48. Bleek to Woldmann, 6 June 1928.

49. Bleek, 'Survey', 78; M. van der Riet, J. van der Riet and D. Bleek. 1940. *More Rock-Paintings in South Africa*. London: Methuen, vii.

50. Stow and Bleek, *Rock Paintings in South Africa*, xxviii; Bleek to Woldmann, 6 June 1928.

51. Stow and Bleek, *Rock Paintings in South Africa*, xxvii–xxviii.

52. Stow and Bleek, *Rock Paintings in South Africa*, Plates 61, 62. See P. Mitchell. 2010. 'Review of *Vols de Vaches à Christol Cave: Histoire Critique d'une Image Rupestre d'Afrique du Sud'. Africa* 80 (4), 664–666, for interrogation on the panel removal from Christol Cave. For a provocative discussion on rock art conservation and the removal of panels, see S. Ouzman. 2006. 'Why "Conserve"? Situating Southern African Rock Art in the Here and Now', in N. Agnew and J. Bridgeland. Eds. *Of the Past, for the Future: Integrating Archaeology and Conservation*. Los Angeles: Getty Institute, 346–352.

53. Stow and Bleek, *Rock Paintings in South Africa*, 57.

54. BC 151, A3.26, 14 pages from front. Stow and Bleek, *Rock Paintings in South Africa*, Plate 9.

55. BC 151, A3.26, 15 pages from front.

56. Iziko South African Museum Precolonial Correspondence. See also P. Vinnicombe. 1976. *People of the Eland: Rock Paintings of the Drakensberg Bushmen as a Reflection of Their Life and Thought*. Pietermaritzburg: University of Natal Press.

57. The Linton panel was removed in 1917 from Linton Farm in the Maclear district of the eastern Cape by Mr G.S.T. Mandy of the Provincial Roads Department to make way for road construction. One of the painted figures from the panel has been adapted for use in the new South African coat of arms. Also on display in the /Qe exhibition is the Zaamenkomst panel, which was removed from Cala near the town of Elliot in the eastern Cape.

58. Stow and Bleek, *Rock Paintings in South Africa*, xxviii.

59. Bleek to Woldmann, 6 June 1928.

60. BC 151, A3.24–A3.26. Other documents relating to rock art include lecture notes, typescripts, picture captions and lists of descriptions of sites, as well as correspondence dealing with the publishing of the two books. See, for example, BC 151, C17, C18, D3, and E5.1.22 to E5.1.26.

61. BC 151, A3.24.

62. At the back of the notebook is what appears to be a list of miscellaneous items and chores written one beneath the other in Dorothea's pencilled scrawl. (BC 151, A3.24, second page from back):

    Watch, watch [both crossed out]

    [Indecipherable word also crossed out]

    ['Bill' or 'sill' also crossed out]

University

Phon. Dip.

Haeckel

Car?

Stockings

63. See respectively, BC 151, A.3.24, first page from front; A3.26, first page from front; and A3.26, 15 pages from front.

64. BC 151, A3.25, first page from front.

65. BC 151, A3.26, 17 pages from front.

66. BC 151, A3.26, 40 pages from back.

67. BC 151, A3.26.

68. BC 151, A3.26, 48 pages from front.

69. BC 151, A3.26, five pages from front.

70. N. Shepherd. 2002. 'Disciplining Archaeology: The Invention of South African Prehistory, 1923–1953'. *Kronos* 28, 127–145.

71. S. Dubow. 2006. *A Commonwealth of Knowledge: Science, Sensibility and White South Africa 1820–2000.* Oxford: Oxford University Press.

72. On copying projects by Frobenius's teams, see J. Wintjes. 2013. 'The Frobenius Expedition to Natal and the Cinyati Archive'. *Southern African Humanities* 25, 167–205. On the political implications and contexts of the prehistorians' visits, see N. Schlanger. 2003. 'The Burkitt Affair Revisited: Colonial Implications and Identity Politics in Early South African Prehistoric Research'. *Archaeological Dialogues* 10 (1), 5–32. See also H. Pager. 1962. English summary in L. Frobenius. *Madsimu Dsangara: Südafrikanische Felsbilderchronik.* (The Forgotten Ones: South African Rock Painting Chronicle)Graz: Akademische Druk, 39–45.

73. Burkitt, *South Africa's Past*, ix.

74. Shepherd, 'Disciplining Archaeology'; Schlanger, 'The Burkitt Affair', 5–32, and responses 33–55, for critical readings of the circumstances surrounding the publishing of these two volumes.

75. S. Dubow. 2000. 'A Commonwealth of Science: The British Association in South Africa, 1905 and 1929', in *Science and Society in Southern Africa.* Manchester: University of Manchester Press.

76. S. Dubow, 'Commonwealth of Science', 85.

77. S. Dubow, 'Commonwealth of Science', 85.

78. S. Dubow, 'Commonwealth of Science', 85–87.

79. Cited in Derricourt, *Inventing Africa*, 35.

80. Bleek to Woldmann, 20 August 1929. BC 210, Box 4.

81. Bleek, 'Survey'.

82. Dubow, 'Commonwealth of Science', 87.

83. Bleek to Woldmann, 28 July 1930. BC 210, Box 4; Bleek, 'Probable Age'; and 'Survey'.

84. Bleek to Woldmann, 28 July 1930.

85. Dubow, 'Commonwealth of Science', 87; Dubow, 'Human Origins'.

86. Dubow, 'Human Origins', 22–23; Derricourt, *Inventing Africa*, 59.

87. Bleek to Woldmann, 28 July 1930.

88. C. van Riet Lowe. 1929. 'Fresh Light on the Prehistoric Archaeology of South Africa'. *Bantu Studies* 3 (4), 386–393. The 1929 trip was funded by Wits University with the support of the SAAAS. It was led by C. van Riet Lowe and yielded a collection of 12 000 specimens, as well as tracings and photographs of engravings and paintings, all deposited at Wits University's Ethnological Museum.

89. Van Riet Lowe, 'Fresh Light', 385. The expedition followed the 'Vaal Valley from Vereeniging to Barkly West, the Riet [River] from Jacobsdal to Klein Philippolis, the Caledon [River] from Wepener to Clarens, with incursions into Basutoland and the Orange Free State generally'.

90. H. Breuil. 1955. *The White Lady of the Brandberg*. London, Trianon Press, 2.

91. Bleek to Woldmann, 3 May 1929. BC 210, Box 4.

92. H. Breuil. 1952. *Four Hundred Centuries of Cave Art*. Transl. M.E. Boyle. Montignac and Dordogne: Centre d'Etudes et de Documentation Prehistoriques.

93. Bleek, 'Survey', 77; Stow and Bleek, *Rock Paintings in South Africa*, xxiv–xxv.

94. Van der Riet, Van der Riet and Bleek, *More Rock-Paintings*, xii–xiv.

95. Van Riet Lowe, 'Fresh Light', 386–393.

96. Bleek, 'Survey', 78.

97. Bleek, 'Survey', 78.

98. Bleek, 'Survey', 78.

99. Bleek, 'Survey', 78. But see A. Flett and P. Letley. 2013. 'Style and Stylistic Change in the Rock Art of the Southeastern Mountains of Southern Africa'. *South African Archaeological Bulletin* 68, 3–14, for a discussion around chronology based on formal qualities of the art.

100. Bleek to Woldmann, 11 April 1927. BC 210, Box 4.

101. S. Marchand. 1997. 'Leo Frobenius and the Revolt against the West'. *Journal of Contemporary History* 32 (2), 153–170.

102. Pager, *Madsimu Dsangara*, 39–45.

103. See Bleek to Woldmann, 5 November 1931. BC 210, Box 4. For background to the Frobenius grant, see Schlanger, 'The Burkitt Affair', 20–23.

104. Report to Secretary of the Interior, 24 August 1929; Bleek to Gill, 29 August 1929; both copies in Iziko South African Museum Precolonial Correspondence.

105. Report to Secretary of the Interior, 24 August 1929; see also Bleek to Gill, 29 August 1929.

106. But Wintjes, 'The Frobenius Expedition', suggests that Frobenius's artists at Cinyati (eBusingata) produced sensitive and comprehensive copies of unfamiliar images that successfully captured the 'pictorial continuity', colour, scale and painterly qualities of the originals, and that can provide crucial information about now damaged sites.

107. Bleek to Woldmann, 26 November 1928.

108. Bleek to Woldmann, 11 April 1927; 20 August 1929; 9 April 1931. BC 210, Box 4.

109. Bleek to Woldmann, 28 July 1930. But see Pager, *Madsimu Dsangara*, 44.

110. Bleek, 'Survey', 81.

111. Bleek, 'Survey', 81–83.

112. Bleek to Woldmann, 28 July 1930. Dorothea argued that engravings needed to be assessed differently: 'Of course the engravings have to be judged completely differently. Some of them are no doubt very old.'

113. Bleek to Woldmann, 28 July 1930.

114. Bleek, 'Survey', 77–78.

115. Bleek, 'Survey', 78.

116. Bleek to Woldmann, 28 July 1930.

117. Bleek to Woldmann, 28 July 1930.

118. Bleek to Woldmann, 20 July 1937. BC 210, Box 4. Dorothea was referring to Frobenius's *Das Urbild: Cicerone zur Vorgeschichtlichen Reichsbildersammlung* (The Primeval Image: Guide to Images from the Prehistoric Realm), a book featuring a selection of rock art copies from around the world that was published in 1936.

119. Bleek to Woldmann, 10 June 1936. BC 210, Box 4.

120. Bleek to Woldmann, 21 February 1936. BC 210, Box 4.

121. Bleek to Woldmann, 28 July 1930.

122. Bleek, 'Survey', 72.
123. R. Dart. 1925. 'The Historical Succession of Cultural Impacts upon South Africa'. *Nature* 115, 425–429; also W. Battiss, *The Amazing Bushman*; D. Bleek. n.d. 'Bushman Paintings: The Neglected Riches of South Africa'. Handwritten notes. Copy of an article written by Dorothea to the *Cape Times* newspaper in which she criticised Battiss's suggestion that the engraved art was created by a 'prehistoric race called Cromagnon, & not the Bushmen'. BC 210, Box 4.
124. Stow and Bleek, *Rock Paintings in South Africa*, xviii.
125. Bleek, 'Bushman Folklore', 311–312.
126. Stow and Bleek, *Rock Paintings in South Africa*, xviii.

Chapter 6

1. D. Bleek. n.d. 'The Record of the Rocks in South Africa'. Undated typescript. Bleek Collection, University of Cape Town Libraries, Manuscripts and Archives Department, hereafter BC 151, E5.1.26, 2.
2. Bleek to Woldmann, 5 November 1931. Käthe Woldmann Papers, University of Cape Town Libraries, Manuscripts and Archives Department, hereafter BC 210, Box 4.
3. For a discussion of the formalising of local knowledge and its representation in scientific terms and taxonomies, see B. Latour. 1987. *Science in Action: How to Follow Scientists and Engineers through Society*. Cambridge, MA: Harvard University Press.
4. For more on fieldwork and networks in developing natural sciences, see N. Jacobs. 2006. 'The Intimate Politics of Ornithology in Colonial Africa'. *Comparative Studies in Society and History* 48, 564–603; J. Camerini. 1996. 'Wallace in the Field'. *Osiris* 11, 44–65. For the development of field networks and research practices in southern and central Africa respectively, see P. Harries. 2007. *Butterflies and Barbarians: Swiss Missionaries and Systems of Knowledge in South-East Africa*. Johannesburg: Wits University Press; L. Schumaker. 2001. *Africanizing Anthropology: Fieldwork, Networks and the Making of Cultural Knowledge in Central Africa*. Durham, NC: Duke University Press.
5. H. Raffles. 2002. 'Intimate Knowledge'. *International Social Science Journal* 173, 325–335; A. Agrawal. 2002. 'Indigenous Knowledge and the Politics of Classification'. *International Social Sciences Journal* 137, 287–297.

6. Camerini, 'Wallace in the Field', 44–65.

7. For evidence of Dorothea's marginality in terms of funding, see Bleek to Woldmann, 11 April 1927. BC 210, Box 4: 'In terms of research, and in particular Bushman research, this takes place on a voluntary basis. As for example my work. Only twice I was given assistance for a few months for research trips.'

8. Bleek to Woldmann, 20 May 1932. BC 210, Box 4; D. Bleek. 1932. 'A Survey of Our Present Knowledge of Rockpaintings in South Africa'. *South African Journal of Science* 29, 72–83.

9. J. van der Riet, M. van der Riet and D. Bleek. 1940. *More Rock-Paintings in South Africa*. London: Methuen. As with the Stow book, this publication featured substantial written input from Dorothea although her name on the title page is secondary to those of her collaborators.

10. Van der Riet, Van der Riet and Bleek, *More Rock-Paintings*, vii–xx.

11. Van der Riet, Van der Riet and Bleek, *More Rock-Paintings*, ix.

12. Areas 3 and 4 referred to the then South West Africa and Southern Rhodesia respectively. Dorothea's summary of the work of these latter two regions was brief and, in the absence of her own fieldwork in the areas, drew on the work of German rock art researchers such as Reinhard Maack, Hugo Obermaier and Hebert Kühn in South West Africa, and on Leo Frobenius in Rhodesia. See H. Obermaier and H. Kühn. 1930. *Bushman Art: Rock Paintings of South-West Africa*. London: Humphrey Milford, Oxford University Press, which includes photographs taken by Maack; L. Frobenius. N.d. *Erythräa, Lander aus Zeiten des Heiligen Konigsmordes*. (Eritrea: Land and Times of Holy Regicide). Berlin-Zurich: Atlantis.

13. Van der Riet, Van der Riet and Bleek, *More Rock-Paintings*, xiv.

14. For Wilhelm and Lucy's interactions using Stow's rock art copies, see A. Bank. 2006. *Bushmen in a Victorian World: The Remarkable Story of the Bleek-Lloyd Collection of Bushman Folklore*. Cape Town: Double Storey, 304–322, 338–339. Bank argues that Dia!kwain's and /Han≠kass'o's responses to copies shown them by Wilhelm Bleek and Lucy Lloyd were 'complex, divergent and often rather misleading', and indicated that their understanding of the art was 'often far from clear and, with very few exceptions, had little or nothing to do with religion or shamanism'. As such, Bank argues, their actual comments do not lend themselves to blanket interpretations of the art as 'essentially shamanistic' as has been widely argued.

15. Van der Riet, Van der Riet and Bleek, *More Rock-Paintings*, xvi.

16. The work of Gertrude Caton-Thompson should be recognised as an exception in this context. See G. Caton-Thompson. 1931. *The Zimbabwe Culture: Ruins and Reactions*. London: Oxford University Press.

17. For a visual record of wives on archaeological expedition, see N. Shepherd. 2002. 'Disciplining Archaeology: The Invention of South African Prehistory, 1923–1953'. *Kronos* 28, 36.

18. In a letter to Käthe Woldmann, Dorothea noted that Frobenius's team comprised 'three ladies and one young man' (Bleek to Woldmann, 20 August 1929. BC 210, Box 4). See also J. Wintjes. 2013. 'The Frobenius Expedition to Natal and the Cinyati Archive'. *Southern African Humanities* 25, 167–205. The Abbé Breuil collaborated with his assistant and translator Elizabeth Boyle. See H. Breuil. 1955. *The White Lady of the Brandberg*. London: Trianon Press. On Mary Boyle, see R. Perschke. Undated poster. *Women Pioneers in Rock Art Research: Mary E. Boyle, Erika Trautmann and Vera C.C. Collum*. Institut für Vor- und Frühgeschichtliche Archäologie und Provinzialrömische Archäologie.

19. Bleek to Woldmann, 11 April 1927.

20. For example, in 1933 Dorothea wrote privately that she did not organise a scientific expedition that year: 'I am getting a bit too old for that.' However, she did travel, with her nieces, to the SAAAS meeting at Barberton. See Bleek to Woldmann, 29 December 1933. BC 210, Box 4.

21. Bleek to Woldmann, 20 May 1932.

22. Bleek to Secretary, National Research Council and Board, 23 August 1938. BC 151, C17.8.

23. Joyce van der Riet to Bleek, 24 February 1932. BC 151, C16.34.

24. Kate Owen, personal communication, 8 June 2007.

25. Bleek to Secretary, National Research Council and Board, 23 August 1938.

26. Van der Riet, Van der Riet and Bleek, *More Rock-Paintings*, xix.

27. Joyce van der Riet to Bleek, 24 February 1932.

28. John Hewitt's landmark contributions to South African archaeology included his descriptions of the 'Wilton' and 'Howieson's Poort' stone-tool cultures (in collaboration with C.W. Wilmot and Reverend A.P. Stapleton respectively). He delivered a paper at the SAAAS meeting in Bulawayo in July 1920, in which he compared aboriginal 'races' of the region on the basis of cultural aspects such as stone tools, pottery fragments and kitchen middens, as well as a section on skulls. See J. Hewitt. 1920. 'Notes Relating to Aboriginal Tribes of the Eastern

Province'. *SA Journal of Science* 17 (1), 304–321; J. Hewitt. 1921. 'On Several Implements and Ornaments from Strandloper Sites in the Eastern Province'. *SA Journal of Science* 18 (1–2), 454–467; J. Hewitt. 1925. 'On Some Stone Implements from the Cape Province'. *SA Journal of Science* 22, 441–453.
29. Joyce van der Riet to Bleek, 24 February 1932.
30. Hewitt to Bleek, 26 February 1932. BC 151, C16.35.
31. Joyce van der Riet to Bleek, 24 February 1932.
32. D. Bleek to Secretary, National Research Council and Board, 1938.
33. Joyce van der Riet to Bleek, 9 March 1932. BC 151, C16.36.
34. For an example of their photographic recordings, see *More Rock-Paintings*, Plates 5A and 4C. For the efficacy of photographic recording of rock art, see comments in Hewitt to Bleek, 26 February 1932.
35. Joyce van der Riet to Bleek, 22 May 1932. BC 151, C16.45.
36. Joyce van der Riet to Bleek, 15 May 1932. BC 151, C16.44: '[W]e have nearly run short of paper & paints & amusing but true both Mollie's & my shoes have worn completely through.'
37. Joyce van der Riet to Bleek, 7 April 1932. BC 151, C16.38. The sisters were likely using their mother's vehicle. For a similar requisitioning of the family motor car for use in scientific inquiry, see A. Bank. 2008. 'The "Intimate Politics" of Fieldwork: Monica Hunter and Her African Assistants, Pondoland and the Eastern Cape, 1931–1932'. *Journal of Southern African Studies* 34 (3), 557–574.
38. Joyce van der Riet to Bleek, 15 April 1932. BC 151, C16.39.
39. For reference to their mother going along on trips, see Mollie van der Riet to Bleek, 25 February 1939. BC 151, C16.56.
40. Joyce van der Riet to Bleek, 24 February 1932.
41. Joyce van der Riet to Bleek, 9 March 1932.
42. Joyce van der Riet to Bleek, 9 March 1932; 21 March 1932, BC 151, C16.37.
43. See M. Tongue. 1909. *Bushman Paintings*. Oxford: Clarendon Press, 23.
44. Van der Riet, Van der Riet and Bleek, *More Rock-Paintings*, site notes to Plate 5A.
45. Joyce van der Riet to Bleek, 24 February 1932.
46. Joyce van der Riet to Bleek, 15 April 1932.
47. My use of the term is drawn from Schumaker, *Africanizing Anthropology*, who uses it to denote the ways in which fieldworkers at the Livingstone Institute inscribed themselves and their particular cultural world views into the processes by which scientific knowledge was constructed in fieldwork.

48. For fieldwork projects involving the assistance of colonial 'others' in which interactions were not always equal or free of conflict, see Harries, *Butterflies and Barbarians*; Camerini, 'Wallace in the Field'; Jacobs, 'Intimate Politics'; Bank, 'The "Intimate Politics"'.

49. Joyce van der Riet to Bleek, 21 March 1932.

50. Joyce van der Riet to Bleek, 23 April 1932. BC 151, C16.40.

51. Joyce van der Riet to Bleek, 21 March 1932; Van der Riet, Van der Riet and Bleek, *More Rock-Paintings*, Plate 6B.

52. Joyce van der Riet to Bleek, 23 April 1932.

53. Joyce van der Riet to Bleek, 15 May 1932.

54. Joyce van der Riet to Bleek, 10 June 1932. BC 151, C16.47.

55. Joyce van der Riet to Bleek, 10 June 1932.

56. Joyce van der Riet to Bleek, 29 April 1932. BC 151, C16.41.

57. See Van der Riet, Van der Riet and Bleek, *More Rock-Paintings*, Plate 7, sketch and maps.

58. Van der Riet, Van der Riet and Bleek, *More Rock-Paintings*, notes to Plate 7.

59. Joyce van der Riet to Bleek, 29 April 1932.

60. See Van der Riet, Van der Riet and Bleek, *More Rock-Paintings*, Plate 4B.

61. Joyce van der Riet to Bleek, 15 April 1932; Van der Riet, Van der Riet and Bleek, *More Rock-Paintings*, Plate 6A.

62. Joyce van der Riet to Bleek, 10 June 1932.

63. Joyce van der Riet to Bleek, 23 April 1932.

64. Joyce van der Riet to Bleek, 4 May 1932. BC 151, C16.42.

65. See Van der Riet, Van der Riet and Bleek, *More Rock-Paintings*, Plate 3.

66. Joyce van der Riet to Bleek, 24 February 1932.

67. Joyce van der Riet to Bleek, 10 May 1932. BC 151, C16.43.

68. See Van der Riet, Van der Riet and Bleek, *More Rock-Paintings*, notes to Plate 17B.

69. Joyce van der Riet to Bleek, 10 May 1932.

70. Joyce van der Riet to Bleek, 10 May 1932.

71. Joyce van der Riet to Bleek, 10 May 1932.

72. Joyce van der Riet to Bleek, 15 May 1932. BC 151, C16.44; Van der Riet, Van der Riet and Bleek, *More Rock-Paintings*, site notes to Plate 17B.

73. Van der Riet, Van der Riet and Bleek, *More Rock-Paintings*, site notes to Plate 17B. For a contemporary exposition of this scene, see J.D. Lewis-Williams and

D. Pearce. 2012. 'Framed Idiosyncrasy: Method and Evidence in the Interpretation of San Rock Art'. *South African Archaeological Bulletin* 67, 75–87; see also F. Thackeray. 1994. 'Animals, Conceptual Associations and Southern African Rock Art: A Multidisciplinary, Exploratory approach', in T. Dowson and J.D. Lewis-Williams. Eds. *Contested Images: Diversity in Southern African Rock Art Research*. Johannesburg: Wits University Press, 232.

74. Bleek, 'Survey', Figures 2, 3 and 7; Van der Riet, Van der Riet and Bleek, *More Rock-Paintings*, Plates 17B–21A from Groenfontein, and Plates 22B–25 from Nooitgedacht.

75. Joyce van der Riet to Bleek, 17 June 1932. BC 151, C16.49; Van der Riet, Van der Riet and Bleek, *More Rock-Paintings*, Plate 5B.

76. Joyce van der Riet to Bleek, 22 May 1932. BC 151, C16.45.

77. Joyce van der Riet to Bleek, 17 June 1932.

78. Joyce van der Riet to Bleek, 15 May 1932.

79. Joyce van der Riet to Bleek, 22 May 1932.

80. Van der Riet, Van der Riet and Bleek, *More Rock-Paintings*, Plates 16B and 17A.

81. Joyce van der Riet to Bleek, 10 June 1932. An oblique reference to the political present can be glimpsed in an anecdote which Joyce included in her letter: 'Mr Maasdorp who owned Doornplaats years ago says that near the homestead he dug up a bushman grave in which he found a skeleton sitting upright with its implements in a pile in front of it. He had to shut in the grave again owing to the troublous times so I suppose it is still there intact. What seems interesting to me is that the bushman should be found *seated*, according to Stow they were buried on *their sides* facing the East – Mr Minnaar, one of another old Graaff Reinet family, also dug up similar seated figures so that it seems that it was the general rule in that district [emphasis in original].' The reference indicates the sisters knew about Stow, his book perhaps featuring in preparatory reading Dorothea might have set for them.

82. Van der Riet, Van der Riet and Bleek, *More Rock-Paintings*, Plates 8B, 9 and 10A.

83. Maria Wilman's book *The Rock-Engravings of Griqualand West and Bechuanaland South Africa* (Cambridge and Kimberley: Deighton Bell and Alexander McGregor Memorial Museum) appeared in 1933.

84. Van der Riet, Van der Riet and Bleek, *More Rock-Paintings*, Plates 11, 12 and 13.

85. Joyce van der Riet to Bleek, 20 June 1932. BC 151, C16.50.

86. Joyce van der Riet to Bleek, 24 June 1932. BC 151, C16.52.

87. Joyce van der Riet to Bleek, 17 June 1932.

88. A. Goodwin and C. van Riet Lowe. 1929. *The Stone Age Cultures of South Africa*. Edinburgh: Neill and Co., 252–253. Hewitt's description of the Wilton paintings reads as follows: 'Amongst the numerous paintings on the inner wall of the rock-shelter are some spirited representations of antelopes in profile. The technique is quite superior, and a number of the antelopes are in two colours, red and creamy white, but there are no group scenes. A very distinctive feature is the treatment of the human figure, the limbs and body being tremendously elongated. These, which are wholly red, may not belong to the same period as the antelope pictures…Thus we arrive at a conclusion which has long been anticipated, but not hitherto so well supported by actual data as now detailed, that the short-headed Bushman made the delicate ostrich-shell beads, the pygmy crescents, and the tiny scrapers, and was also the author of rock paintings of superior and characteristic technique.' For reference to the stone-tool 'industries' associated with the shelter, see M. Burkitt. 1928. *South Africa's Past in Stone and Paint*. Cambridge: Cambridge University Press. See also Van der Riet, Van der Riet and Bleek, *More Rock-Paintings*, Plate 8A.

89. Joyce van der Riet to Bleek, 17 June 1932.

90. Joyce van der Riet to Bleek, 30 July 1932. BC 151, C16.53; Van der Riet, Van der Riet and Bleek, *More Rock-Paintings*, Plates 1 and 2.

91. Joyce van der Riet to Bleek, 17 June 1932.

92. BC 151, C16.51.

93. W. Bleek and L. Lloyd. 1938. *Das wahre Gesicht des Buschmannes in seinen Mythen und Märchen*. Trans. Käthe Woldmann. Basel: Kommissionverlag Zbinden & Hügin; Bleek to Woldmann, 5 November 1931, 16 September 1938 and elsewhere in BC 210, Box 4.

94. BC 151, C17.1–C17.76.

95. Bleek to Secretary of the Research Grant Board, 12 March 1938. BC 151, C17.6; Van der Riet, Van der Riet and Bleek, *More Rock-Paintings*, xx. In the 1940s, Goodwin would establish the South African Archaeological Society, with Dorothea a founder member. See Shepherd, 'Disciplining Archaeology', 139.

96. Bleek to Scott, 7 September 1939. Letter in the collection of Patricia Scott Deetz.

97. Dorothea with her nieces Marjorie and Dorothy went with Goodwin to the Barberton SAAAS conference in 1933. They drove up in the Hillman Wizard that Dorothea owned at the time. See P. Scott Deetz and M. Scott Roos. 2010. 'Memories of Growing Up with "Aunt D"', email communication.

98. J. White (Methuen) to D. Bleek, 24 February 1938. BC 151, C17.1.
99. Bleek to Methuen, 31 December 1938. BC 151, C17.14.
100. J. White (Methuen) to D. Bleek. 24 November 1938. BC 151, C17.13.
101. Other titles available at the time in similar large format with colour reproductions included her earlier publication G. Stow and D. Bleek. 1930. *Rock Paintings in South Africa from Parts of the Eastern Province and Orange Free State*. London: Methuen; Obermaier and Kühn, *Bushman Art*.
102. J. White (Methuen) to D. Bleek, 24 November 1938.
103. See Dorothea's acknowledgement in her Introduction, where she thanks 'Mr A.J.H. Goodwin very heartily for his help in taking the paintings to England and seeing the publishers for me, and for much good advice'.
104. Bleek to Methuen, 3 February 1939. BC 151, C17.51.
105. J. White (Methuen) to D. Bleek, 5 December 1938. BC 151, C17.15.
106. Bleek to Methuen, 28 April 1939. BC 151, C17.34; J. White to D. Bleek, 10 May 1939. BC 151, C17.35; Bleek to Methuen, 25 May 1939. BC 151, C17.36.
107. Van der Riet, Van der Riet and Bleek, *More Rock-Paintings*, xiii.
108. Bleek to Mrs Ginn and Miss Mollie van der Riet, 4 January 1939. BC 151, C16.54.
109. Van der Riet, Van der Riet and Bleek, *More Rock-Paintings*, xx, Plates 27 and 28, for copies by Marjorie Bright and Sheila Fort.
110. Bleek to Mrs Ginn and Miss Mollie van der Riet, 4 January 1939. For Wilhelm Bleek's suggestions in regard to 'indication and description of the locality', see W. Bleek, 'Remarks', 13.
111. Mollie van der Riet to Miss Bleek, 13 February 1939. BC 151, C16.55.
112. Joyce Ginn to Miss Bleek, n.d. BC 151, C16.57.
113. Mollie van der Riet to Miss Bleek, 25 February 1939; E.J.T. Pringle to Miss Van der Riet, 6 April 1939. BC 151, C16.59.
114. Joyce Ginn to Miss Bleek, n.d.
115. Mollie van der Riet to Miss Bleek, 28 February 1939. BC 151, C16.56.
116. Van der Riet, Van der Riet and Bleek, *More Rock-Paintings*, Plate 6B.
117. Mollie van der Riet to Miss Bleek, 20 May 1939. BC 151, C16.60.
118. Van der Riet, Van der Riet and Bleek, *More Rock-Paintings*, Plate 6B, 'Remarks'.
119. Mollie van der Riet to Miss Bleek, 26 May 1939. BC 151, C16.61.
120. Bleek to Woldmann, 19 April 1939. BC 210, Box 4; Sketchbooks and rock art tracings. BC 151, G3.1.1–G3.1.8.

121. Methuen to Bleek, 20 June 1939. BC 151, C17.37.

122. J. White (Methuen) to Bleek, 28 November 1939. BC 151, C17.43; J. White to Bleek, 4 December 1939. BC 151, C17.44; Methuen to Bleek, 21 December 1939. BC 151, C17.45; Bleek to Methuen, 23 January 1940. BC 151, C17.491.

123. National Research Council and Board to Bleek, 16 March 1940. BC 151, C17.56.

124. Bleek to Methuen, 11 January 1940. BC 151, C17.46. Marjorie and her husband, Richard Thring Scott, were at the time living on a smallholding they had purchased near Wellington, outside Cape Town. (Patricia Scott Deetz, personal communication, 26 July 2010.)

125. J. White to Bleek, 12 January 1940. BC 151, C17.47.

126. J. White to Bleek, 12 January 1940.

127. J. White to Bleek, 19 January 1940. BC 151, C17.48, C17.54.

128. Bleek to Methuen, 11 July 1940. BC 151, C17.61.

129. J. White to Bleek, 14 June 1940. BC 151, C17.60.

130. J. White to Bleek, 14 June 1940.

131. Bleek to Methuen, 11 July 1940.

132. J. White to Bleek, 15 August 1940. BC 151, C17.62.

133. Bleek to Bullard, Ling & Co., 27 January 1941. BC 151, C17.66.

134. BC 151, C17.67 and C17.68; Bleek to Methuen, 4 April 1941. BC 151, C17.72.

135. J. White (Methuen) to Bleek, 17 January 1941. BC 151, C17.67; Attwell & Co. to Bleek, 30 January 1941. BC 151, C17.69; Bleek to Methuen, 7 February 1941. BC 151, C17.71

136. http://uboat.net/allies/merchants/534.html (accessed 25 May 2010).

137. J. White (Methuen) to Bleek, 17 January 1941.

138. Bleek to Methuen, 4 April 1941.

139. Eddie to Bleek, 7 August 1941. BC 151, C18.45; copies at G3.2.1–G3.3.137.

140. For Nooitgedacht, see Van der Riet, Van der Riet and Bleek, *More Rock-Paintings*, Plates 22B, 23, 24 and 25; BC 151, G3.2.1. For Groenfontein, see Plates 17B–21A; BC 151, G3.3.31–G3.3.41.

141. Van der Riet, Van der Riet and Bleek, *More Rock-Paintings*, Plate 28; BC 151, G3.3.13–G3.3.17.

142. BC 151, C18.1–C18.86.

143. This body, administered by the Union Education Department, took over the functions of the National Research Board and Council sometime in 1946. See Secretary for Education to D. Bleek, 15 July 1946. BC 151, C18.75.

144. BC 151, C18.85.
145. S. Drinker. 1948. *Music and Women: The Story of Women and Their Relation to Music*. New York: Coward McCann; Van der Riet, Van der Riet and Bleek, *More Rock-Paintings*, Plate 7. Dorothea described the plate as 'the illustration of some myth'. It had been copied from a rock shelter on the northern side of the Great Fish River 'twenty-seven miles north-west of Grahamstown along the Cradock Road', on the farm Mountain Top. It was reproduced as Figure 4 in her 'Survey'.

Chapter 7

1. Bleek Collection, University of Cape Town Libraries, Manuscripts and Archives Department, hereafter BC 151, 2008 additions #183, 184. Newspaper clipping preserved inside funeral programme.
2. Bleek to Doke, 27 May 1932. BC 151, 2008 additions #176.
3. For Wilhelm Bleek's attitude towards 'bushmen' as a dying race, see R. Thornton. 1983. '"This Dying Out Race": W.H.I. Bleek's Approach to the Languages of Southern Africa'. *Social Dynamics* 9 (2), 1–10.
4. BC 151, A1.2.2. P. Skotnes. Ed. 2007. *Claim to the Country: The Archive of Wilhelm Bleek and Lucy Lloyd*. Cape Town: Jacana, 40. Wilhelm Bleek and Lucy Lloyd had almost completed sorting out their 'card entries' at Wilhelm's death. See also J. Engelbrecht. 1956. 'Introduction', in D. Bleek. *A Bushman Dictionary*. New Haven, CT: American Oriental Society, v–x.
5. See D. Bleek. 1928. *The Naron: A Bushman tribe of the Central Kalahari*. London: Cambridge University Press, 3. Dorothea placed the 'tribe' speaking this language 'between the Black Nossop and the eastern border of the Protectorate south of Oas'. She classified /Nusan alongside /Xam in her Southern group of languages. The provenance of Krönlein's samples included in Wilhelm Bleek's vocabulary remains vague. In notes bound into the volume, Wilhelm Bleek explained that the samples were obtained from an 'Oorlam' who had employed a member of the /Nusan bushman people, and had lived among the 'nations' inhabiting the dry deserts between the Auhoup and Nossop rivers stretching over to the Winterberg. 'Oorlam' was the name given to hybrid communities who migrated from the Cape colonial frontier into the south-western parts of southern Africa during the nineteenth century. But based

on his knowledge in 1862, Wilhelm Bleek pronounced the examples of /Nusan vocabulary to be 'authentic'. On Bleek and Krönlein, see A. Bank. 2006. *Bushmen in a Victorian World: The Remarkable Story of the Bleek-Lloyd Collection of Bushman Folklore*. Cape Town: Double Storey, 32–35.

6. BC 151, A1.3.1–A3.3.4.

7. For background on the manuscript dictionaries compiled by Bleek and Lloyd, see Bank, *Bushmen in a Victorian World*, 32–41 and Chapter 3.

8. BC 151, A1.3.1, 133, Vol. I A–W, for reference to notebook pages, e.g. 'tsŏă!ē Stoffel's father's mother's father 361,5'. Also Vol. II Y–F [beginning with /Xam sound yă]; Vol. III !; Vol. IV //–⊙, as in labial 'kiss' sound.

9. W. Bleek. 1857. 'Hottentot Dialects: A Vocabulary of the Dialects of the Hottentots and Bushmen'. Grey Collection, National Library of South Africa, Cape Town. See also Bleek, *Dictionary*, xi.

10. Wilhelm Bleek's activities on the day of his death are narrated in a letter written by Jemima Bleek to Sir George Grey a few months after Wilhelm's death. The letter is transcribed in Skotnes, *Claim to the Country*, 281–287.

11. See A. Zimmerman. 2001. 'Looking Beyond History: The Optics of German Anthropology and the Critique of Humanism'. *Studies in History and Philosophy of Biological and Biomedical Sciences* 32 (3), 390–393.

12. For a review of Doke's career, see R. Herbert. 1993. 'Not With One Mouth'. *African Studies* 52 (2), 1–4.

13. Bleek to Kirby, 18 December 1933. Kirby Collection, University of Cape Town Libraries, Manuscripts and Archives Department, hereafter BC 750, Correspondence A.

14. Bleek to Kirby, 18 December 1933. In the same letter, Dorothea observed that the distinction between musical and hunting bows might not be as large as ethnographers supposed. For the *!goin !goin*, see W. Bleek and L. Lloyd. Ed. 1911. *Specimens of Bushman Folklore*. London: George Allen & Co., 352–355. See also D. Hansen. 1996. 'Bushman Music: Still an Unknown', in P. Skotnes. Ed. *Miscast: Negotiating the Presence of the Bushmen*. Cape Town: UCT Press, 297–305.

15. Bleek to Woldmann, 13 July 1936. Käthe Woldmann Collection, University of Cape Town Libraries, Manuscripts and Archives Department, hereafter BC 210, Box 4.

16. Westermann to Bleek, 14 August 1933. BC 151, C16.6; see also Bleek to Lestrade, 8 November 1944. BC 151, C19.1. See also Dorothea's incomplete bibliography.

BC 151, D3.24.3. For more on Westermann's career and the International Institute of African Languages and Cultures, see S. Pugach. 2012. *Africa in Translation: A History of Colonial Linguistics in Germany and Beyond, 1814–1945*. Ann Arbor: University of Michigan Press, 127–128, 163–169, 186–195.

17. Bleek to Lestrade, 8 November 1944; Bleek to Maingard, 11 July 1945. BC 151, C16.14.

18. BC151, D3.24.3.

19. See Bleek, *Dictionary*, iii.

20. Dorothea's summary of the project is set out in her 1945 application to the National Research Board for funding to publish the work. See Bleek to Maingard, 11 July 1945. For a list of authors included in the final manuscript, see Bleek to Marquard, 1 May 1946. BC 151, C19.14.

21. Engelbrecht, 'Introduction', viii.

22. For an idea of her orthography requirements, see Bleek to Lestrade, 25 November 1944. BC 151, C19.4.

23. P. Scott Deetz. 2007. *Catalog of the Bleek-Lloyd Collection in the Scott Family Archive*. Williamsburg, VA: Deetz Ventures, Inc., 53; also Engelbrecht, 'Introduction'.

24. Bleek to Woldmann, 21 February 1936. BC 210, Box 4.

25. Bleek to Woldmann, 22 January 1930. BC 210, Box 4.

26. For an annotated reproduction of the entire series, see J. Hollmann. Ed. 2005. *Customs and Beliefs of the /Xam Bushmen*. Johannesburg: Wits University Press.

27. Bleek to Woldmann, 9 April 1931.

28. D. Bleek. 1931. 'Baboons'. *Bantu Studies* 5, 167–179.

29. Bleek to Woldmann, 22 January 1930.

30. D. Bleek. 1932. 'The Lion, Part 2'. *Bantu Studies* 6, 47–63; D. Bleek. 1932. 'Game Animals, Part 3'. *Bantu Studies* 6, 233–249.

31. D. Bleek. 1932. 'Omens, Wind-Making, Clouds, Part 4'. *Bantu Studies* 6, 323–342; D. Bleek. 1933. 'The Rain, Part 5'. *Bantu Studies* 7, 297–306; D. Bleek. 1933. 'Rain-Making, Part 6'. *Bantu Studies* 7, 375–392.

32. D. Bleek. 1935. 'Sorcerors, Part 7'. *Bantu Studies* 9, 1–47; D. Bleek. 1936. 'More about Sorcerors and Charms, Part 8'. *Bantu Studies* 10, 130–161. See also discussion and annotations in Hollmann, *Customs and Beliefs*, 199–272.

33. D. Bleek. 1936. 'Special Speech of Animals and Moon Used by the /Xam Bushmen'. *Bantu Studies* 10, 163–199.

34. H. Phillips. 1993. *The University of Cape Town 1918–1948: The Formative Years.* Cape Town: UCT Press, 28, for photograph of a Nama-speaker using the kymograph in UCT's new phonetics laboratory in 1929. For more on laboratory techniques employed at the *Seminar für Kolonialsprachen* in Hamburg, see Pugach, *Africa in Translation*, 126–139.

35. Maingard to Bleek, 5 April 1938. BC 151, C16.7.

36. Bleek to Kirby, 1 October 1935. BC 750, Correspondence A.

37. Bleek to Maingard, 14 October 1935. BC 151, C16.6.

38. Bleek to Kirby, 6 November 1935. BC 750, Correspondence A. In correspondence with Kirby around other matters, Dorothea ended her letter by wondering whether Maingard was sick since he had not replied to her letter asking for his opinion on 'some pages of my attempt at a dictionary'.

39. Maingard to Bleek, 24 November 1936. BC 151, 2008 additions #178.

40. For more on Donald Bain and the bushman 'exhibit' at the Empire Exhibition, see R. Gordon. 1999. '"Bain's Bushmen": Scenes at the Empire Exhibition, 1936', in B. Lindfors. Ed. *Africans on Stage: Studies in Ethnological Show Business.* Bloomington: Indiana University Press, 266–289.

41. For a discussion on the research programme at the 'laboratory in the desert' and its contribution to defining bushman as a physical type, see C. Rassool and P. Hayes. 2002. 'Science and the Spectacle: //Khanako's South Africa, 1936–1937', in W. Woodward, P. Hayes and G. Minkley. Eds. *Deep hiStories: Gender and Colonialism in Southern Africa.* New York: Rodopi, 117–164. See also Gordon,' "Bain's Bushmen" '.

42. *Bantu Studies* 9, 253–278.

43. Bleek to Woldmann, 18 February 1938. BC 210, Box 4.

44. Bleek to Kirby, 20 April 1937. BC 570, Correspondence A.

45. In 1946, Dorothea was still trying to contact Mabel through the International Red Cross. Whether she was successful is not known. See Bleek to Woldmann, 11 January 1946. BC 210, Box 4. She had also lost contact with a cousin whom she thought was living in Dornach, Switzerland, where Woldmann lived.

46. Bleek to Doke, 4 and 10 September 1940. BC 151, 2008 additions #180, 181.

47. Bleek to Doke, 27 April 1943. BC 151, 2008 additions #182.

48. Maingard to Bleek, 10 July 1944. BC 151, C16.8. The wording in his letter suggests he was replying to a direct question from Dorothea as to whether he was able to continue advising her.

49. Maingard to Bleek, 10 July 1944.
50. Maingard to Bleek, 26 September 1944. BC 151, C16.10.
51. Bleek to Lestrade, 8 November 1944.
52. Bleek to National Research Board, n.d. BC 151, C19.6; Bleek to Maingard, 11 July 1945.
53. Bleek to Marquard, 1 May 1946.
54. Bleek to Wilman, 25 April 1934. Kimberley Africana Library. M. Wilman. Ethnology file. Ms 76.
55. Bleek to Lestrade, 8 November 1944. Bleek to Maingard, 18 May 1945. BC 151, C16.12.
56. Bleek to Maingard, 18 May 1945.
57. Bleek to Lestrade, 25 November 1944.
58. Previously Department of Bantu Studies. See Maingard to Bleek, 3 July 1945. BC 151, C16.13.
59. Previously Research Grant Board. See Maingard to Bleek, 3 July 1945; Bleek to Maingard, 11 July 1945; Bleek to National Research Board, n.d.
60. Maingard to Bleek, 19 July 1945. BC 151, C16.15.
61. Scott Deetz, *Catalog*, 53–54.
62. Scott Deetz, *Catalog*, 53–54.
63. Scott Deetz, *Catalog*, 55.
64. Scott Deetz, *Catalog*, 55.
65. Bleek to Marquard (OUP), 1 May 1946. BC 151, C19.14; Bleek to Lovedale Press, 23 July 1946. BC 151, C19.15.
66. Maingard to Bleek, 28 September 1946. BC 151, C16.16.
67. Shepherd (Lovedale) to Bleek, 6 August 1946. BC 151, C19.16; Marquard to Bleek, 17 October 1946. BC 151, C19.17.
68. Schapera to Bleek, 5 November 1946. BC 151, C19.18; 3 April 1947. BC 151, C19.21; Harris to Schapera, 22 March 1947. BC 151, C19.22.
69. Harris to Schapera, 22 March 1947.
70. Bleek to Schapera, 14 May 1947. BC 151, C19.24.
71. Bleek to Maingard, 7 April 1947. BC 151, C16.18; 14 May 1947.
72. P. Scott Deetz and A. Scott Roos. 2010. 'Memories of Growing Up with "Aunt D"', email communication.
73. Scott Deetz, *Catalog*, 54–55. Also see Scott Deetz and Roos, 'Memories'.
74. Scott Deetz and Roos, 'Memories'. Dorothy died on 19 January at the age of 31.
75. Scott Deetz and Roos, 'Memories'.

76. Bleek to Schapera, 19 June 1947. BC 151, C19.27.

77. Schapera to Bleek, 14 October 1947. BC 151, C19.29.

78. Bleek to Schapera, 14 October 1947.

79. Schapera to Bleek, 23 December 1947. BC 151, C19.31; Bleek to Schapera, 27 December 1947. BC 151, C19.32.

80. Bleek to Harris, 27 December 1947. BC 151, C19.33, C19.34.

81. Harris to Bleek, 16 July 1948. BC 151, C19.35. Harris wrote from the University of Pennsylvania that there were 'many difficulties in getting satisfactory characters, and the ones used here are the best that we could arrange', even though one or two of them 'do not have exactly the form which you would want'.

82. BC 151, C19.37–C19.47.

83. See Scott Deetz, *Catalog*, 51: 'Scott was elected a Fellow of the Royal Entomological Society in 1953, a great honor that she valued highly throughout her life. When she retired in December 1978 as a Senior Chief Research Officer with the CSIR [Council for Scientific and Industrial Research] she was Curator of the National Collection of Freshwater Invertebrates at the Albany Museum in Grahamstown. She had by then published 22 scientific papers on Trichoptera and had a total of 35 publications. She continued her research and published a further 13 papers on Trichoptera before her death in 1998 at the age of 85.'

84. Maingard to Scott, 13 December 1949. BC 151, C16.23.

85. Hause to Maingard, 20 February 1950. BC 151, C16.25.

86. Scott Deetz, *Catalog*, 53–54. Dick's last diary entry on 5 February 1951 records: 'Marj home to lunch – she is trying to see Knott-Craig about Aunt's dictionary, as have had no reply to our letters to the US.'

87. Hause to Scott, 12 August 1951. BC 151, C19.41.

88. Z. Harris. 1952. 'Discourse Analysis'. *Language* 28 (1), 1–30.

89. Hause to Scott, 4 October 1951. BC 151, C19.42.

90. For Maingard's withdrawal, see Scott to Harris, 1 March 1950. BC 151, C19.39.

91. Engelbrecht to Scott, 11 April 1952. BC 151, 2008 additions #190. J. Engelbrecht. Ed. 1952. *Zulu Legends*. Cape Town: Van Schaik.

92. BC 151, 2008 additions #191–192.

93. Engelbrecht to Scott, 16 July 1952. BC 151, 2008 additions #189–194.

94. Engelbrecht to Scott, 31 August 1952. BC 151, 2008 additions #192.

95. Engelbrecht, 'Introduction'.

96. C. Doke. 1957. 'A *Bushman Dictionary* Review'. *African Studies* 16 (2), 124–125.

97. Doke, 'Review', 124–125.

98. Based on Worldcat search through University of Minnesota Twin Cities Libraries, 24 May 2010.

99. Bleek to Woldmann, 11 April 1927. BC 210, Box 4.

100. Dornach remains the centre of the international anthroposophical movement. The original Goetheanum was destroyed in an arson attack on 31 December 1922. The Second Goetheanum was designed by Steiner and completed in 1928 after his death.

101. Bleek to Woldmann, 8 February 1932. BC 210, Box 4.

102. Woldmann's collection at UCT confirms that she was a dedicated follower of anthroposophist philosophies and teachings, BC 210. For a contemporary view on Steiner, see P. Staudenmaier and P. Zegers. 2007. 'Anthroposophy and Ecofascism'. *Communalism*. http://www.communalism.net/index.php?option=com_content&view=article&id=193:anthroposophy-and-ecofascism-&catid=42:fashion-beauty&Itemid=34 (accessed 26 May 2010).

103. Bleek to Woldmann, 8 February 1932.

104. Uehli wrote prolifically on anthroposophist theories. His interest in the source of Germanic *Geist* or spirit saw him seeking to uncover a link between ancient Nordic and Germanic mythologies. His 1926 book on the topic has been described as 'the major anthroposophist statement on the topic' published after Steiner's death. A reading of Uehli's journal articles (most often published in *Das Goetheanum*) and books has led US historian Peter Staudenmaier to argue that Uehli, like other anthroposophists of his day, 'engaged extensively with racial theorists of his time'. See P. Staudenmaier. 2014. *Between Occultism and Nazism: Anthroposophy and the Politics of Race in the Fascist Era*. Leiden: Brill, 89.

105. Steiner's references to lost continents were his elaborations of the esoteric cosmology espoused in the writings of the theosophist Helena Petrovna Blavatsky, H. Blavatsky. 1888. *The Secret Doctrine: The Synthesis of Science, Religion and Philosophy*. London: Theosophical Publishing; R. Steiner. [1904] 1911. *The Submerged Continents of Atlantis and Lemuria, Their History and Civilisation*. Trans. M. Gysi. Chicago: Rajput Press.

106. Bleek to Woldmann, 29 December 1933. BC 210, Box 4.

107. 'Descendenz' in original. See Bleek to Woldmann, 22 January 1930.

108. Bleek to Woldmann, 22 January 1930.

109. Bleek to Woldmann, 22 January 1930. For a discussion on settler and colonial responses to poisoned arrows, see D. Bunn. 1996. 'The Brown Serpent of the Rocks: Bushman Arrow Toxins in the Dutch and British Imagination, 1735–1850', in B. Cooper and A. Steyn. Eds. *Transgressing Boundaries: New Directions in the Study of Culture in Africa.* Cape Town: UCT Press, 59–85.

110. Bleek to Woldmann, 22 January 1930.

111. Bleek to Woldmann, 20 May 1932. BC 210, Box 4. Karutz has been described as the 'most prolific anthroposophist racial theorist during the interwar period'. See Staudenmaier, *Between Occultism and Nazism*, 90. Karutz favoured a 'spiritual ethnology based on the root race doctrine', and wanted to protect anthropology as a discipline from a 'sociological flood of materialist thinking'. See Staudenmaier and Zegers, 'Anthroposophy and Ecofascism'.

112. Bleek to Woldmann, 20 May 1932; for Woldmann's visit to South Africa, Bleek to Woldmann, 11 April 1927.

113. Bleek to Woldmann, 20 May 1932. Steiner used the phrase 'atavistic clairvoyance' to refer to primitive minds at the initial level of development. The appearance of 'clairvoyance' in contemporary times meant that the person had inherited or carried the faculty over from earlier times. It was not an indication of advanced thinking, but of thinking that had 'lagged behind'. See R. Steiner. 1914. 'The Presence of the Dead on the Spiritual Path'. Lecture given in Berlin. http://wn.rsarchive.org/Lectures/Dates/19140418p01.html (accessed 3 June 2010).

114. E. Uehli. 1936. *Atlantis und das Rätsel der Eiszeitkunst: Versuch einer Mysteriengeschichte der Urzeit Europas* (Atlantis and the Enigma of Ice Age Art: An Attempt to Understand the Mystery of Prehistoric Europe). Stuttgart: Hoffmann. Uehli's was one of two anthroposophist books on 'Atlantis' published in Nazi Germany exploring the relationship between race and 'different levels of evolutionary development and the unfolding of consciousness'. See Staudenmaier, *Between Occultism and Nazism*, 164–165.

115. Bleek to Woldmann, 13 July 1936.

116. Bleek to Woldmann, 24 October 1931. BC 210, Box 4. Moldenhauer has been described as one of the anthroposophist theorists of the 1930s who developed Steiner's 'race doctrines' in the context of the Third Reich. See Staudenmaier, *Between Occultism and Nazism*, 163–164.

117. Erythräea is the ancient name for the body of water between the Horn of Africa and the Arabian Peninsula (now identified as the Gulf of Aden). It featured in the 'root races' geography of anthroposophical thought.
118. Bleek to Woldmann, 5 November 1931. BC 210, Box 4.
119. Bleek to Woldmann, 6 March 1936. BC 151, Box 4. This comment was pointed out to me by Hannelore van Rhyneveld (personal communication, March 2008) as the only reference she could find to Nazism in the letters.
120. Bleek to Woldmann, 26 December 1930. BC 210, Box 4.
121. See, for example, Bleek to Woldmann, 24 September 1931. BC 210, Box 4, where, in a discussion on her submissions to *Bantu Studies*, she commented: 'There is such a lot of originality among the small people.' In relation to rock art, see Bleek, *The Naron*, 41.

Bibliography

Aaron, D. Ed. 1978. Studies in Biography, Harvard English Studies 8.

Adhikari, M. 2010. *The Anatomy of a South African Genocide: The Extermination of the Cape San Peoples*. Cape Town: UCT Press.

Agrawal, A. 2002. 'Indigenous Knowledge and the Politics of Classification'. *International Social Sciences Journal* 137, 287–297.

Bagshawe, J. 1925. 'The Peoples of the Happy Valley, Part II'. *Journal of the Royal African Society* 24, 117–130.

Balfour, H. 1909. 'Preface', in M. Tongue, *Bushman Paintings*. London: Clarendon Press.

Bank, A. 2008. 'The "Intimate Politics" of Fieldwork: Monica Hunter and Her African Assistants, Pondoland and the Eastern Cape, 1931–1932'. *Journal of Southern African Studies* 34 (3), 557–574.

Bank, A. 2006. *Bushmen in a Victorian World: The Remarkable Story of the Bleek-Lloyd Collection of Bushman Folklore*. Cape Town: Double Storey.

Bank, A. 2006. 'Anthropology and Fieldwork Photography: Dorothea Bleek's Expedition to the Northern Cape and the Kalahari, July to December 1911'. *Kronos* 32, 77–113.

Bank, A. 2002. 'From Pictures to Performance: Early Learning at the Hill'. *Kronos* 28, 66–101.

Bank, A. 2000. 'Evolution and Racial Theory: The Hidden Side of Wilhelm Bleek'. *South African Historical Journal* 43 (1), 163-178.

Bank, A. and L. Bank. Eds. 2013. *Inside African Anthropology: Monica Wilson and Her Interpreters*. Cambridge: Cambridge University Press.

Barnard, A. 2004. 'Coat of Arms and the Body Politic: Khoisan Imagery and South African National Identity'. *Ethnos* 69 (1), 5–22.

Battiss, W. 1952. *Bushman Art*. Pretoria: Red Fern Press.

Battiss, W. 1939. *The Amazing Bushman*. Pretoria: Red Fern Press.

Beard, M. 2000. *The Invention of Jane Harrison*. Cambridge, MA, and London: Harvard University Press.

Bennun, N. 2004. *The Broken String: The Last Words of an Extinct People*. London: Viking.

Birkett, D. and J. Wheelwright. 1990. ' "How Could She?" Unpalatable Facts and Feminists' Heroines'. *Gender and History* 2 (1), 49–56.

Blake, S. 1992. 'A Woman's Trek: What Difference Does Gender Make?', in N. Chaudhuri and M. Strobel. Eds. *Western Women and Imperialism: Complicity and Resistance*. Bloomington and Indianapolis: Indiana University Press.

Blavatsky, H. 1888. *The Secret Doctrine: The Synthesis of Science, Religion and Philosophy*. London: Theosophical Publishing.

Bleek, D. 1936. 'Special Speech of Animals and Moon Used by the /Xam Bushmen'. *Bantu Studies* 10, 163–199.

Bleek, D. 1936. 'More about Sorcerors and Charms, Part 8'. *Bantu Studies* 10, 130–161.

Bleek, D. 1935. 'Sorcerors, Part 7'. *Bantu Studies* 9, 1–47.

Bleek, D. 1933. 'Rain-Making, Part 6'. *Bantu Studies* 7, 375–392.

Bleek, D. 1933. 'The Rain, Part 5'. *Bantu Studies* 7, 297–306.

Bleek, D. 1932. 'A Survey of Our Present Knowledge of Rockpaintings in South Africa'. *South African Journal of Science* 29, 72–83.

Bleek, D. 1932. 'Omens, Wind-Making, Clouds, Part 4'. *Bantu Studies* 6, 323–342.

Bleek, D. 1932. 'Game Animals, Part 3'. *Bantu Studies* 6, 233–249.

Bleek, D. 1932. 'The Lion, Part 2'. *Bantu Studies* 6, 47–63.

Bleek, D. 1931. 'Baboons'. *Bantu Studies* 5, 167–179.

Bleek, D. 1931. 'The Hadzapi or Watindega of Tanganyika Territory'. *Africa* 4 (3), 273–286.

Bleek, D. 1928–1930. 'Bushman Grammar: A Grammatical Sketch of the Language of the / Xam-ka-!k'e'. *Zeitschrift fürEingeborenen-Sprachen* 19, 81–98; 20, 161–174.

Bleek, D. 1929. *Comparative Vocabularies of Bushman Languages*. London: Cambridge University Press.

Bleek, D. 1929. 'Bushman Folklore'. *Africa* 2 (3), 302–313.

Bleek, D. 1928. *The Naron: A Bushman Tribe of the Central Kalahari*. London: Cambridge University Press.

Bleek, D. 1928. 'Bushmen of Central Angola'. *Bantu Studies* 3 (2), 105–125.

Bleek, D. 1927. 'The Distribution of Bushman Languages in South Africa'. *Festschrift Meinhof*, Hamburg, 55–64.

Bleek, D. Ed. 1923. *The Mantis and His Friends: Bushman Folklore Collected by the Late Dr. W.H.I. Bleek and the Late Dr. Lucy C. Lloyd*. Cape Town: Maskew Miller.

Bleek, E. and D. Bleek. 1909. 'Notes on the Bushmen', in M. Tongue. 1909. *Bushman Paintings*. London: Clarendon Press.

Bleek, W. 1875. 'Second Report Concerning Bushman Researches'. Presented to the Cape Parliament.

Bleek, W. 1874. 'Remarks by Dr Bleek'. *Cape Monthly Magazine* 9, 11–13.

Bleek, W. and L. Lloyd. Ed. 1911. *Specimens of Bushman Folklore*. London: George Allen & Co.

Bleek, W. and L. Lloyd. Eds. 1938. *Das wahre Gesicht des Buschmannes in seinen Mythen und Märchen*. Trans. K. Woldmann. Basel: Kommissionverlag Zbinden & Hügin.

Blundell, G. 2004. *Nqabayo's Nomansland: San Rock Art and the Somatic Past*, Studies in Global Archaeology 2, Sweden: Uppsala University.

Blundell, G., C. Chippindale and B. Smith. Eds. 2010. *Seeing and Knowing: Understanding Rock Art With and Without Ethnography*. Johannesburg: Wits University Press.

Blunt, A. 1994. *Travel, Gender and Imperialism: Mary Kingsley and West Africa*. New York and London: Guilford Press.

Breuil, H. 1955. *The White Lady of the Brandberg*. London: Trianon Press.

Breuil, H. 1952. *Four Hundred Centuries of Cave Art*. Trans. M. E. Boyle. Montignac and Dordogne: Centre d'Études et de Documentation Préhistoriques.

Brody, H. 2013. *Tracks across Sand: The Dispossession of the ‡Khomani San of the Southern Kalahari*. London: Face to Face Media.

Bunn, D. 1996. 'The Brown Serpent of the Rocks: Bushman Arrow Toxins in the Dutch and British Imagination, 1735–1850', in B. Cooper and A. Steyn. Eds. *Transgressing Boundaries: New Directions in the Study of Culture in Africa*. Cape Town: UCT Press, 59–85.

Bunzl, M. and H. Glenn Penny. 2003. 'Introduction: Rethinking German Anthropology, Colonialism, and Race', in M. Bunzl and H. Glenn Penny. Eds. *Worldly Provincialism: German Anthropology in the Age of Empire*. Ann Arbor: University of Michigan Press, 1–30.

Burkitt, M. 1928. *South Africa's Past in Stone and Paint*. Cambridge: Cambridge University Press.

Camerini, J. 1996. 'Wallace in the Field'. *Osiris* 11, 44–65.

Carstens, P., G. Klinghardt and M. West. 1987. *Trails in the Thirstland: The Anthropological Field Diaries of Winifred Hoernlé*. Cape Town: Centre for African Studies.

Caton-Thompson, G. 1931. *The Zimbabwe Culture: Ruins and Reactions*. London: Oxford University Press.

Cavanaugh, C. and R. Warne. 2000. Eds. *Telling Tales: Essays in Western Women's History*. Vancouver and Toronto: UBC Press.

Challis, S. 2012. 'Creolisation on the Nineteenth-Century Frontiers of Southern Africa: A Case Study of the AmaTola "Bushmen" in the Maloti-Drakensberg'. *Journal of Southern African Studies* 38, 265–280.

Chaudhuri, N. and M. Strobel. 1992. *Western Women and Imperialism: Complicity and Resistance*. Bloomington and Indianapolis: Indiana University Press.

Chippindale, C. and P. Taçon. Eds. 1998. *The Archaeology of Rock-Art*. Cambridge: Cambridge University Press.

Christol, F. 1897. *Au Sud de l'Afrique*. Paris: Berger-Levrault.

Clifford, J. 1990. 'Notes on Field(notes)', in R. Sanjek. Ed. *Fieldnotes: The Makings of Anthropology*. Ithaca, NY: Cornell University Press, 47–70.

Comaroff, J. and J. Comaroff. 1991. *Of Revelation and Revolution: Christianity, Colonialism and Consciousness in South Africa*. Chicago: University of Chicago Press.

Coombes, A. 2004. *History After Apartheid: Visual Culture and Public Memory in a Democratic South Africa*. Johannesburg: Wits University Press.

Coplan, D. 2003. 'Land from the Ancestors: Popular Religious Pilgrimage along the South Africa–Lesotho Border'. *Journal of Southern African Studies* 29 (4), 984–990.

Crais, C. 1992. *The Making of the Colonial Order: White Supremacy and Black Resistance in the Eastern Cape, 1770–1865*. Johannesburg: Wits University Press.

Cushman, M. 1944. *Missionary Doctor: The Story of Twenty Years in Africa*. New York: Harper, 152–153.

Dart, R. 1925. 'The Historical Succession of Cultural Impacts upon South Africa'. *Nature* 115, 425–429.

Davison, P. 2001. 'Typecast – Representations of the Bushmen at the South African Museum'. *Public Archaeology* 1, 3–20.

Deacon, J. 2005. 'Foreword', in J. Hollmann. Ed. *Customs and Beliefs of the /Xam Bushmen*. Johannesburg: Wits University Press, xiii-xv.

Deacon, J. 1986. ' "My Place is the Bitterpits": The Home Territory of Bleek and Lloyd's /Xam San Informants'. *African Studies* 45, 135–155.

Deacon, J. and T. Dowson. Eds. 1996. *Voices from the Past: /Xam Bushmen and the Bleek and Lloyd Collection*. Johannesburg: Wits University Press.

De Kock, W. Ed. 1968. *Dictionary of South African Bibliography*, Vol. I. Johannesburg: National Council for Social Research, 80–85.

Denbow, J. 1984. 'Prehistoric Herders and Foragers of the Kalahari: The Evidence for 1500 Years of Interaction', in C. Schrire. Ed. *Past and Present in Hunter Gatherer Studies*. London: Academic Press, 175–193.

Derricourt. 2011, R. *Inventing Africa: History, Archaeology and Ideas*. New York: Pluto Press.

De Villiers, J. 2012. *Tamme's Country: An Intertextual Reading of the !Kun-Lloyd Archive*. Unpublished MA dissertation, University of the Western Cape.

Di Gregorio, M. 2002. 'Reflections of a Nonpolitical Naturalist: Ernst Haeckel, Wilhelm Bleek, Friedrich Müller and the Meaning of Language'. *Journal of the History of Biology* 35, 79–109.

Doke, C. 1957. 'A Bushman Dictionary Review'. African Studies 16 (2), 124–125.

Doke, C. 1933. 'Preliminary Investigation into Native Languages'. Bantu Studies 7.

Dowson, T., S. Ouzman, G. Blundell and A. Holliday. 1994. 'A Stow Site Revisited: Zastron District, Orange Free State', in T. Dowson and J.D. Lewis-Williams. Eds. Contested Images: Diversity in Southern African Rock Art Research. Johannesburg: Wits University Press, 177–188.

Drinker, S. 1948. Music and Women: The Story of Women and Their Relation to Music. New York: Coward McCann.

Driver, D. 1995. 'Lady Anne Barnard's Cape Journals and the Concept of Self-Othering'. Pretexts: Studies in Literature and Culture 5, 46-65.

Dubow, S. 2006. A Commonweath of Knowledge, Science, Sensibility and White South Africa 1820–2000. Oxford: Oxford University Press.

Dubow, S. 2000. 'A Commonwealth of Science: The British Association in South Africa, 1905 and 1929', in Science and Society in Southern Africa. Manchester: University of Manchester Press.

Dubow, S. 2004. 'Earth History, Natural History and Prehistory at the Cape, 1860–75'. Comparative Studies in Society and History 46, 207–233.

Dubow, S. 1996. 'Human Origins, Race Typology and the Other Raymond Dart'. African Studies 55 (1), 1–30.

Dubow, S. 1995. Illicit Union: Scientific Racism in Modern South Africa. Johannesburg: Wits University Press.

Du Plessis, M. 2014. 'The Damaging Effects of Romantic Mythopoeia on Khoesan Linguistics'. Critical Arts 28 (3), 569–592.

Du Plessis, M. 2014. 'A Century of the "Specimens of Bushman Folklore": 100 Years of Linguistic Neglect', in J. Deacon and P. Skotnes. Eds. The Courage of //Kabbo: Celebrating the 100th Anniversary of the Publication of 'Specimens of Bushman Folklore'. Cape Town: UCT Press.

Eberhard, E. 1996. 'Wilhelm Bleek and the Founding of Bushman Research', in J. Deacon and T. Dowson. Eds. Voices from the Past: /Xam Bushmen and the Bleek and Lloyd Collection. Johannesburg: Wits University Press, 49–65.

Edwards, E. 2001. Raw Histories: Photographs, Anthropology and Museums. Oxford: Berg.

Edwards, E. 1997. 'Making Histories: The Torres Strait Expedition of 1898'. Pacific Studies 20 (4), 13–34.

Elphick. R. 1985. Khoikhoi and the Founding of White South Africa. Johannesburg: Ravan Press.

Engelbrecht. J. 1956. 'Introduction', in D. Bleek. A Bushman Dictionary. New Haven, CT: American Oriental Society.

Engelbrecht, J. Ed. 1952. Zulu Legends. Cape Town: Van Schaik.

Etherington, N. 2011. 'Barbarians Ancient and Modern'. American Historical Review 116 (1), 31–57.

Fabian, J. 2000. Out of Our Minds: Reason and Madness in the Exploration of Central Africa. Berkley: University of California Press.

Finkel, M. 2009. 'The Hadza'. National Geographic 216 (6), 94–104.

Flett, A., and P. Letley. 2013. 'Style and Stylistic Change in the Rock Art of the Southeastern Mountains of Southern Africa'. South African Archaeological Bulletin 68, 3–14.

Flett, A., and P. Letley. 2007. 'Brother Otto Mäeder: An Examination and Evaluation of His Work as a Rock Art Recorder in South Africa'. Southern African Humanities 19, 103–121.

Fountaine, M. 1980. *Love among the Butterflies: The Travels and Adventures of a Victorian Lady*. Boston: Little, Brown.

Frobenius, L. 1909. *The Childhood of Man*. Trans. A. Keane. London: Seely & Co.

Frobenius, L. N.d. *Erythräa, Länder aus Zeiten des Heiligen Königsmordes*. Berlin-Zurich: Atlantis.

Glenn Penny, H. 2008. 'Traditions in the German Language', in H. Kuklick. Ed. *A New History of Anthropology*. Oxford: Blackwell, 79–95.

Godby, M. 1996. 'Images of //Kabbo', in P. Skotnes. Ed. *Miscast: Negotiating the Presence of the Bushmen*. Cape Town: UCT Press, 115-128.

Goodwin, A., and C. van Riet Lowe. 1929. *The Stone Age Cultures of South Africa*. Edinburgh: Neill and Co.

Gordon, R. and S. Sholto Douglas. 2000. *The Bushman Myth: The Making of a Namibian Underclass*. Boulder, CO: Westview Press.

Gordon, R. 1999. ' "Bain's Bushmen": Scenes at the Empire Exhibition, 1936', in B. Lindfors. Ed. *Africans on Stage: Studies in Ethnological Show Business*. Bloomington: Indiana University Press, 266–289.

Gordon, R. 1987. 'Remembering Agnes Winifred Hoernlé'. *Social Dynamics* 13 (1), 68–72.

Gordon, R. 1984. 'The !Kung in the Kalahari Exchange: An Ethnohistorical Perspective', in C. Schrire. Ed. *Past and Present in Hunter Gatherer Studies*. London: Academic Press, 195–224.

Guenther, M. 1999. *Tricksters and Trancers: Bushman Religion and Society*. Bloomington: Indiana University Press.

Guenther, M. 1996. 'From "Lords of the Desert" to "Rubbish People": The Colonial and Contemporary State of the Nharo of Botswana', in P. Skotnes. Ed. *Miscast: Negotiating the Presence of the Bushmen*. Cape Town: UCT Press, 323.

Guenther, M. 1994. 'The Relationship of Bushman Art to Ritual and Folklore', in T. Dowson and J.D. Lewis-Williams. Eds. *Contested Images: Diversity in Southern African Rock Art Research*. Johannesburg: Wits University Press, 257–273.

Güldemann, T. 2006. 'The San Languages of Southern Namibia: Linguistic Appraisal with Special Reference to J.G. Krönlein's Nuusaa Data'. *Anthropological Linguistics* 4, 369–395.

Güldemann, T. 2005. 'Introduction', in J. Hollmann. Ed. *Customs and Beliefs of the /Xam Bushmen*. Johannesburg: Wits University Press, 385–387.

Güldemann, T. Ed. 2000. *The ///ke or Bushmen of Griqualand West: Notes on the Language of the ///ke or Bushmen of Griqualand West by Dorothea F. Bleek*. Working Paper 15, Khoisan Forum. Köln: Institut für Afrikanistik.

Hammond-Tooke, D. 1997. *Imperfect Interpreters: South Africa's Anthropologists, 1920–1990*. Johannesburg: Wits University Press.

Hansen, D. 1996. 'Bushman Music: Still an Unknown', in P. Skotnes. Ed. *Miscast: Negotiating the Presence of the Bushmen*. Cape Town: UCT Press, 297–305.

Harries, P. 2007. *Butterflies and Barbarians: Swiss Missionaries and Systems of Knowledge in South-East Africa*. Johannesburg: Wits University Press.

Harries, P. 2000. 'Field Sciences in Scientific Fields: Ethnology, Botany and the Early Ethnographic Monograph in the Work of H-A Junod', in S. Dubow. Ed. *Science and Society in Southern Africa*. Manchester: University of Manchester Press.

Harries, P. 1991. 'Exclusion, Classification and Internal Colonialism: The Emergence of Ethnicity among the Tsonga-Speakers of South Africa', in L. Vail. Ed. *The Creation of Tribalism in Southern Africa*. Los Angeles: University of California Press, 85–87.

Harris, Z. 1952. 'Discourse Analysis'. *Language* 28 (1), 1–30.

Hart, L. 2002. *The San (Bushman) Photographs of Dorothea Bleek: The Complete 312 Images.* BC 151, University of Cape Town: Manuscripts and Archives Department.

Hartmann, W., J. Silvester, and P. Hayes. Eds. 1998. *The Colonising Camera: Photographs in the Making of Namibian History.* Cape Town: UCT Press.

Hayes, P. and A. Bank. Eds. 2001. 'Judging Books by Their Covers'. *Kronos* 27, Visual History Special Issue, 1–14.

Heine, B. and C. König. 2008. 'What Can Linguistics Tell Us about Early Khoekhoe History?' *Southern African Humanities* 20, 235–248.

Henry, L. 2007. 'A History of Removing Rock Art in South Africa'. *South African Archaeological Bulletin* 62 (185), 44–48.

Herbert, R. 2002. 'The Socio-history of Clicks in Southern Bantu', in R. Mesthrie. Ed. *Language in South Africa.* Cambridge: Cambridge University Press, 297–315,

Herbert, R. 1993. 'Not With One Mouth'. *African Studies* 52 (2), 1–4.

Hewitt, J. 1925. 'On Some Stone Implements from the Cape Province'. *SA Journal of Science* 22, 441–453.

Hewitt, J. 1921. 'On Several Implements and Ornaments from Strandloper Sites in the Eastern Province'. *SA Journal of Science* 18 (1–2), 454–467.

Hewitt, J. 1920. 'Notes Relating to Aboriginal Tribes of the Eastern Province'. *SA Journal of Science* 17 (1), 304–321.

Hewitt, R. 1986. *Structure, Meaning and Ritual in the Narratives of the Southern San.* Hamburg: Helmut Buske.

Hollmann, J. Ed. 2005. *Customs and Beliefs of the /Xam Bushmen.* Johannesburg: Wits University Press.

Huss, B. and O. Mäeder. 1925. 'The Origin of the Bushman Paintings at the Kei River'. *South African Journal of Science* 22, 496–503

Impey, S. 1926. *Origin of the Bushmen and the Rock Paintings of South Africa.* Johannesburg: Juta.

Jacobs, N. 2006. 'The Intimate Politics of Ornithology in Colonial Africa'. *Comparative Studies in Society and History* 48, 564–603.

Jeater, D. 1995. 'The Fruits of the Tree of Knowledge: Power versus Pollution in Official Attitudes towards African Vernaculars in Southern Rhodesia, 1890–1993'. Seminar paper, Wits Institute for Advanced Social Research.

Jeater, D. 1994. 'The Way You Tell Them: Language, Ideology and Development Policy in Southern Rhodesia'. Paper presented at the Journal of Southern African Studies Conference on 'Paradigms Lost, Paradigms Regained? Southern African Studies in the 1990s'.

Jolly, P. 1996. 'Between the Lines: Some Remarks on "Bushman" Ethnicity', in P. Skotnes. Ed. *Miscast: Negotiating the Presence of the Bushmen.* Cape Town: UCT Press, 197–209.

Jolly, P. 1998. 'Modelling Change in the Contact Art of the South-Eastern San, Southern Africa', in C. Chippindale and P. Taçon. Eds. *The Archaeology of Rock-Art.* Cambridge: Cambridge University Press, 247–267.

Kaplan, J. 1978. 'The "Real Life" ', in D. Aaron. Ed. *Studies in Biography*, Harvard English Studies 8, 1–8.

Kleingeld, P. 1999. 'Six Varieties of Cosmopolitanism in Late Eighteenth-Century Germany'. *Journal of the History of Ideas* 60 (3), 505–524.

Krige. E. 1960. 'Agnes Winifred Hoernlé: An Appreciation'. *African Studies* 19 (3), 138–144.

Krog, A. 2003. *A Change of Tongue.* Cape Town: Struik.

Kuklick, H. 2011. 'Personal Equations: Reflections on the History of Fieldwork, with Special Reference to Sociocultural Anthropology'. *Isis* 102 (1), 2.

Kuper, A. 2005. *The Reinvention of Primitive Society: Transformations of a Myth*. London and New York: Routledge.

Kuper, A. 1999. 'South African Anthropology: An Inside Job', in *Among the Anthropologists: History and Context in Anthropology*. London: Athlone Press, 45–70.

Kuper, H. 1984. 'Function, History, Biography: Reflections on Fifty Years in the British Anthropological Tradition', in G. Stocking. Ed. *Functionalism Historicised: Essays on British Social Anthropology*. Madison: University of Wisconsin Press, 192–213.

Landau, P. 2010. *Popular Politics in the History of South Africa, 1400–1948*. Cambridge: Cambridge University Press.

Larson, F. 2007. 'Anthropology as Comparative Anatomy: Reflecting on the Study of Material Culture during the Late 1800s and the Late 1900s'. *Journal of Material Culture* 12 (1), 89–112.

Latour, B.1987. *Science in Action: How to Follow Scientists and Engineers through Society*. Cambridge, MA: Harvard University Press.

Lee, H. *Virginia Woolf*. London· Vintage, 1997.

Legassick, M. and C. Rassool. 2000. *Skeletons in the Cupboard: South African Museums and the Trade in Human Remains, 1907–1917*. Cape Town and Kimberley: Iziko and McGregor Museum.

Leibhammer, N. 2009. 'Originals and Copies: A Phenomenological Difference', in P. Mitchell and B. Smith. Eds. *The Eland's People: Essays in Memory of Patrica Vinnicombe*. Johannesburg: Wits University Press, 43–59.

Leśniewski, M. 2010. 'Guns and Horses, c 1750 to c 1850: Korana – People or Raiding Hordes?' *Werkwinkel Journal of Low Countries and South African Studies* 5 (2), 11–16.

Lestrade, G. 1934. 'European Influences upon the Development of Bantu Language and Literature', in I. Schapera. Ed. *Western Civilisation and the Natives of South Africa*. London: Routledge, 105–127.

Lewis-Williams, J.D. 2013. 'From Illustration to Social Intervention: Three Nineteenth-Century /Xam Myths and Their Implications for Understanding San Rock Art'. *Cambridge Anthropological Journal* 23 (2), 241–262.

Lewis-Williams, J.D. 2009. 'Patricia Vinnicombe: A Memoir', in P. Mitchell and B. Smith. Eds. *The Eland's People: Essays in Memory of Patricia Vinnicombe*. Johannesburg: Wits University Press, 13–27.

Lewis-Williams, J.D. 2008. 'A Nexus of Lives: How a Heretical Bishop Contributed to Our Knowledge of South Africa's Past'. *Southern African Humanities* 20, 463–475.

Lewis-Williams, J.D. 2002. *A Cosmos in Stone: Interpreting Religion and Society through Rock Art*. Oxford: AltaMira Press.

Lewis-Williams, J.D. Ed. 2000. *Stories that Float from Afar: Ancestral Folklore of the San of Southern Africa*. Cape Town: David Philip.

Lewis-Williams, J.D. 1996. '"The Ideas Generally Entertained with Regard to the Bushmen and Their Mental Condition"', in P. Skotnes. Ed. *Miscast: Negotiating the Presence of the Bushmen*. Cape Town: UCT Press, 307–310.

Lewis-Williams, J.D. 1984. 'Ideological Continuities in Prehistoric Southern Africa: The Evidence of Rock Art', in C. Schrire. Ed. *Past and Present in Hunter Gatherer Societies*. London: Academic Press.

Lewis-Williams, J.D. 1981. *Believing and Seeing: Symbolic Meanings in Southern San Rock Art*. London: Academic Press.

Lewis-Williams, J.D. and D. Pearce. 2012. 'Framed Idiosyncrasy: Method and Evidence in the Interpretation of San Rock Art'. *South African Archaeological Bulletin* 67, 75–87.

Lewis-Williams, J.D. and S. Challis. 2011. *Deciphering Ancient Minds: The Mystery of San Bushman Rock Art*. London: Thames & Hudson.

Lewis-Williams, J.D. and T. Dowson. Eds. 1994. 'Aspects of Rock Art Research: A Critical Retrospective', in T. Dowson and J.D. Lewis-Williams. Eds. *Contested Images: Diversity in Southern African Rock Art Research*. Johannesburg: Wits University Press, 201-221.

Lloyd, L.1889. *A Short Account of Further Bushman Material Collected. Third Report Concerning Bushman Researches*. London: David Nutt.

Loubser, J. 2010. 'Layer by Layer: Precision and Accuracy in Rock Art Recording and Dating', in G. Blundell, C. Chippindale and B. Smith. Eds. *Seeing and Knowing: Understanding Rock Art With and Without Ethnography*. Johannesburg: Wits University Press, 149–165.

Loubser, J. and G. Laurens. 1994. 'Depictions of Domestic Ungulates and Shields: Hunter/Gatherers and Agro-Pastoralists in the Caledon River Valley Area', in T. Dowson and J.D. Lewis-Williams. Eds. *Contested Images: Diversity in Southern African Rock Art Research*. Johannesburg: Wits University Press, 83–118.

Mandela, N. 2010. *Conversations with Myself*. London: Pan Macmillan.

Marchand, S. 1997. 'Leo Frobenius and the Revolt against the West'. *Journal of Contemporary History* 32 (2), 153-170.

Marks, S. Ed. 1987. *Not Either an Experimental Doll: The Separate Worlds of Three South African Women*. Bloomington: Indiana University Press.

Marshall Thomas, E. 1959. *The Harmless People*. New York: Knopf.

Martin, M. 1996. 'Bringing the Past into the Present: Facing and Negotiating History, Memory, Redress and Reconciliation at the South African National Gallery'. South African Museums Association conference, Durban.

Maynes, M., J. Pierce and B. Laslett. 2008. *Telling Stories: The Use of Personal Narratives in the Social Sciences and History*. Ithaca, NY, and London: Cornell University Press.

Mazel, A. 2009. 'Unsettled Times: Shaded Polychrome Paintings and Hunter-Gatherer History in the Southeastern Mountains of Southern Africa'. *Southern African Humanities* 21, 85–115.

McGranaghan, M., S. Challis and J.D. Lewis-Williams. 2013. 'Joseph Millerd Orpen's "A Glimpse into the Mythology of the Maluti Bushmen": A Contextual Introduction and Republished Text'. *Southern African Humanities* 25, 137–166.

Meskell, L. 2009. 'Contextualising *People of the Eland*', in P. Mitchell and B. Smith, *The Eland's People: Essays in Memory of Patrica Vinnicombe*. Johannesburg: Wits University Press, 29-41.

Mesthrie, R. 2002. 'South Africa: A Sociolinguistic Overview', in R. Mesthrie. Ed. *Language in South Africa*. Cambridge: Cambridge University Press, 11–26.

Mguni, S. 2012. 'Five Years of Southern African Rock Art Research', in P. Bahn, N. Franklin and M. Strecker. Eds. *Rock Art Studies News of the World IV*. Oxford: Oxbow Books, 99–112.

Mitchell, P. 2010. Review: *Vols de Vaches à Christol Cave: Histoire Critique d'une Image Rupestre d'Afrique du Sud. Africa* 80 (4), 664–666.

Mitchell, P. 2009. 'Hunter-Gatherers and Farmers: Some Implications of 1,800 Years of Interaction in the Maloti-Drakensberg Region of Southern Africa'. *Senri Ethnological Studies* 73, 15–46.

Mitchell, P. and S. Challis. 2008. 'A First Glimpse into the Maloti Mountains: The Diary of James Murray Grant's Expedition of 1873–1874'. *Southern African Humanities* 20 (1), 401–463.

Mitchell, P. and B. Smith. Eds. 2009. *The Eland's People: New Perspectives in the Rock Art of the Maloti-Drakensberg Bushmen: Essays in Memory of Patricia Vinnicombe*. Johannesburg: Wits University Press.

Mitchell, W. 1994. 'Imperial Landscape', in W. Mitchell. Ed. *Landscape and Power*. Chicago: University of Chicago Press, 4–34.

Moran, S. 2009. *Representing Bushmen: South Africa and the Origin of Language*. Rochester: University of Rochester Press.

Morris, D. 2008. 'Driekopseiland Rock Engraving Site, South Africa: A Precolonial Landscape Lost and Re-membered', in A. Gazin-Schwartz and A. Smith. Eds. *Landscapes of Clearance: Archaeological and Anthropological Perspectives*. Walnut Creek, CA: Left Coast, 87–111.

Mostert, N. 1992. *Frontiers: The Epic of South Africa's Creation and the Tragedy of the Xhosa People*. London: Pimlico.

Obermaier, H. and H. Kühn. 1930. *Bushman Art: Rock Paintings of South-West Africa*. London: Humphrey Milford, Oxford University Press.

Orpen, J. 1874. 'A Glimpse into the Mythology of the Maluti Bushmen'. *Cape Monthly Magazine* 9, 1–11.

Ouzman, S. 2006. 'Why "Conserve"? Situating Southern African Rock Art in the Here and Now', in N. Agnew and J. Bridgeland. Eds. *Of the Past, for the Future: Integrating Archaeology and Conservation*. Los Angeles: Getty Institute, 346–352.

Ouzman, S. 2005. 'The Magical Arts of a Raider Nation: Central South Africa's Korana Rock Art'. *South African Archaeological Society Goodwin Series* 9: 101–113.

Ouzman, S. 1998. 'Towards a Mindscape of Landscape: Rock-Art as Expression of World-Understanding', in C. Chippindale and P. Taçon. Eds. *The Archaeology of Rock-Art*. Cambridge: Cambridge University Press, 30–41.

Pager, H. 1971. *Ndedema: A Documentation of the Rock Paintings of the Ndedema Gorge*. Graz: Akademische Druck.

Pager, H. 1962. English summary in L. Frobenius. *Madsimu Dsangara: Südafrikanische Felsbilderchronik*. Graz: Akademische Druk, 39–45.

Parkington, J. 2007. '//Kabbo's Sentence', in P. Skotnes. *Claim to the Country: The Archive of Wilhelm Bleek and Lucy Lloyd*. Cape Town and Athens, OH: Jacana and Ohio University Press, 75–89.

Pearce, D. 2012. 'Ethnography and History: The Significance of Social Change in Interpreting Rock Art', in B. Smith, K. Helskog and D. Morris. Eds. *Working with Rock Art: Recording, Presenting and Understanding Rock Art Using Indigenous Knowledge*. Johannesburg: Wits University Press.

Penn. N. 1996. ' "Fated to Perish": The Destruction of the Cape San', in P. Skotnes. Ed. *Miscast: Negotiating The Presence of the Bushmen*. Cape Town: UCT Press, 81–91.

Perham, M. 1974. *African Apprenticeship*. New York: Homes & Meier.

Perschke, R. Undated poster. *Women Pioneers in Rock Art Research: Mary E. Boyle, Erika Trautmann and Vera C.C. Collum*. Institut für Vor- und Frühgeschichtliche Archäologie und Provinzialrömische Archäologie.

Phillips, H. 1993. *The University of Cape Town 1918–1948: The Formative Years*. Cape Town: UCT Press.

Pratt, M. 1992. *Imperial Eyes: Travel Writing and Transculturation*. London: Routledge.

Pugach, S. 2012. *Africa in Translation: A History of Colonial Linguistics in Germany and Beyond, 1814–1945*. Ann Arbor: University of Michigan Press.

Quigley, C. 2001. *Skulls and Skeletons: Human Bone Collections and Accumulations*. Jefferson, NC: McFarland.

Raffles, R. 2002. 'Intimate Knowledge'. *International Social Science Journal* 173, 325–335.

Rassool, C. 2015. 'Re-storing the Skeletons of Empire: Return, Reburial and Rehumanisation in Southern Africa'. *Journal of Southern African Studies* 41 (3), 659–660.

Rassool, C. 2004. 'The Individual, Auto/biography and History in South Africa'. Unpublished PhD thesis, University of the Western Cape, 248.

Rassool, C. 2002. 'Beyond the Cult of "Salvation" and "Remarkable Equality": A New Paradigm for the Bleek-Lloyd Collection'. *Kronos* 32, 251.

Rassool, C. and P. Hayes. 2002. 'Science and the Spectacle: //Khanako's South Africa, 1936–1937', in W. Woodward, P. Hayes and G. Minkley. Eds. *Deep hiStories: Gender and Colonialism in Southern Africa*. New York: Rodopi.

Romero, P. Ed. 1992. *Women's Voices on Africa: A Century of Travel Writings*. Princeton, NJ, and New York: Markus Wiener.

Rosenthal, E. and A. Goodwin. 1953. *Cave Artists of South Africa*. Cape Town: A.A. Balkema.

Ross, R. 2004. 'Hermanus Matroos, aka Ngxukumeshe: A Life on the Border'. *Kronos* 30, 47–69.

Sadr, K. 2008. 'Invisible Herders? The Archaeology of Khoekhoe Pastoralists'. *Southern African Humanities* 20, 179–203.

Sadr, K. and F. Fauvelle-Aymar. Eds. 2008. 'Khoekhoe and the Origins of Herding in Southern Africa'. *Southern African Humanities* 20 (1), 93–132.

Sanders, E. 1996. 'The Hamitic Hypothesis: Its Origin and Functions in Time Perspective'. *Journal of African History* 10 (4), 521–532.

Saunders, C. 1988. *The Making of the South African Past: Major Historians on Race and Class*. Cape Town: David Philip.

Schapera, I. 1930 [1980]. *The Khoisan Peoples of South Africa*. London: Routledge.

Schapera, I. 1927. 'The Tribal Divisions of the Bushmen'. *Man* 27, 68–73.

Schapera, I. 1926. 'A Preliminary Consideration of the Relationship between the Hottentots and the Bushmen'. *South African Journal of Science* 23, 833–866.

Schapera, I. 1925. 'Some Stylistic Affinities of Bushman Art'. *South African Journal of Science* 22, 504–515.

Schestokat, K. 2003. *German Women in Cameroon: Travelogues from Colonial Times*. New York: Peter Lang,

Schlanger, N. 2010. 'Manual and Intellectual Labour in Archaeology: Past and Present in Human Resource Management', in S. Koerner and I. Russell. Eds. *Unquiet Pasts: Risk Society, Lived Cultural Heritage, Re-designing Reflexivity*. London: Ashgate, 161–171.

Schlanger, N. 2003. 'The Burkitt Affair Revisited: Colonial Implications and Identity Politics in Early South African Prehistoric Research'. *Archaeological Dialogues* 10 (1), 5–32.

Schoeman, K. Ed. 1997. *A Debt of Gratitude: Lucy Lloyd and the 'Bushman Work' of G.W. Stow*. Cape Town: South African Library.

Schrire, C. 1996. 'Native Views of Western Eyes', in P. Skotnes. Ed. Miscast: *Negotiating the Presence of the Bushmen*. Cape Town: UCT Press, 343–353.

Schumaker, L. 2001. *Africanizing Anthropology: Fieldwork, Networks and the Making of Cultural Knowledge in Central Africa*. Durham, NC: Duke University Press.

Scott Deetz, P. 2007. *Catalog of the Bleek-Lloyd Collection in the Scott Family Archive*. Williamsburg, VA: Deetz Ventures, Inc.

Scott Deetz, P. and M. Scott Roos. 2010. 'Memories of Growing Up with "Aunt D"', email communication.

240

Segal, B. 1935. 'A Possible Base for "Bushman" Paint'. *Bantu Studies* 9, 49–51.

Shepherd, N. 2003. ' "When the Hand that Holds the Trowel is Black": Disciplinary Practices of Self-Representation and the Issue of "Native" Labour in Archaeology'. *Journal of Social Archaeology* 3 (3), 334–352.

Shepherd, N. 2002. 'Disciplining Archaeology: The Invention of South African Prehistory, 1923–1953'. *Kronos* 28, 127–145.

Shostak, M. 1989. ' "What the Wind Won't Take Away": The Genesis of *Nisa: The Life and Words of a !Kung Woman*', in Personal Narratives Group. *Interpreting Women's Lives, Feminist Theory and Personal Narratives*. Bloomington: Indiana University Press.

Skotnes, P. 2008. *Unconquerable Spirit: George Stow's History Paintings of the San*. Johannesburg: Jacana.

Skotnes, P. 2007. Ed. *Claim to the Country: The Archive of Wilhelm Bleek and Lucy Lloyd*. Cape Town and Athens, OH: Jacana and Ohio University Press.

Skotnes, P. 2002. 'The Politics of Bushman Representation', in P. Landau and D. Kaspin. Eds. *Images and Empires: Visuality in Colonial and Postcolonial Africa*. Los Angeles and London: University of California Press, 253–274.

Skotnes, P. 1996. 'The Thin Black Line: Diversity and Transformation in the Bleek and Lloyd Collection and the Paintings of the Southern San', in J. Deacon and T. Dowson. Eds. *Voices from the Past: /Xam Bushmen and the Bleek and Lloyd Collection*. Johannesburg: Wits University Press, 234–244.

Skotnes, P. Ed. 1996. *Miscast: Negotiating the Presence of the Bushmen*. Cape Town: UCT Press.

Skotnes, P. and M. Fleishman. 2002. *A Story is the Wind: Representing Time and Space in San Narratives*. Cape Town: LLAREC.

Smith, B., J.D. Lewis-Williams, G. Blundell and C. Chippindale. 2000. 'Archaeology and Symbolism in the New South African Coat of Arms'. *Antiquity* 74, 467–468.

Smith, D. 2010. *Young Mandela*. London: Weidenfeld & Nicolson.

Solomon, A. 2006. 'Roots and Revolutions: A Critical Overview of Early and Late San Rock Art Research'. *Afrique & Histoire* 2 (6), 77–110.

Solomon, A. 1996. 'Some Questions about Style and Authorship in Later San Paintings', in P. Skotnes. Ed. *Miscast: Negotiating the Presence of the Bushmen*. Cape Town: UCT Press, 291–295.

Solomon, A. 1994. ' "Mythic Women": A Study in Variability in San Rock Art and Narrative', in T. Dowson and J.D. Lewis-Williams. Eds. *Contested Images: Diversity in Southern African Rock Art Research*. Johannesburg: Wits University Press, 331–371.

Staudenmaier, P. 2014. *Between Occultism and Nazism: Anthroposophy and the Politics of Race in the Fascist Era*. Leiden: Brill.

Steiner, R. [1904] 1911. *The Submerged Continents of Atlantis and Lemuria, Their History and Civilisation*. Trans. M. Gysi. Chicago: Rajput Press.

Steinmetz, G. 2007. *The Devil's Handwriting: Precoloniality and the German Colonial State in Qingdao, Samoa, and Southwest Africa*. Chicago: University of Chicago Press.

Stocking, G. 1992. *The Ethnographer's Magic and Other Essays in the History of Anthropology*. Madison: University of Wisconsin Press.

Stow, G. 1905. *The Native Races of South Africa: A History of the Intrusion of the Hottentots and Bantu into the Hunting Grounds of the Bushmen, the Aborigines of the Country*. London: Swan Sonnenschein.

Stow, G. and D. Bleek. Ed. 1930. *Rock Paintings in South Africa from Parts of the Eastern Province and Orange Free State*. London: Methuen.

Swanepoel, N., A. Esterhuysen and P. Bonner. Eds. 2008. *Five Hundred Years Rediscovered: Southern African Precedents and Prospects*. Johannesburg: Wits University Press.

Szalay, M. Ed. 2002. *The Moon as Shoe: Drawings of the San*. Zurich: Scheidegger and Spiess.

Teukolsky, R. 2009. 'Primitives and Post-Impressionists: Roger Fry's Anthropological Modernism', in *The Literate Eye: Victorian Art Writing and Modernist Aesthetics*. Oxford: Oxford University Press, 192–233.

Thackeray, F. 1994. 'Animals, Conceptual Associations and Southern African Rock Art: A Multidisciplinary, Exploratory Approach', in T. Dowson and J.D. Lewis-Williams. Eds. *Contested Images: Diversity in Southern African Rock Art Research*. Johannesburg: Wits University Press, 223–235.

Thornton, R. 1983. 'Narrative Ethnography in Africa, 1850–1920: The Creation and Capture of an Appropriate Domain for Anthropology'. *Man* 18 (3), 502–520.

Thornton, R. 1983. ' "This Dying Out Race": W.H.I. Bleek's Approach to the Languages of Southern Africa'. *Social Dynamics* 9 (2), 1–10.

Tomaselli, K. 2005. *Where Global Contradictions Are Sharpest: Research Stories from the Kalahari*. Amsterdam: Rosenberg Publishers.

Tongue, M. 1909. *Bushman Paintings*. London: Clarendon Press.

Trail, A. 2002. 'The Khoesan Languages', in R. Mesthrie. Ed. *Language in South Africa*. Cambridge: Cambridge University Press, 42–43.

Tucker, A. 1913. 'Richtersveld: The Land and Its People'. Public lecture delivered in Johannesburg.

Tylor, E. 1871 [1920]. *Primitive Culture*. London: John Murray.

Uehli, E. 1936. *Atlantis und das Rätsel der Eiszeitkunst: Versuch einer Mysteriengeschichte der Urzeit Europas*. Stuttgard: Hoffmann.

Van der Riet, J., M. van der Riet and D. Bleek. 1940. *More Rock-Paintings in South Africa*. London: Methuen.

Van Riet Lowe, C. 1929. 'Fresh Light on the Prehistoric Archaeology of South Africa'. *Bantu Studies* 3 (4), 386–393.

Vinnicombe, P. 1976. *People of the Eland: Rock Paintings of the Drakensberg Bushmen as a Reflection of Their Life and Thought*. Pietermaritzburg: University of Natal Press.

Vossen, R. Ed. 2013. *The Khoesan Languages*. Oxford: Routledge.

Wanless, A. 2007. *The Silence of Colonial Melancholy: The Fourie Collection of Khoisan Ethnologica*. Unpublished DPhil thesis, University of the Witwatersrand.

Webster, C. 2000. 'The Portrait Cabinet of Dr Bleek: Anthropometric Photographs by Early Cape Photographers'. *Critical Arts* 14 (1), 1–14.

Weinberg, P. 1997. *In Search of the San*. Johannesburg: Porcupine Press.

Weintroub, J. 2013. 'On Biography and Archive: Dorothea Bleek and the Making of the Bleek Collection'. *South African Historical Journal* 65 (1), 70–89.

Weintroub, J. 2006. ' "Some Sort of Mania": Otto Hartung Spohr and the Making of the Bleek Collection'. *Kronos* 32, 114–138.

Weintroub, J. 2006. *From Tin Trunk to World Wide Web: The Making of the Bleek Collection*. Unpublished MPhil dissertation, University of Cape Town.

Wessels, M. 2010. *Bushman Letters: Interpreting /Xam Narratives*. Johannesburg: Wits University Press.

Wessels, M. 2008. 'New Directions in/Xam Studies: Some of the Implications of Andrew Bank's *Bushmen in a Victorian World: The Remarkable Story of the Bleek-Lloyd Collection of Bushman Folklore*'. *Critical Arts* 22 (1), 69–82.

Whitman, J. 1984. 'From Philology to Anthropology in Mid-Nineteenth-Century Germany', in G. Stocking. Ed. *Functionalism Historicised: Essays on British Social Anthropology*. Madison: University of Wisconsin Press.

Willcox, A. 1956. *Rock Paintings of the Drakensberg, Natal and Griqualand East*. London: Max Parrish.

Wilman, M. 1933. *The Rock-Engravings of Griqualand West and Bechuanaland South Africa*. Cambridge and Kimberley: Deighton Bell and Alexander McGregor Memorial Museum.

Wilmsen, E. 2002. 'Primal Anxiety, Sanctified Landscapes: The Imagery of Primitiveness in the Ethnographic Fictions of Laurens van der Post'. *Visual Anthropology* 15, 143–201.

Wilmsen, E. 1989. *Land Filled with Flies: A Political Economy of the Kalahari*. Chicago: University of Chicago Press.

Wintjes, J. 2013. 'The Frobenius Expeditionto Natal and the Cinyati Archive'. *Southern African Humanities* 25, 167–205.

Wintjes, J. 2011. 'A Pictorial Genealogy: The Rainmaking Group from Sehonghong Shelter'. *Southern African Humanities* 23, 17–54.

Witz, L. 2006. 'Transforming Museums on Postapartheid Tourist Routes', in I. Karp, C. Kratz, L. Szwaja and T. Ybarra-Frausto. Eds. *Museum Frictions: Public Cultures/Global Transformations*. Durham, NC: Duke University Press, 115–123.

Woolf, V. 1942. 'The Art of Biography', in *The Death of the Moth and Other Essays*. New York: Harcourt Brace Jovanovich, 187–197.

Yates, R., A. Manhire and J. Parkington. 1994. 'Rock Painting and History in the South-Western Cape', in T. Dowson and J.D. Lewis-Williams. Eds. *Contested Images: Diversity in Southern African Rock Art Research*. Wits University Press, 29–60.

York Mason, A. 1933. 'Rock Paintings in the Cathkin Peak Area, Natal'. *Bantu Studies* 7, 131–159.

Zemon Davis, N. 1995. *Women on the Margins: Three Seventeenth-Century Lives*. Cambridge, MA: Harvard University Press.

Zimmerman, A. 2001. *Anthropology and Antihumanism in Imperial Germany*. Chicago and London: University of Chicago Press.

Zimmerman, A. 2001. 'Looking Beyond History: The Optics of German Anthropology and the Critique of Humanism'. *Studies in History and Philosophy of Biological and Biomedical Sciences* 32 (3), 385–411.

COLLECTIONS

The Bleek Collection, University of Cape Town Libraries, Manuscripts and Archives Department, BC 151.

Percival Kirby Papers, University of Cape Town Libraries, Manuscripts and Archives Department, BC 750.

Käthe Woldmann Papers, University of Cape Town Libraries, Manuscripts and Archives Department, BC 210.

Iziko South African Museum Precolonial correspondence.

Maria Wilman Collection, McGregor Museum (MMKD).

M. Wilman Collection, Kimberley Africana Library.

Patricia Scott Deetz private collection.

Grey Collection, National Library of South Africa.

Index

Printed and bound by CPI Group (UK) Ltd, Croydon, CR0 4YY

09/06/2025

14685804-0003